ALLAN JONES

CAN'T STAND UP FOR FALLING DOWN

BLOOMSBURY PUBLISHING

LONDON · OXFORD · NEW YORK

BLOOMSBURY PUBLISHING
Bloomsbury Publishing Plc
50 Bedford Square, London, WC1B 3DP, UK

BLOOMSBURY, BLOOMSBURY PUBLISHING and the
Diana logo are trademarks of Bloomsbury Publishing Plc

First published in Great Britain 2017
This edition published 2018

A catalogue record for this book is available from the British Library

All articles appear here with the kind permission of Uncut/Time Inc

Library of Congress Cataloguing-in-Publication data has been applied for

ISBN: TPB: 978-1-4088-8591-8; eBook: 978-1-4088-8593-2; PB: 978-1-4088-8592-5

2 4 6 8 10 9 7 5 3 1

Typeset by Newgen Knowledge Works Pvt Ltd., Chennai, India
Printed and bound in Great Britain by CPI Group (UK) Ltd, Croydon CR0 4YY

To find out more about our authors and books visit
www.bloomsbury.com and sign up for our newsletters

CONTENTS

INTRODUCTION

It happens like this: in April 1974, *Melody Maker* advertises a vacancy for a new "junior reporter/feature writer". In this by-gone time, *Melody Maker* is a genuinely big deal – the UK's best-selling music paper, with weekly sales of 200,000 and counting. Eager young scribes all over the country are probably already stapling together their painstakingly-composed reviews of albums like *Aqualung, Brain Salad Surgery*, and *In The Wake Of Poseidon* – the kind of overblown prog rock guff too often (for my liking) championed by *MM*. These earnest appreciations are no doubt even now being stuffed into envelopes and addressed to editor Ray Coleman at the paper's swanky Fleet Street offices. This is probably the chance a lot of people have been waiting for.

Anyway, my girlfriend Kathy sees the ad in a London listings magazine, reads it all the way through and laughs when she gets to the bit about the kind of new recruit *MM* is apparently looking for. Now *that* sounds like me, she says. Why not apply? Go on, take a look. I do and it does, which makes me laugh, too, because it turns out they are after someone who's 21 or younger, a music fan, and is, in their words, "highly opinionated". And what's this at the end of the ad? "No previous journalistic experience necessary."

That gets my attention.

Well, I'm 21, evidently a hurdle cleared there. I've also got a lot of records. I similarly have a lot of opinions, often brashly expressed even when I don't know what I'm talking about. As for journalistic experience, I don't have any. I *do* have a small belief that I can probably manage to write something more complicated than a ransom note. But it's not like I have some long-smouldering ambition to write seriously – about music or anything else. And that includes writing for *Melody Maker*, even though I've been reading it for years – it's just never crossed my mind. In fact, the whole idea of making even a half-hearted bid for the job seems suddenly preposterous. What am I thinking of? I'd surely stand more chance of being taken on by the circus as a moustachioed strongman or a whip-cracking lion-tamer. On the other hand, nine months after leaving art school in South Wales and moving to London with only a vague idea of what I'm going to do next, I've ended up working in the mail order department of a posh bookshop near Piccadilly Circus where my mind has started to unravel. It's not like I've got a whole lot going for me at the moment. No one's caught me sobbing at my desk yet, or stabbing myself in the leg with a letter opener, but you never know what's around the next corner.

I decide to apply.

I don't, for obvious reasons, have any kind of CV or clippings of local paper scoops, and it doesn't occur to me to knock up some sample reviews to offer up as palpable evidence of my wit, insight and general musical knowledge. So I write a letter that tells whoever reads it that I'm a typical small-town music fan of the time, the kind that as a teenager in the late Sixties spends hours in the local record shop – in my case, a place called Derrick's which is about as big as a minicab office but astonishingly well-stocked. In shops like these all the best new records are on tempting display, racks of them, their sleeves handled as tenderly as religious relics. *Melody Maker*, I explain, was an essential guide to what was worth listening to among all these releases. You could have put together a pretty good record collection back then by paying reasonable attention to the recommendations of writers like Richard Williams and Michael Watts. I did, anyway. In fact, I read every issue of *MM* from cover to cover, at least twice over, hungry for everything in it, thus including the jazz section, Folk News, the loon pants ads at the back and the enormous classified section that lurks there also – a vast marketplace for jobbing musicians (did "A Able Accordionist" ever find the gig he was looking for?).

For years, I go on, *MM* is just about indispensible. But something's recently changed: in 1972, the ailing *New Musical Express* is given weeks to improve circulation or face closure. The paper's editor Alan Smith and his deputy Nick Logan boldly recruit new writers from London's underground press who bring a new acerbity to its pages, and an irreverence and general liveliness that suddenly makes *MM* seem regrettably stuffy, sober and staid – its more temperate approach to just about everything makes it seem dull against its rival's colourful outspokenness. There are still plenty of great writers on *MM*, I say, but what makes new *NME* stars like Nick Kent and Charles Shaar Murray stand out, apart from their writing, of course, is that they look so much the part. The picture by-lines of *MM* staff do little to flatter them. Richard Williams and his frankly scary moustache have both gone by 1974, but long-serving Features Editor Chris Welch still beams from *MM's* pages like someone who's just won a marrow in a raffle, while Assistant Editor Mick Watts' picture makes him look frighteningly like the infamous international terrorist, Carlos The Jackal. Kent on the other hand looks enough like a rock star to pass for one of Roxy Music's itinerant early bass players and Charlie Murray with his shades, afro and leather jackets wouldn't be out of place in a band shot of The MC5. My point is that *MM* right now could do with livening up. I go on about this at some length, get quickly and hopelessly worked up, and with a bravado I don't for a moment really feel, sign off the letter with the following message: "Melody Maker needs a bullet up the arse. I'm the gun, pull the trigger." I post the thing before I have second thoughts.

A week later, I get a letter from Ray Coleman, along with a totally flabbergasting invitation: can I come in to *MM* HQ for an interview? Hey, *what?* How did this happen? Has no one else applied for the job? Come the appointed day, I turn up at *MM's* offices in Fleet Street, convinced there's been a mistake that will belatedly be recognised upon my arrival, at which point I fully expect to be sent politely packing with apologies for whatever misunderstanding has occurred. In the event, I am ushered into the presence of the fabled Coleman, the editor who's turned *MM* into such a sales juggernaut. He's a man in his late-thirties, balding with fuzzy sideburns, large heavy-rimmed glasses and the reassuring manner of an avuncular oncologist or much-loved family vet, although the jarring colour clash of what he's wearing – a purple suit, bright yellow tie and lime green shirt – makes him look like the manager of a Miami car wash franchise. He's quite a sight. God knows what he makes of me with my scarves, bracelets, earring and one of my old glam rock jackets with padded shoulders, sequins and zips up the inside of both sleeves. Whatever, he's warm and courteous and we chat pleasantly about art school and music for around half an hour, with Ray gently prompting sometimes

3

outrageous opinions from me that seem to amuse him. And that's pretty much it. I hadn't been expecting to sit a written exam or anything, but I'm still surprised that Ray hasn't asked me to present so much as a shopping list as evidence that I can actually, you know, write. Instead, he thanks me for dropping in – as if I've just strolled by and popped in to see him on a whim – shows me to the door and says he'll be in touch.

Two weeks later I still haven't heard from him and presume I've made such a hapless impression that he's simply forgotten me. I can only imagine they've done the sensible thing and given the job to some ingratiating little swot with a taste for bands that wear wizard's capes, which would of course have left me with no hard feelings whatsoever, absolutely none. Then one afternoon at the bookshop I get a call from someone who says she's Ray's secretary. She wants to know why I haven't replied to Ray's letter offering me the job. *Ray's letter offering me the job?* Well, that's a letter I haven't seen. Do I even in fact still want the job, she's asking? *Do I still want it?* Does love break your heart? Does one thing follow another? *Do I still want the job?* Of course I still fucking want it.

And so on Tuesday, June 4, I turn up for my first day at work as *Melody Maker's* new junior reporter/feature writer, hoping for the best. The first few weeks are like being picked up by a tornado and landing in somewhere that isn't Kansas anymore. It takes me about an afternoon to realise that, compared to the mass of musical knowledge shared by the *MM* staff I've just joined, I know less than fuck all about very little. Everyone's friendly enough, although I get the impression that Mick Watts, the writer I'm most in awe of, is convinced Ray's only given me a job out of pity or, even more likely, in a moment of spit-dribbling lunacy. I'm immediately put on the junior reporter Chitlin' Circuit, so low on the editorial totem pole that I'm actually part of its foundations. But I'm uncomplaining as they send me off to interview sundry hit parade regulars of the day. Memorably, I turn up in Slough one day to interview The Bay City Rollers to find them lolling around a hotel suite looking like they're fresh out of the showers or a communal bath, drying off with towels around their waists like something out of *Spartacus* while their creepy-looking manager answers my questions on their mute behalf. I'm frankly happy at this point

4

to be doing *anything*. But I'm also starting to wonder how long I'm going to be stuck as the office dogsbody. It's right about now I get an unexpected crack at Leonard Cohen, and the picture gets a lot prettier. Mick Watts is soon enough offering me much sage advice, for which I am immediately grateful, even as I continue to treat him with appalling flippancy. Mick sends me off in quick succession to interview Bryan Ferry, Van Morrison, Ray Davies and Frank Zappa. Things are looking up. Not much later I go on tour with a band for the first time. Excitingly, the band is Roxy Music. For the next few years after this, I'm constantly bombing up and down Britain's motorways and back roads in a variety of leaky vans, clapped-out charabancs and beat-up tour buses. When I'm not here, I'm there, everything at times a blur. When Richard Williams replaces Ray as *MM* editor in August 1978, he sends me even further afield, as if he can't decide what to do with me and settles for keeping me out of the office for as long as possible. I am apparently regarded as a 'disruptive influence'. For nearly 18 months I only sleep on planes, like a character in a Warren Zevon song. I spend hours, days, weeks, with people whose music I dig, and even find entertainment in the company of people whose music I wouldn't feed to a starving dog. Let it be enough for me to say that, all things considered, I have the time of my fucking life, although the deadlines are sometimes horrifying and I didn't expect to be punched quite so much.

After I become editor of *MM* in 1984 – in another totally unexpected turn of events – the trips, jaunts and long-haul jolly-ups inevitably begin to dwindle. One a year, none a year – it happens that quickly. I'm more likely now to be found trying to look at least awake, if not fully alert, in meetings with various publishing types, rather than doing drugs with Lou Reed, knocking about with Joe Strummer, getting plastered with Nick Lowe, being set on fire by The Damned or beaten up by Black Sabbath's Tony Iommi. It's a change of pace, at least. But by 1996, a dire combination of Britpop's beer-fart blare and the publishing plans for *MM* that make me fear for its future convince me it's time to go. That summer, I spend a week in Nashville with Kurt Wagner's 13-piece country-soul collective Lambchop and come back with an idea for the magazine that becomes *Uncut*, a new music monthly that I quit *MM* to edit. A few weeks before the first

5

issue comes out in May 1997, we're in the office when the subject of an Editor's Letter to introduce the new magazine comes up. Alan Lewis, the editorial director we've been working with (an old *MM* man who is also former editor of both *Sounds* and *NME* and more recently had a hand in launching *Loaded*), has an idea. He suggests that instead of the usual homely welcome to readers, I should write up some of the stories I collected over my years at *MM*. These have become quite a repertoire by now, one that I am prone to windily recount in the pub, especially if old cronies like *MM* photographer Tom Sheehan, an accomplice on many of these adventures, or news editor Carol Clerk are at uproarious hand to turn the anecdotal flow into something more torrential. I'm not sure how many stories I've actually got, but decide to give it a go anyway. I start writing a column called Stop Me If You've Heard This One Before that quickly turns into a regular back page feature and runs for the next 15 years. It seems I have a lot of stories.

A selection of those many yarns are now collected in *Can't Stand Up For Falling Down*. Some of them appear more or less as they originally ran in *Uncut*, others have been remixed, touched up here and there, parts of them rewritten, expanded and arranged in the order these things happened. The source for them all, of course, are the stories, interviews and on-the-road reports I wrote for *MM*. The bulk of them come from that wild early time on the paper, from 1974 to 1984, when every day was a new adventure and you never wanted the nights to end. This roughly coincides with what has subsequently become known as a golden age for music weeklies, a gilded time. I'm not sure anyone in the thick of things back then regarded it as any kind of 'age' so much as a particularly riotous phase some of us were going through and were determined to enjoy before it was all too quickly over. I was just happy and amazed to be a small part of it all.

Am I nostalgic for the time that inspired most of the stories in *Can't Stand Up For Falling Down*? I guess in many ways I am. For a start, there was still a thriving weekly music press back then, before it was first marginalised, then increasingly ignored and eventually almost completely abandoned. And who in their right mind wouldn't prefer a world that still counted among its living many of the people who appear in these pages, including Lou Reed, Leonard Cohen,

David Bowie, Joe Strummer, Warren Zevon, Lee Brilleaux, John Martyn, Alex Harvey, Townes Van Zandt, Lemmy, Gene Clark, Mick Ronson, John Peel and even Sid Vicious? Like the weekly music press itself, they are all gone now.

As for what follows, we start somewhere near the beginning.

LEONARD COHEN

London, June 1974

A few weeks after I join the hallowed ranks of what used to be *Melody Maker*, I'm on my own one afternoon in the office. Everyone else is either being wined and dined at some no doubt lavish record company lunch, of which in those days there were plenty, or down the pub drinking like Vikings – a daily ritual for the paper's sub-editors.

The common feeling among the senior staff at *Melody Maker* at the time is that my recent appointment by editor Ray Coleman is either further evidence of Ray's unravelling sanity or the result of a ghastly administrative error. To their horror – especially the horror of uncommonly suave assistant editor Michael Watts, famed in the *MM* office for his cravats, safari suits and gourmet luncheons – I can barely type and the abstract codifications of shorthand look like indecipherable hieroglyphics to me. As for actual, you know, journalistic experience, as already mentioned, I don't have any. Unlike, I am given to understand, my estimable new colleagues, who are universally skilled in ways Mick seems already convinced I'll never be.

As far as Mick's concerned, it seems to me, I'd be of more use to *MM* if I was a veteran of some local paper, a *Bugle*, *Gazette* or *Chronicle*, where I might have honed my journalistic skills reporting from the front lines of village fetes, town planning meetings, the openings of floral gardens, council estate murders—heady stuff like that. This is the sturdy stock from which *MM* usually recruits its new writers. Mick seems to regard me, therefore, as an opportunistic little chancer who's somehow hoodwinked Ray into giving me a job for which I am uniquely unqualified. Eager, perhaps, but doomed all the same. Furthermore, I get the feeling Mick thinks there's some budding junior reporter out there, a Jimmy Olsen-type, a kid with rosy-cheeked promise, currently stuck doing the pop column for some far-flung provincial rag who was surely destined for greater things here at *MM* until I minced along to bamboozle him out of his rightful inheritance, with my fancy art school patter and glam rock shoulder pads.

"If you're still here by the end of the month, it'll be a miracle," Mick informs me on my first day. And for the next couple of weeks he throws me scraps. I'm grateful for anything he tosses my way, but it's not quite what I expected and I'm beginning to feel like I'm being groomed for an early exit. Cheers, Mick!

Anyway, I'm dropping off something at Mick's empty desk when his phone rings and doesn't stop for about five minutes, someone clearly calling with urgent things to discuss with the absent assistant editor. I pick up the phone. It's someone from CBS about the interview with Leonard Cohen – *Leonard Cohen*! – that Mick's been trying to set up since shortly before fire was invented. Can I now tell Mick that Cohen's currently at a hotel in Chelsea and is happy to meet him tomorrow morning? I'm given a time and address, which I promise to pass onto Mick, dutiful servant that I am.

Except, I don't tell Mick about the call. He doesn't come back to the office that afternoon, and I don't make much of an effort to find out how I can get in touch with him. Instead, I turn up for the interview myself, feeling, as a long-time fan about to meet one of his heroes, slightly weak in the region of my knees as I tap lightly on his hotel door, which now opens.

"I'm Leonard Cohen," he announces with a warm smile. A handsome man, impeccably dressed in a smart grey suit. "Welcome."

He invites me into a modest room with windows overlooking Sloane Square and flowers on a small table. I notice now that he's barefooted. He takes a seat, feet on the bed. I remind him that the last time he appeared in *Melody Maker*, remarks he'd made about his own low opinion of his music had been luridly accompanied by headlines announcing his retirement. Since he is in London finishing an album he tells me will be called either *New Skin For The Old Ceremony* or *Return Of The Broken Down Nightingale*, he's clearly not retired. What's the story?

"I have read over the years so much negative criticism of my work and of my position, so much satire, so much humorous indifference to where I stand," he says, "that on the public level and in social inter-course with strangers I tend to dismiss myself and not take my work very seriously.

"I think that interview was just a way of saying goodbye for a while, a temporary cheerio, nothing tragic. I seem, however, to have given this impression to people that I've been recovering from some serious illness, which I am happy to say has not been the case.

"The image I've been able to gather of myself from the press is of a victim of the music industry, a poor sensitive chap who has been destroyed by the very forces he started out to utilise. But that is not so, never was. I don't know how that ever got around. I would also contest the notion that I am or was a depressed and extremely frail individual, also that I am sad all the time.

"There is a perception, too, of my songs as depressing, but I think that's not the case. One side of the third album I find a little burdened and melodramatic. I think that's the fault of the songs and of the singer. It's a failure of that particular album, but it's not a characteris-tic of the work as a whole."

It seemed to me, and I hoped not fancifully, that his music was less 'depressing' than emblematic of an urgent inclination to create art that was fit for a world in which people died and calamity was wholesale, in which circumstance it would hardly be cheerful. I told him as much.

"I'm very pleased with that observation," he says. "That is defin-itely the most important aesthetic question of these days. Can art, or what we call entertainment, confront or incorporate the experience of man today? There's a lot of evidence for a negative answer. I skirt around that question myself, very often. One feels often inadequate in the face of massacre, disaster and human humiliation. What, you think, am I doing, singing a song at a time like this? But the worse it gets, the more I find myself picking up a guitar and playing that song.

"It is, I think, a matter of tradition. You have a tradition on the one hand that says, if things are bad we should not dwell on the sadness, that we should play a happy song, a merry tune. Strike up the band and dance the best we can, even if we are suffering from concussion.

"And then there's another tradition, and this is a more Oriental or Middle Eastern tradition, which says that if things are really bad, the best thing to do is sit by the grave and wail, and that's the way you are going to feel better. I think both these efforts are intended to lift the spirit. And my own tradition, which is the Hebraic tradition, suggests that you sit next to the disaster and lament. The notion of the lamentation seemed to me to be the way to do it. You don't avoid the situation – you throw yourself into it, fearlessly."

Before I go, I ask him to sign my copy of his novel *Beautiful Losers*. He takes the book and looks at it, as if he hasn't seen one in a while, then notices a passage I've underlined and reads it aloud.

"'How can I begin anything new with all of yesterday inside me... how can I exist as the vessel of yesterday's slaughter?' Not bad," he laughs. "I wonder," he smiles, returning the book and walking me to the door, "who I was when I wrote that."

I stand in the hotel corridor as the door to the room behind me closes. Panic almost immediately consumes me. Have I really just interviewed Leonard Cohen? What did I ask him? I can't remember. My mind's a complete blank. Did he even show an interest in anything I said? Yes, I think he did. But maybe he didn't. I don't know. Perhaps he had merely endured my presence, a notable stoic, too polite to show me the door, however inane my questions. I have to lean against the nearest wall, breathing hard. Fuck. I don't remember getting into this kind of state after recently interviewing, I don't know, Gary Glitter or the blokes from Mud. But, then, they didn't write "Suzanne", "So Long, Marianne" or "Famous Blue Raincoat". I'm seized now by another worry. What if the tape recorder hasn't worked? Oh, God. I find a quite corner in a nearby pub and check the thing. I've used a side and half of a C90 cassette. What if I play it back and there's nothing but static? I press play, and there's Cohen's voice. The volume's a bit low, there's some traffic noise in the background, but nothing to worry about. That's a relief. I have a drink to calm down and a couple more to steel me for my return to the *Melody Maker* office. I am in little doubt that I am shortly going to face the proverbial music, which I suspect will be a positively Wagnerian noise, a furious racket, Mick Watts its demonic conductor.

He's at his desk at the far end of the office when I get back, head down over some copy he's hacking lumps out of, clearly not in the best of moods.

"This better be good," he says without looking up. He's obviously spoken to someone at CBS and predictably taken a somewhat dim view of my apparently errant behaviour. I decide to play the indignant innocent (I've had some practise). So I describe my increasingly frantic attempts yesterday to track him down – a huge exaggeration, since I made only one half-arsed call. I tell him I was eventually so worried – positively besides myself – that *MM* would lose a valuable exclusive I decided to do the interview myself, thus saving the fucking day! Don't I deserve some credit for showing a little initiative here? Mick just snorts, which has a significantly dampening effect on my wavering bravado. It's like he's already decided to ditch the entire feature. I tell him that if he'll give me a chance to actually write the thing, he might, you know, want to run it after all.

Mick now appears to be thinking something over.

"Write it up, then" he says of my interview. "But be advised," he adds with grave emphasis, "that if it's rubbish, you're fucked."

I spend what's left of the afternoon transcribing the tape of the interview and the rest of the night writing up the feature. It's on his desk when he arrives the next morning, wearing some kind of fucking poncho. He picks up the copy I've left on his desk and tosses it into an in-tray, hardly overflowing, where it sits for the rest of the morning and most of the afternoon. He still hasn't read it when I have to go out – I think I have an interview to do with Showaddywaddy or The Rubettes, somebody like that, my typical beat at the time. Anyway, it's late when I get back to the office. There's just Mick and *MM*'s great jazz writer, Max Jones, busy with his weekly expenses. Mick is packing up for the day, getting ready to go. I'm now desperate to know if he's read the Leonard Cohen piece.

"Oh, that," he says, as if I've just brought up something trivial, a wholly petty matter, not the feature my future at *Melody Maker* is apparently riding on. He seems more preoccupied, in fact, with the evidently trickier-than-it-looks task of getting the top on the Tupperware container in which he brings his pre-prepared lunches to work. His indifference to my anxiety makes me want to blow up his car. "Yes, I think we can use it," he adds, rather airily, stuffing the Tupperware container into his big leather shoulder bag. "Some of it, anyway."

He's got his poncho on now. He waves good night to Max on his way out, then pauses at the door. "Bryan Ferry's got a new album coming out," he says then. "You should interview him."

Since I can't imagine he's talking to Max, who's sorting through a pile of crumpled receipts and sundry bar-bills from places like Ronnie Scott's club, I guess Mick is talking to me. This is unexpected. Bryan Ferry! I want to give a little whoop, but settle for looking suitably humble (a tough one) and grateful (not so hard). So does Mick see me in some sudden new light? I have no idea. But I do get an impression – vague as it might be – that I may after all be here a bit longer than Mick had ominously predicted on my first day.

"See you in the morning," he says. And he does, and for a lot more after that.

Tony Iommi

Iommi Mansions, Warwickshire, July 1974

No doubt picking up the karmic tab for sins committed in a multiplicity of former lives, I'm deemed by the *Melody Maker* features desk to be the most suitable person on the editorial staff to write a piece on Black Sabbath, for which I'm supposed to interview their guitarist, Brummie bruiser Tony Iommi. The interview is duly arranged for 2:30pm on Friday, at the offices of his record company. Come that particular woebegone morn, I get a call from the record company. According to what they have to say, Tony won't be travelling down to London from his country pile in the Midlands. Can I do the interview over the phone? This doesn't seem to me to be anything approaching a problem. I dial the number they've given me.

BRRRRRINNNNG!!!!

"Er... 'ello."

Is this Tony Iommi?

"Er... yes."

Are you sure?

"How d'yer mean?"

Uh, you answered the phone and when I asked you if you were Tony Iommi, you hesitated. Like you weren't sure who you were.

"Are you taking the fucking piss, mate?"

I assure him I'm not.

"That's all right, then."

I ask him why he's up there and I'm down here, when down here together is where we both should be.

"Say that again."

Why couldn't you get down here today, Tony?

"Well," says Iommi, in a voice so curiously faint I wonder what end of the receiver he's talking into, "we... er... we were all over at Ozzy's last night, rehearsing."

And how do you feel today?

"Bloody groggy, to be honest with yer."

I sympathise and ask if we can start the interview, keen to get this over with.

"All right," he says. "But I'm a bit untogether, like. Can't quite think."

We start anyway. The American rock magazine *Creem* has just voted Black Sabbath the world's greatest punk band, the term "punk" belonging then to a different lexicon than the 1977 version. There's a silence as Tony takes this in.

"Does that mean they think we're rubbish?"

No!

"It sounds like they think we're crap."

They like you.

"Doesn't sound like it ter me," he says, sounding a bit morose.

But they've just given you an award!

"Are you sure they weren't just taking the piss?"

I am fairly sure, but decide to move on. Next question.

"NO," Tony says, and I can imagine his little head shaking, foot-stamping possibly to follow as he works himself into a petulant strop. "I don't think so. I'm not in the mood. I can't get it together enough to answer any questions. I'm feeling a bit, yer know..."

Groggy?

"Absolutely."

So where do we go from here?

"Could you come up here?" he suggests as my heart sinks faster than the Titanic, plans for the weekend scuppered and all that. "Have a cuppa and a bit of a chat," he adds, as if I'll find this irresistible.

All of which explains why the following afternoon I found myself sitting outside a railway station somewhere in the Midlands, avoiding the increasingly hostile stares of a crowd of incredibly drunken wedding guests, two of which were squaring up for a scrap, with several others urging them on while a woman in a paisley trouser suit threw up in a flower bed. I've been here for – what? – an hour at least, waiting for Iommi and I'm starting to nod off when there's an

15

almighty retching roar – the sound of something turbo-charged with smoking brakes. It's Iommi, of course, screaming into the station car park and screeching to a halt, looking belligerent behind the wheel of something sleek.

"Gerrin," he says.

We then take off like something NASA might like to know more about, hurtling out of the car park and around the first bend of a narrow country road on two wheels, me still struggling with a seat belt when the door on my side of the car flies open.

"Pull it shut... with that piece of string!" Iommi shouts over the infernal howl of wind, horsepower, gears and the shrill screaming panic of his hysterical passenger, who for a moment is convinced he's going to be catapulted out of the car through the open door into the wild blue yonder that's passing by at some speed. Not long after this, me still clutching the door shut, we pull up outside Iommi Mansions. What we have here is a genuinely imposing country house, a kind of castle really, with turrets and the like, the only thing missing from the scene a drawbridge and moat. After the high-speed terrror of the drive from the station, everything seems unexpectedly tranquil. There's birdsong, a breeze whispering gently through the trees and... uh, oh. What's *this*? Two rather fierce German Shepherds – dogs as big as bungalows – are prowling the lawn, teeth-bared and growling.

"Show no fear and they won't hurt yer," Tony tells me. "Just walk to the door, slowly."

I do. The door is a bloody great oak thing that Iommi pushes open with some effort, shoulder to the wood. I step inside, out of the sunlight and into the gloom of a long hallway lined on each side with suits of armour. The next thing I know, I'm sprawled on what I take to be a carpet but turns out to be a flayed horse's skin. I've tripped over its head and can see its teeth and eyes, now gleaming in the light streaming through the door behind me.

"A present from Ozzy," Iommi explains, nodding at the horse hide while he helps me to my feet. "Killed it and skinned it for me when he was working in a slaughterhouse."

We retire to the parlour, where we are served tea and biscuits and talk about Black Sabbath and their music.

"I just write the riffs," Tony tells me. "If you want to know what the songs are about, you'll have to talk to Geezer." Geezer is Geezer Butler, Sabbath's bass player. "Geezer's got an incredible mind Geezer has."

We sip our tea and I ask Tony what he thinks he might be doing if he wasn't in a band.

"The way I was going, I'd probably be in prison," he says, enjoying a digestive. "Same with Ozzy. He was always in fights and gangs. Then he found, with music, there was another side to life."

Pretty soon, it's time to go. I head back down the long dark hallway to the front door. Tony's walking behind me and, as I pull the door open, I hear him muttering something about the dogs. But it's too late. I step out onto the lawn, blinking in the late afternoon sunlight, and freeze in something approaching terror. One of the German Shepherds is heading for me at a ferocious clip, streaking across the lawn, a flash of fur, a hint of teeth, a canine missile now launching itself at me. The thing is actually mid-flight when I'm barged out of the way by the intrepid Iommi, who catches the flying mutt in a head-lock, wrestles it to the ground and stuns it into submission with a punch between the eyes.

"Sorry about that," he says. "I thought the dogs were around the other side of the house."

I give him a weak grin and head for the car. The next time I see Iommi, the fist he's just used to batter the hapless hound now whimpering at his feet will be heading in my direction. And, boy, will it hurt when it hits me.

VAN MORRISON

Knebworth, July 1974

It's Friday afternoon in the *Melody Maker* office and most of the editorial staff are already in the pub. I, however, am on the phone, chatting to Speedy Keen, who wrote and sang Thunderclap Newman's 'Something in the Air'. I've just written something in *MM* about Speedy's 1973 solo album, *Previous Convictions*, a record he thought no one had even heard, and he's called me up to ask me if I'd like to meet him for a chat and a drink the following week (at Track studios, incidentally, where in a couple of years he'll produce Johnny Thunders & The Heartbreakers *LAMF*). I do, of course, and we eventually have a lively time. Anyway, a shadow falls across my desk so I tell him I have to go, because elaborately-coiffed assistant editor Mick Watts is looming over me and from the weird little hand signals he's making I can only presume he has urgent business to discuss. I put the phone down and brace myself for whatever's coming next.

Mick perches on the edge of my desk in an unusually familiar manner, legs crossed like a secretary waiting for me to dictate a letter. His chumminess makes me immediately wary. What is he up to? My jaw rather drops when he says he'd like me to interview Van Morrison. Van Morrison! When? Where? Well, Van's playing the first Knebworth Festival tomorrow, part of a line-up that also includes The Allman Brothers, Tim Buckley, The Mahavishnu Orchestra, The Doobie Brothers and The Sensational Alex Harvey Band. I can interview Van after his set. *Far out!* Of course, in my excitement it doesn't occur to me that I'm probably far from Mick's first choice for this particular gig, and that everyone else he's asked has obviously found a convenient excuse to avoid what's likely to be an agonisingly

18

unpleasant encounter with the notoriously ill-tempered, permanently morose and legendarily grumpy Morrison. In other words, I'm being thrown in as bait. But who cares? There's a slight problem, though. I've promised Richard Ogden, who goes on to run Paul McCartney's business empire but at the time is a freelance PR building up his own small company, that I'll go with him tonight to see one of his bands. In Swansea. I don't want to let him down, but anyway he quickly checks the train times from Swansea to London and reckons we can get a pre-dawn train the next day, from South Wales. According to Richard, we'll be back in London with time to spare for me to get to Soho, where I need to catch the official Warner Bros coach to Knebworth.

As a plan, it's pretty much a disaster. The train's inevitably delayed and by the time I get to the Warner's office the coach has gone. I now don't have a ticket, pass or anything else that might get me into the festival. And something else strikes me: I don't have a fucking clue where Knebworth actually is. I can see my Van Morrison interview going up in smoke and Mick Watts advancing menacingly towards me through the flames that even now are incinerating my future employment. My immediate response is hysteria, quickly followed by uncontrollable howling. However help is at hand. Richard Ogden now volunteers to drive me to Knebworth. We actually get there at some speed, Richard displaying a hitherto unremarked instinct for avoiding traffic jams, snarl-ups and assorted tail-backs. How do we then get into the festival without tickets, passes or any kind of official identification? Richard blasts through a couple of checkpoints at a fair clip, as if we are on urgent business and can't be stopped, and at the third we're waved straight through with no questions asked. If anyone gets in our way, we just shout at them and act like we own the place. This seems to work, as shortly we are inside the festival's security perimeter, wading through a growing crowd and just coming over a sort of hill – with the stage way down there at the bottom of this sweeping natural bowl – when Tim Buckley's voice comes floating across the morning.

It's a moment I'll never forget: he's singing "Buzzin' Fly". I feel like dropping to my knees in awe.

"Thanks," he's telling the crowd now, finishing his set as the Warner Bros coach pulls into the backstage car park (arriving late due to the hideous traffic congestion that Richard miraculously managed to avoid). Still, everyone's here now and suddenly there seems also to be an enormous amount of free booze around, courtesy of Warner's at-the-time legendary hospitality. I have a few beers then neck a bottle of wine. The Sensational Alex Harvey Band appear, play a blinding set, and take the festival, as they say, by storm. I go backstage to their trailer to help them celebrate. Much whiskey is heartily consumed, most of it knocked back with true Celtic gusto and much laughter. Which is interrupted by two pot-bellied, walrus-moustached, baseball-capped Americans who announce themselves as members of The Doobie Brothers' road crew. They want us out of the trailer. Why? Because there are obviously so many fucking Doobie Brothers that they need this trailer as well as their own deluxe motor home.

Alex, who's had a few, gives them the Gorbals' eye.

"Tell the fuckin' Doobie Brothers that if they want this fuckin' caravan, they'll have to fight us for it wi' fuckin' knives," he tells the roadies, which sort of puts an end to the Doobies moving in *here*.

We get back to toasting SAHB's knock-out festival appearance. Not much later I'm chatting to a member of the Allmans' crew, who gives me a hit on a joint and a few more after that, which presumably explains why I wake up under a truck that I've evidently crawled under for a bit of shade and a quick nap after such an early start. I come to with a start. What's that music? It sounds like Bob Dylan and The Band. Fuck! It *is* Dylan and The Band. I'm suddenly convinced they've been helicoptered in for an unannounced appearance and are now on stage at Knebworth! But, rushing to the press pit at the front of the stage, which is bewilderingly empty apart from Mick Watts, who's enjoying a piece of quiche and a glass of Chablis, I realise what I'm listening to is the recent Dylan live album, *Before the Flood*, being played over the festival PA. Not long after this Van Morrison plays and as soon as he's finished his set I'm being marched across the backstage area to Van's trailer by Mick Watts and a couple of people from Warner's London office, like I'm part of a hostage exchange or something. Someone taps a bit nervously on the door of the trailer and on muffled command from inside pushes the door open and me inside.

Anyway, here's Van in his caravan, sitting in this – I dunno – *kitchenette*, or whatever it is. I reach out to shake his hand and he looks at me like I've just sold his children into slavery. I get an inkling then – and it's a heart-sinking moment – that things are not going to proceed smoothly. I set up my tape recorder on the table between us. He pushes it away. I push it back. He gives me a piggy little look and pushes the tape recorder away again, but not as far as last time. I leave it where it is, otherwise we're going to be here all night. I open my notebook and over the next 20 minutes I ask twice as many questions, which Van variously ignores or answers with not much more than a shrug, an occasional grunt, a few exasperated groans and a great deal of contempt. All the while, he's smacking a can against the metal rim of the table in front of him.

Smack, he goes.

Smack.

Smack.

Smack, again.

Smacksmacksmacksmack.

Smack.

By now I want to smack *him*, although professional courtesy for the moment prevails.

Smack.

But only just.

I ask him another question and this time get a nod in response, which seems to be a bit of a breakthrough. I ask him if he wants to elaborate on the nod.

"No," he says, somewhat less than cheerily. "I'm just agreeing with you."

Not much later, I've had as much as I can stand of Van's sullen belligerence and tell him that if he doesn't want to talk, fine. I'll go. I have better things to do, after all, than sit in this puddle of misery at the black whim of his moodiness.

"That's not my problem," he says. And smack goes the can.

I pack up my notebook and tape recorder.

"What are you doing?" he asks.

I tell him since there's no point going on like this, I might as well bid farewell, hit the highway, the breeze, whatever. See what's shaking in the backstage bar.

He's quiet for a moment.

Then, "Let's start again," he says.

I grab the opportunity like a drowning man getting a second chance at a life-belt. Halfway through my first question, however, Van starts making a noise like a kettle coming to the boil that makes him sound like he's having a fit.

"Where... where," he asks, and it seems like an effort getting the words out, "*where* are these questions *coming from*?"

A love of his music is my rather feeble, if honest, answer, but he's not impressed. He's smacking the can against the table again, drifting into a long difficult silence.

"This isn't... it's just not happening," he says finally, but he's talking to himself. I'm already at the door.

"Are you going to print any of this?" he asks, not that he probably cares.

One day, maybe. Who knows?

RAY DAVIES

London, September 1974

In those bygone times of lively nightly carousing, I usually ended up at Dingwalls Dancehall in Camden. Back then, it was one of the few places in London you could get a drink after normal closing time, and so a favourite of the pub rock crowd, most of whom would, in a couple years, find a home at Stiff Records. On any given night, you'd run into, say, Jake Riviera, Dave Robinson, Nick Lowe with Dave Edmunds in boisterous tow, Dr Feelgood's Lee Brilleaux (if he was in town), Ian Dury with his minder, Fred "Spider" Rowe, and sundry other notorious bar jockeys, including Mick Farren, Larry Wallis, Boss Goodman, Sean Tyla and Lemmy.

On this night, I turn up with my friend of colourful reputation, BP Fallon. Beep is a legendary Sixties scenester who I ran into backstage at a Roy Harper gig at Kingston Polytechnic in southwest London about a month before. I recognise him from a photo in *Melody Maker* showing him interviewing John and Yoko at the Amsterdam Hilton, where they were holding their first Bed-In. This resulted in Lennon digging Beep enough to later invite him onto *Top of the Pops* as a member of The Plastic Ono Band, with Beep 'playing' bass on 'Instant Karma!'. That night, backstage with Harper, I introduce myself and very quickly I'm regaled by many hilarious tales of Beep's time as "media consultant" for King Crimson, Marc Bolan at the height of T Rex-mania, and Led Zeppelin – stories he tells in a hipster Esperanto of his own sublime invention, quite unlike anything I've ever heard. Anyway, on this particular night at Dingwalls, most of the usual crowd are there and also, on his own, standing at the end of the bar – and I get very excited about this – is Ray Davies.

"Do you want me to introduce you?" Beep, who I have come to realise knows everybody, asks. I do! And so we make our way down the bar to Ray, who has the distracted air of someone trying to remember where he is and what he's doing there.

"Ray!" Beep says, hand outstretched for a handshake that doesn't come as Ray instead regards us somewhat warily, but at least without fleeing the premises as a victim of unwanted attention. Finally, he looks at Beep and smiles, as if he's recognised someone he hasn't seen in a while, and Beep introduces me as a new writer on *Melody Maker*, only a few months on the job, and a great admirer of The Kinks and all their works. To my spluttering surprise, Beep's now telling Ray how wonderfully cool it would be if Ray did an interview with me for *Melody Maker* – or as Beep puts it, "Get together for a spot of verbal".

Ray gives this some thought, and says, "Why not?" He scribbles something on a scrap of paper and hands it to me. "Call this number and ask for Claire," he says. "She'll sort something out."

I'm lost for words, so mutely thank him and Beep and I are about to head back down the bar when Ray, clearly curious, says to Beep, "What was your name again?"

"BP Fallon," Beep says. "At your service," he adds, with a gallant bow.

Didn't Beep say he knew Ray? It now strikes me they've never met before.

"I didn't say I *knew* him," Beep says. "I just asked if you wanted me to introduce you to him."

I'm not sure it'll get me anywhere, but still I call the number Ray's given me and speak to Claire, as instructed. A couple of days later I turn up at Konk, The Kinks' north London studio, expecting to find Ray. Just before I arrive, however, he goes out for a walk, promising to return shortly. It's the last anyone sees of him that day. I'm luckier on my next visit. Ray's waiting for me in a basement room, looking washed-out, fretful and unhappy after a long day in the studio. He's leaning against a snooker table as big as a football field.

"Fancy a game?" Ray says. I've never played, and tell him as much.

"What a sheltered life you must've led," he says, as if I'm now in his eyes some lisping little Fauntleroy when he would have much preferred me to have grown up surrounded by whippets and Woodbine smoke.

24

"Not to worry," he says, encouragingly. "I'm sure you'll pick it up quickly enough."

I accept his invitation to 'break', badly miscue the white ball, which hits three separate cushions but misses every other ball on the table and disappears into what apparently is called a 'pocket', one of six on the table.

"That'll be four away, then," he says, clearly dismayed by my ineptitude. Anyway, it seems I've handed Ray an advantage he now exploits ruthlessly, 'breaking' the reds, and racing into an early lead before missing an easy 'pot', allowing me back on the table.

While he's been knocking balls hither and yon on the smooth baize, we've been talking about his rock musical *Starmaker*, recently broadcast by Granada TV to poor reviews from people who these days regularly bemoan Ray's theatrical ambitions and just want him to get back to what he's always been so great at, which is the writing of classic, three-minute pop singles.

He's back on the table now, following another of my disastrously errant shots, and he quickly dispatches a red, followed by the black. He then stares at the table for what seems a very long time.

"A lot of people think I'm completely on the wrong track these days," he says, potting another red. "They think I should never have stopped writing three-minute story-songs like 'Waterloo Sunset', 'Autumn Almanac' and 'Dead End Street'. But I've written so many of them," he says, sinking the blue. "I mean, like, 18 or 20 hit singles. I've lost count. But you can't keep doing that. People are going to lose interest in you if you just keep doing the same thing, over and over, which is what I felt I was doing. The formula begins to reveal itself. The magic goes. It did for me, anyway.

"I have a talent, I know," he says, re-spotting the blue, "for writing a certain kind of song. I think I've learned enough about the craft of song-writing to always be able to write a song. They may not always be hits, but they're usually pretty good. But where do I take that talent? I need to take it somewhere else, hence my little efforts like *Starmaker*. I know I'm upsetting a lot of people who want something else from me. Some of them are in my own band. One of them is my own brother. They think I should be writing two hit singles a year and a hit album we can take on the road. But that's not what I want to do anymore.

"I wonder these days what my place is," he says. "Our band's never really fit in. We're not a pretty band. We're not really a heavy rock band. We're not flash musicians. I don't know what we are. I don't know who I am. Sometimes I feel I don't even exist. There are just so many questions I don't know the answers to," he says. "Right now, I don't even know if I'm winning or losing," he goes on. And I know he's not talking about the game we're playing, which he goes on to win by clearing the table before laying down his cue and telling me he has nothing more to say for the moment.

ROXY MUSIC

Cardiff, September 1974

I'm sitting on a train at Paddington Station that's about to leave for South Wales, waiting nervously for Simon Puxley, Roxy Music's permanently-harassed "media consultant" who's supposed to be coming with me to Cardiff, where tonight Roxy are opening their Country Life tour at the Capitol Theatre.

Whistles blow, doors slam, the train shudders, stalls and starts again. I'm convinced that Simon's missed the train when the compartment door flies open and Simon falls through it, more flustered than ever. He's red-faced, breathing heavily, jacket askew and wearing what looks like someone else's hair. Still wheezing, he shoves a couple of bags into the luggage rack and with rather more delicacy hangs from the rack a large suit holder which he carefully straightens out, his fingers running over its surface as if it's some legendary religious icon, something for which he'd give up his life rather than surrender to the hands of strangers or anyone else who might want to get their mitts on it.

I wonder what priceless treasure the hanger might contain and whistle, impressed, when Simon tells me it's Bryan Ferry's New Stage Outfit. The bespoke manufacture of this has only just been completed, presumably in a last-minute flurry of nipping and tucking, so that Simon could pick it up on his way to Paddington and deliver it to Bryan in Cardiff, where it will be unveiled tonight. Simon's just settling into his seat, with his breathing getting back to normal, when the carriage door is again thrown open. A looming scarecrow of a man, in a filthy overcoat with eyes as wild as his hair, starts shouting at us in the manner of some demented old seadog.

"Do you have change to spare for a shipwrecked man?" asks the vision in the doorway, who now staggers forward into the carriage, his attention caught by Bryan's New Stage Outfit that's swinging from the luggage rack and which he beadily eyes-up, as if he may make off with it. Simon looks like he's going to faint.

"A few coppers, if you please," the impoverished mariner pleads.

Simon can't get his wallet out quick enough, the crusty old timer's eyes now a-glint as Simon peels off a couple of fivers, which he greedily grabs and noisily kisses before ramming them into the pockets of his soiled and threadbare trousers. He then fishes in the pocket of his overcoat and pulls out a can of beer, already open, which he pours on the hapless Puxley's head, as if in some kind of arcane anointment, while simultaneously making some gesture over Simon's head that I take to be the sign of the evil eye, or something similar. We get to Cardiff without further incident, and pre-gig find ourselves backstage with Roxy in a crowded dressing room. There's no sign of Bryan, however, or his New Stage Outfit.

"Look for the nearest mirror," Andy Mackay says. "He'll be in front of it."

Later, as I stand at the side of the stage and their taped intro fades to silence, Phil Manzanera leads the band into their opening number, 'Prairie Rose', which no one's heard because it's from the unfinished new album, *Country Life*, which should have been out by now. It's great, but where's Bryan? And what will he be wearing when finally we get to see him in his new gear? There's a movement now on the far side of the stage, which I take to be Bryan getting ready for his grand entrance. And – indeed – here he comes, sauntering in semi-darkness to the microphone in the centre of the stage. The lights go up as he hits his spot, and there's a gasp as Ferry is revealed in all his intended magnificence. And Jesus. What the fuck is he wearing?

It looks, from where I'm standing, like a gaucho outfit, and it *is* – billowing white blouse, black pantaloons held up by a thick length of rope and tucked into dinky wee boots, the whole thing topped off with a black sombrero, rakishly tilted over his eyes. So this is what Puxley's hauled all the way from London, amid much fretting. It's not a look, I probably needn't add, that would catch on. Frankly, if you walked into your local pub dressed like Ferry that night, people would first laugh and then pick you up and throw you under a bus for looking like such a twat.

I'm speechless and still trying to find my voice the next afternoon, when I meet Ferry in his hotel room to hear some rough mixes of the new album. Compared to some of the places I've lived, Ferry's suite is positively palatial, although he's unhappy with it. "One looks at a room like this," he says airily, "and one rather thinks it looks like a council flat."

He puts a tape in his cassette player and introduces 'The Thrill of It All' which, when it's finished, will be *Country Life's* opening track. What follows is extraordinary. I think I can hear Manzanera's guitar somewhere in the mix, but the rest is a howling blizzard of apocalyptic noise, a great churning thing, redolent of malfunctioning machinery.

I tell Ferry I've never heard anything quite like it.

"Er, neither have I," he says, fussing with the cassette player. "I think there's something wrong with the tape actually."

And there is. Ferry ejects the cassette and is immediately swathed in about three miles of unravelled tape, great mangled spools of the stuff spilling into his lap. He looks stricken, like someone for whom the world is simply too complicated to safely negotiate.

"I just don't know what to say," he admits forlornly, staring at the ruined cassette, disconsolate and baffled. Neither did I.

KC AND THE SUNSHINE BAND

London, October 1974

Ask me now, as you inquisitively might, and I couldn't tell you exactly how I ended up in Ilford on this wet Wednesday night. Possibly, I've drifted off in a *Melody Maker* editorial meeting, while jovial Chris Welch, *MM's* Bunter-esque features editor and a man of such relentless good cheer I sometimes want to set him on fire, goes through the contents of next week's issue (including a predictable menu of windy prog-rockers I'd similarly like to turn a flamethrower on). Yes, this was the likely case, with one of my reveries about turning Jethro Tull to toast interrupted by the blunt reality of being told to hot-foot it to Ilford that night, the rain-swept streets of which I am now forlornly traipsing, to do a story on KC and The Sunshine Band. They of course go on to have monster disco hits, like 'That's the Way (I Like It)', which sell millions, but have recently had a rather more modest chart success in the UK with something called 'Queen of Clubs'. Anyway, on the back of this they've been flown in from Miami for a hastily arranged British tour, whose demented itinerary has seen them hurtling around the country with haphazard abandon. Tonight, they're booked to play three shows, someone clearly keen to cash in on their current hit. The first of them is at The Greengate in Ilford, outside of which I am presently standing, getting very wet indeed and cursing bun-eating Chris Welch with all the venom I can muster, which is plenty.

The Greengate is advertised as an "entertainment complex", which in terms of 1970s architecture means it looks like something built by the Soviets out of reinforced concrete on the outskirts of far-off Stalingrad, in anticipation of the arrival of the Wehrmacht. The neon sign I'm now looking at promises STAR CABARET AND

LIVE ENTERTAINMENT, which tonight, I guess, means KC and the boys. There's no one at the box office, so cub reporter instinct takes me to the stage door where a couple of roadies of surprisingly advanced age are humping gear from the back of something that looks like it might have seen service as a field ambulance in the Spanish Civil War. I ask one of them if KC and the gang are inside the venue and, between wheezes that make me think I should call a doctor, he's able to tell me they're not. So where are they? The roadies aren't sure.

"They could be at The Speakeasy," says one.

"That was last night," says the other.

"Where are we now?"

"Ilford."

"Then the band are in Leytonstone."

This is all very confusing so I go back around the front, where a surprisingly large queue has miraculously formed, hunched in the rain like penitents. Just to be sure I'm where I'm supposed to be, I ask them if they're here to see KC and The Sunshine Band, which they are. This actually comes as a surprise to one girl who'd been under the impression her boyfriend's brought her to see Cockney Rebel. An argument noisily ensues as she gives him what you'd have to call a piece of her mind.

An hour later, The Greengate is packed. It's not a pretty sight. I'm not sure if glam ever took off in Ilford, but this crowd looks drab even for the era – everyone looks like they're recovering from rickets or something. The girls are either oddly matronly or slightly mad-looking, giggling together and dancing in bunches like the pygmies of distant Borneo. The boys all look like squaddies and wear jackets with lapels of such width and heft, a small gust of wind could see a few of them airborne. The stage doors where I'd earlier met KC's roadies actually open onto the dance floor and I wander over to them just as the Sunshine Band and a weary-looking KC arrive, looking totally disorientated, as if nothing for them is real anymore. Someone asks for the dressing rooms and there's a communal gasp of exhausted disbelief when they're told by the Greengate's manager that there isn't one and they'll have to use his flat, which is above the club and looks, when we get there, like a shrine to Formica, or the bachelor pad of a serial killer. The band change into their stage duds, moving slowly like people who've lost the will to live. I'm approached by someone who introduces himself as the tour's promoter – a man by the name of Maurice. Something about him hints of an era of Brylcreem and Babycham, un-tipped cigarettes and white fivers. I wouldn't describe him as shifty, but I find myself checking my pockets every time he comes near me.

"This band," Maurice tells me, waving a hand in the direction of KC and co, "is going to be the Band of '75. Like Lennon, like McCartney," Maurice goes on, "they write all their own material." He gives me a wink, signifying I don't know what.

"Right, lads," he now shouts at KC and his baffled troupe, "time to make some money."

Thirty minutes later, the band are back in the flat after a short sprint from the stage, through the crowd, into the rainy night, around the corner and upstairs to their temporary quarters. They're already packing for the next gig, at Crackers, a disco in Wardour Street.

"You won't get many bands coming here if you don't provide dressing rooms," Maurice admonishes the Greengate's manger, who clearly can't wait to get these people out of his apartment, presumably so he can restock the fridge with heads and other body parts.

"Actually," he tells Maurice, "I'm thinking of having a caravan placed out the back somewhere. Do you think that would do?"

We get repeatedly lost on our way to Crackers, the band arriving just before they're due on stage. They play for about 20 minutes in front of a crowd who are either heavily-anaesthetised or simply dead, which is also the state of the band who, once finished, collectively slump in a room not much bigger than a cupboard. KC's being helped out of the protective corset he's been wearing since an emergency appendectomy just before the tour started. He shows me his scars, still fresh.

"I have to wear the corset so I don't sorta flop out when I'm on stage," he explains, rather too vividly.

Maurice arrives rubbing his hands, a sound like chalk on cardboard. "Great show, boys, great show, everybody loved you," he says. "You might even get paid."

This gets him a look from everyone.

"Only joking," he cackles, "only joking." Why he says this twice, I don't know, since no one laughed the first time.

LEMMY

London, January 1975

Because I've got long hair when I join what used to be *Melody Maker* everyone assumes without asking that I must be a fan of Hawkwind, the popular space rockers. So I'm duly dispatched on a late January day to interview Lemmy, legendary bass player with the psychedelic warriors. He turns up at an office in the Harrow Road, a mess of warts, whiskers and loudly creaking leather. He's wearing a WW2 German helmet that's sprayed silver, which he promptly turns upside down on the table between us. Inside the helmet there's a bag full of amphetamine sulphate, which certainly catches my attention. He then produces a knife, and plunges it into the toot. With an astonishingly steady hand for someone who looks like he hasn't slept since before the earth cooled, he lifts the knife blade towards me, a miniature Matterhorn of sulphate at its end.

"Not too early for you, I hope," he says, and it isn't. Some days, it never is.

"Good man," Lemmy says, as I hoover up the speed.

Lemmy does an almighty nose-full himself, introducing obvious havoc to what I take to be his already unsettled chemobiological infrastructure.

"Just what the doctor ordered," he says, loosening his grip on the arms of the chair he's sitting in. I was beginning to wonder if he might be fired from it, as if from a cannon, at any moment.

"Care for another?" he asks, clearly at home among the merry twang of amphetamine mayhem. As ever, I am sacrificially sociable and Lemmy and I are now talking at once, and not necessarily to each other. After a while, he calls something of a halt to all this gibbering nonsense.

"Aren't you supposed to be interviewing me?" he asks, and he has a point.

Now that I'm listening to what he's telling me, he appears to be talking about the lethal possibilities of sound, the destructive potential of noise, its capacity for subjugation, the brainwashing of entire populations by sinister sonic manipulation.

"Sound," he's saying, "if used at the proper frequency, can render all your people – turn them, like – into *zombies*. Living dead. With no will of their own. You'll get, if you're a conquering power and you attack with sound, all the cheap slave labour you need. You could conquer a whole country, bring the population to heel, take over everything. And," he says with a flourish, "there'd be no cities to rebuild. Because there'd be no need to drop tons of bombs or blow everything up. You just sort of deafen everybody and they all go a bit fucking ga-ga, and you're in. Probably take about ten minutes," he goes on, "if that."

He gives me a conspiratorial wink.

"Keep it to yourself," he continues, "but the government's already been looking into this. They've got hundreds, literally *hundreds*, of speakers all over Neasden."

Neasden?

He nods, glancing around the room as if for evidence of surveillance, covert eavesdropping, cameras, bugs, Gene Hackman in a cupboard with a tape recorder, reels whirring, everything we say being taken down, to be held against us no doubt in some sinister tribunal, people without faces and voices like British Rail announcements condemning us to harrowing fates.

"Neasden," he says, with an air of finality that puts a perhaps welcome end to this topic of conversation. Lemmy moves on to fresh anecdotal pastures even as I'm wondering how on earth we ever got onto the subject of sonic distortion in Neasden in the first place. He's now telling me about The Rockin' Vicars, with whom he used to play in the mid-'60s.

"We played Yugoslavia, once," he says. "We were guests of honour at a dinner hosted by Tito."

I wonder what Lemmy and the Yugoslavian president and former partisan leader might have spent dinner talking about – Tito's political philosophy of "positive neutralism", perhaps, or profit sharing workers' councils, unrest in Bosnia-Herzegovina, demonstrations in Montenegro and Macedonia.

So, Lemmy, what did you say to the great man at the dinner?

"I said, 'Pass the fuckin' peas, Tito!'"

And what did Tito have to say by way of reply to this colourful request?

"He looked at me," Lemmy recalls, "and said, 'Call me Josip.' He was a great lad!"

At this, Lemmy starts to guffaw. The guffaw then takes on a life of its own and he starts to twitch, spasm and generally convulse. He's wheezing now, like something struggling for its life, not enough air in its lungs to keep going, a bone-rattling procedure that's followed by a phlegm-loosening bout of coughing that will surely have him turning first purple then pale in the arms of paramedics.

At about the same time, I'm suddenly aware of a hideous cackling laugh, like something you might find described in the stage directions of *Macbeth*. Worryingly, it's coming from me. Evidently, what started out as a somewhat meagre anecdotal scrap has turned into a finely-honed account of one of the century's most highly amusing encounters – a wry yarn, the telling of which would embarrass the practised humorous story-telling of comic titans like Woodhouse, Waugh and SJ Pearlman, people like that.

"'Pass the fuckin' peas, Tito,'" Lemmy says again, snatching at the words between explosive outbursts of uncontrollable mirth, and by now we are weak to the point of collapse.

"Let's go for a fuckin' drink," Lemmy now suggests, wiping tears from his eyes.

I tell him I can't.

"Why the fuck not?" he wants to know.

I have to get back to the office, I explain, where I am duly expected within the hour by kipper-tied editor Ray Coleman. After an unfortunate incident at the *Melody Maker* Christmas party, only weeks ago, during which I drunkenly fell over in the editor's office, gashing my head on his desk and then bleeding profusely all over his shag-pile carpet before being carried out on a stretcher to a waiting ambulance, I am under what they call a bit of a cloud. Ray is more explicit: until I exhibit a lot more sense than recklessness, I am officially "on probation". I'm not sure exactly what this means, and at least Ray has stopped short of having me electronically tagged, but probation sounds grim enough for me to take his serial warnings about my future conduct more seriously than in the recent past.

"Fair enough, mate," Lemmy says when I explain all this to him. "If you really have to get back to work, no bother, man. I don't want to twist your arm or get you into trouble. You've got responsibilities, things to do. If you've got to get back, you've got to get back. Shall I get someone to call you a cab?"

Maybe a quick one, then, I say, knowing I'll regret it.

"Absolutely," Lemmy grins. "Just a quick one, and we'll be on our way."

He leans over for the speed.

"One for the road?"

The next thing I remember, we're in a bar with a lot of people who are even more out of it than we are. Then it's dark outside, and there's talk of a party somewhere. After that, things get sort of hazy. The party takes on an epic momentum that carries me with it, all thought of getting back to the *MM* office long gone. In fact, by the time I get home, it's February.

JOHN MARTYN

Leeds, February 1975

A day that ends in mayhem starts pleasantly with lunch at the Savoy with Billy Swan, who's had a hit recently with a great record called 'I Can Help'. Over generous portions from the most expensive menu I've ever seen, washed down with a couple of bottles of wine that each cost more than I earn for a week's toil for *Melody Maker*, Billy tells me fantastic stories about growing up with rock 'n' roll in Cape Girardeau, Missouri, where he used to see Jerry Lee Lewis and Charlie Rich in local beer joints.

By the time we get to coffee and brandies, Billy's on a hilarious roll. He finishes with a flourish: a story about Phil Spector driving Billy, Kris Kristofferson and Carly Simon up to his Hollywood mansion and playing them rough mixes of John Lennon's *Imagine*, which Spector had just produced.

"I couldn't believe it," Billy says with a smile I can still remember. "I thought I'd died and gone to heaven."

There's still some brandy left in the bottle when I have to leave my lunch with Billy. I'm due in Leeds later today to interview John Martyn, who's meant to be recording a live album that night, at a show he's playing at the university. We get to Leeds around seven in the evening and drive onto the university campus, where someone helpful in a very short skirt shows us to Martyn's dressing room.

I knock on the door, provoking a great bellowing from inside. I push the door open and walk into the smallest dressing room I've ever seen, before or since. Martyn's slumped in a corner looking like he's been drinking since the dawn of time or slightly earlier.

"Who the fuck are you?" he wants to know, bubbles of spit in the corner of his mouth.

I start to tell him that I'm from *Melody Maker*, here to interview him, when some fucking oaf blindsides me, smashing me into a wall before trying to hang me from a coat hook.

"If you're Chris Welch, I'm going to fucking kill you," I am now being told. Turns out the bearded, balding maniac I'm staring in the eye is virtuoso bassist Danny Thompson, now playing with Martyn after years with folk super group Pentangle.

Danny's about to introduce his fist to my face when Martyn gets unsteadily to his feet and punches the bass player in the region of his kidneys. This makes Danny grunt, but doesn't put him off.

"Let him the fuck go," Martyn tells Thompson gruffly. "He's not the one you want."

Danny lets me go and retreats to the other side of the small unpleasant room, which I now realise is stocked with so much booze it looks like an off-license store room or a bootlegger's lock-up.

"Sorry about that," Martyn says then. "He thought you were someone else."

I can hear Thompson sort of growling, and decide on the spot that if the belligerent fucker comes near me I'm going to stick a finger in one of his eyes – I'm not fussed which one – and we'll see where we go from there. But who am I kidding? If he comes roaring at me again, he'll probably end up slapping me around the room until I weep for mercy. I give him a bit of a look anyway, just to keep him on his toes.

Martyn then claps me somewhat thunderously on the shoulder and offers me a drink, which I accept. No point holding grudges. I knock it back quickly before accepting another one.

I remind Martyn that I'm here to do an interview with him. He is struggling to process this information when the dressing room door flies open and this sort of scruffy fucking troll staggers in, swigging vigorously from a bottle of Crème de Menthe. This is former Free guitarist Paul Kossoff, who will apparently be playing tonight with Martyn, Thompson and drummer John Stevens.

"Who's this cunt?" Kossoff asks Martyn, pointing at me.

"He's from *Melody Maker*," Martyn tells Kossoff. "But he's not Chris Welch."

Kossoff looks at Martyn like he's being spoken to in a language he doesn't understand and heads back out the door. I'm still trying to get Martyn to sit down and talk when about 15 minutes later, the dwarf-like Kossoff returns, bleeding from the nose and lip and wailing like the recently bereaved.

"Fuck's going on now?" Martyn asks, which provokes a tale of considerable woe, Kossoff now telling us he's been set upon by homicidal students from whose clutches he has been lucky to escape still alive. Martyn's on his feet in a flash, Danny Thompson, too – the bassist snaps an arm off a chair, brandishing it like a club. Martyn's got a bottle he might break over someone's head.

"Show us these fuckers," Martyn tells Kossoff, who leads us out of the building, into the student's union bar.

"That's the one!" Kossoff now shouts, finger accusingly aimed at a skinny little twat, holding his girlfriend's hand like she's about to run off, and looking at us fearfully as we approach like he thinks he's going to be kidnapped by a death squad and driven off to a dank room in a remote location where terrible things will happen to him.

"He's the one that hit me," Kossoff fairly shrieks.

Martyn, moments ago ready for havoc, pauses now.

"He's not a fucking GANG," he says of the trembling student. "What's going on?"

Turns out Kossoff drunkenly groped this bloke's girlfriend and the bloke's given Kossoff a shove that's sent the guitarist tumbling down some steps. All talk of a gang attack is pathetic bollocks.

"You cunt," Martyn shouts at Kossoff, smacking him extremely hard in the face. The short-arsed former guitar hero is further surprised when Danny Thompson fetches him what I'm delighted to describe as a pretty painful thwack to the side of the head with the arm of the chair he snapped off in the dressing room.

This makes Kossoff cry, at which point Martyn and Thompson stalk off, laughing like people who are mad.

The general weirdness that attaches itself to Martyn like static follows him on to the stage. The music he plays with Thompson and John Stevens is often sublime. Even Kossoff makes a reasonable contribution. Martyn's patter between songs, however, is testing in the extreme. There's a lot of sniggering buffoonery, hysterical giggling and an extravagant amount of swearing. Martyn carries on conversations with himself in a variety of what you can only presume are meant to be comic voices culled from *The Goons* and *Monty Python* that leave you wondering how many people live in his fucking head. Back in the band's dressing room after the show, I'm sitting with Martyn, finally getting around to the interview, when Paul Kossoff walks up to Martyn and breaks a beer bottle over his head, glass shattering everywhere.

"Everybody OUT," Martyn screams, grabbing Kossoff in what looks like a near-fatal head-lock. "I'm going to give this cunt the kicking he's been asking for."

The room clears pretty sharpish at this point, and several of us stand in the corridor listening to Martyn and Kossoff go at it like rutting elks, the most alarming sounds of destruction and violent combat reaching us from the other side of the door – a symphony of bone-cracking, head-banging, furniture-breaking, glass-shattering detonations. This goes on for a while, then Martyn opens the door, blood all over the front of his shirt, holding Kossoff like laundry which he then drops to the floor and kicks.

"Shall we finish that fucking interview now?" Martyn asks me, and minutes later he's waxing lyrical about the influence of Davy Graham on his music, as if this sort of thing happens every night when he's on tour. Which it probably does.

DAVE BROCK

Devon, February 1975

In the time of which I'm writing, I seem to have become *Melody Maker's* unofficial Hawkwind correspondent, sent hither and yon on a fairly regular basis to cover the band. They're great blokes, though, and they always have great drugs. I'm therefore fairly uncomplaining when I'm dispatched to cover them. Today, I'm in Devon to talk to the band's Dave Brock, who lives on a ten-acre farm down here. As you join us, Dave's just invited me into his farmhouse, a dark and homely space. There are low beams, a fire aglow in a friendly hearth, and we sit at a large kitchen table while Dave talks me through Hawkwind's colourful history, rolling a joint as he goes. He's talking about the old days in Notting Hill when he passes the joint to me. I have a few tokes and nearly pass out. But Dave keeps talking and rolling joints, and the afternoon slips by rather pleasantly, at least up to the point when the Milawi Tripweed, or whatever it is we're smoking, has delivered us both to a state of somewhat stoned beffudlement. I'm feeling pretty fucked in other words, and Dave for his part looks like he couldn't remember his own name if you held a blowtorch to his trousers. We go, at Dave's suggestion, for a brief stroll around the farm. The sun is beginning to set beyond the rolling hills and a breeze picks up, a chill in the late afternoon air. I find myself taking deep breaths of the latter as soon as we're outside, in an attempt to clear my head that doesn't work. I am still stoned to the point of eerie somnambulism, with only some deeply-rooted native memory of a time when I could walk unaided without falling over, reminding me that it's by putting one foot in front of the other that I can get from here to what you might call there. Frankly, I feel like I'm underwater, and can't quite

41

work out why I'm not wet. Dave, meanwhile, is pointing at something in the distance and appears to be telling me about it, but I can't make out a word. I begin to drift, as if toward some light, probably the source of everything. Dave's now leaning against a wooden fence, with his back to a pasture where animals I can't put a name to are grazing in the last of the failing sun. I am now disturbed by something large and incredible moving slowly towards Dave, who's got his back to whatever beast of the field has stirred itself and is even now at Dave's shoulder. A lurking thing I'm fairly mesmerised by, but of whose presence Dave remains blissfully ignorant. I just wish I could remember what kind of animal it is. The aforementioned breeze is stronger now, and Dave's Viking locks are being borne, as it were, aloft – flaxen wisps, lifting on the wind. The beast notices this and with a flash of teeth as big, it seems to me, as tombstones takes what I am sure is a bite at them, actually missing Dave's wafting hair, but not by much. It snorts then, and stamps the ground with one of its four hoofed feet.

It's a *horse*! Thank God, I've been able to put a name to it! Anyway, this horse, a handsome fellow, is again snapping at Dave's hair. Dave continues telling me whatever it is he's telling me, still quite unaware, as far as I can tell, of the horse behind him (which takes another nip at his floating tresses). Uh-oh! Our equine pal now has a fair mouthful of Dave's lank locks between its teeth and is beginning to chew. Yes, the horse is *chewing Dave's hair*.

"What's that, man?" I can hear as if from a distance Dave asking me, vaguely quizzical, his mind apparently elsewhere – among the star fields of Orion, perhaps. Somewhere out there beyond the singular cusp of things, anyway, where the sweet winds blow. I make a flailing gesture, indicating I don't know what, in the general direction of the valiant Hawklord.

"What is it, man?" a little impatient this from Dave. "What?"

The horse is still chomping hungrily at Dave's hair.

I point again, willing myself to speak, but all I can manage is an incommunicative grunt while the horse still chews. I wave my arms like a castaway on a beach, trying to flag down a passing aircraft.

"What is it, man?" Dave asks a third time, still quite dreamily.

I find my voice suddenly, although it seems weirdly disconnected, as if I am talking to myself down a phone.

"Th-that horse," I'm telling him, Dave looking at me as if I am talking about things of which he has no knowledge – horses among other things being presumably scarce out there in Orion's star belt.

"Horse?" he says. "What horse?"

"Th-the one behind you!"

"The horse behind me?" Dave muses, clearly finding it difficult to come to terms with this unlikely event. "What's it doing?"

"*It-it's eating your hair!*"

Dave now glances over his shoulder and, yep, there's that pesky horse dining out on Dave's hair.

"Wow," he says. "It is."

There's a moment's silence as we think this over.

"Amazing," Dave says then.

And from where I'm barely standing, it is.

Joe Strummer

London, February 1975

In the film I'm watching that you can't see, Joe Strummer is 22 years old, duck-walking across the bare boards of something called The Charlie Pigdog Club, dressed in a baggy white suit and making more noise than the end of *The Wild Bunch*. The band playing behind him is an early version of the since-fabled 101'ers. There's about 10 of them – bass, guitars, four or five saxes, someone shaking maracas, future Clash collaborator Tymon Dogg on the fiddle. But it's Strummer you can't take your eyes off. He's amazing, even then, already on the road to legend, a myth in the making but right now tearing into a caterwauling version of Van Morrison's garage band classic, 'Gloria', The 101'ers on their way to the climax of a show that ends up with sirens, flashing lights and the local constabulary pulling the plug on the band while Strummer thrashes away on a battered guitar even as the lights come up, oblivious to everything but the noise he's making.

At this point in time, I haven't seen Joe for nearly two years. But imagine him for a moment the way I remember him at 20. Let's say, then, that it's early 1973, the start of my last term at art school in Newport, South Wales. Joe, who everyone knows then as Woody, has fetched up here after dropping out of London's Central School of Art. Around this time he's got a job digging graves for the council, or something like that, and is otherwise a regular in the college canteen and at the students' union building – a dilapidated place on Stow Hill, not far from where I'm living at the time with my girlfriend Kathy, who Woody asks to cut his hair. For as long as we've known him, Woody has sported an ungainly frizzy thatch that makes him look like the unnecessary additional percussionist in a tank-top-wearing white funk band. So Kathy gives Woody his first rockabilly haircut, a tonsorial improvement that makes him walk with a newly-affected tough guy swagger.

At the student's union, a regular bunch of us that sometimes includes Woody, usually gather on a Tuesday night to watch *The Old Grey Whistle Test* in an upstairs room where we sit on beer crates because there are no chairs and argue about the bands on the show. I have an opinion about everyone we see, not always complementary. I am, in other words, a lippy sod and people are often incensed by my more unreasonable ranting, especially when it's about groups who are favourites of theirs but not mine. Amazingly, in a little over a year from now, *Melody Maker* will actually be paying me for such opinions. Who could have seen *that* coming at the time or, rather more notably, the fact that Woody would go on to become who he did? Back then, he was just someone with a donkey jacket and a shovel, digging holes for the dead. Anyway, one night Woody drops by my digs with a bottle of vodka. He's keen, he says, to find out a bit more about some of the music I've been talking up so brashly. Ever the gobby evangelist, I pull out some records I think he should hear and start playing them. There's not a lot he immediately likes. I can't for instance get him to listen to The Velvet Underground at all, and he's not keen on The Stooges. I play him 'TV Eye' from *Funhouse* and he feigns acute distress, screwing up his face in an approximation of horror that makes me laugh out loud. He's similarly unimpressed by The MC5. He also hates glam, thinks Lou Reed is nothing more than a decadent slut, decides Roxy Music are the sequinned spawn of a shrieking she-devil—and the very mention of David Bowie makes him look like he's going to spew, although this could be the vodka, which we are drinking straight from the bottle and probably too quickly. I play him 'Watch That Man' from *Aladdin Sane*, which he grudgingly acknowledges actually rocks, but he's more comfortable still with *Exile on Main Street* and we play the first side over and over, no argument between us over the likes of 'Rocks Off', 'Shake Your Hips' (which he will one day cover with The 101'ers) and 'Tumbling Dice'. *Highway 61 Revisited* also gets a bit of a leathering, with 'Just Like Tom Thumb's Blues' a mutual favourite. We're on common ground, too, with Chuck Berry, Little

Richard and Jerry Lee, and he especially likes an album showcasing the blues harmonica-playing of Little Walter that I've recently found in a great second hand record shop where I used to spend a lot of time and money, a funky place at the top of Commercial Road, the gateway to an area of Newport called Pill, a place then of ill-repute, shall we say – rough pubs and drug dealers, that sort of thing.

There's a college band at the time called The Rip-Off Park All-Stars that Woody's keen to join, although as yet he can't play anything. They split up before he can, but are quickly reincarnated as The Vultures, with Woody on guitar and vocals. The Vultures are brash and noisy and still playing around Newport when I leave in the summer of 1973, moving to London and losing touch with Woody in the process. But by the end of 1974, he's also in London. He's done a little busking here and around Europe and now apparently he's got a band. By now, I'm working for *Melody Maker* and that's where he calls me one afternoon and asks if I'll come and see them. They're called The 101'ers, he says. They don't have much money, barely any equipment and they're not great musicians, he adds, as if this may count against them in the prevailing climate of hot-shot musical virtuosity – all those prog-rock symphonies, dry ice and wizards' capes, much admired at the time but shortly to be soundly discredited. I tell him I'm not much bothered with musical etiquette. If he can promise me noise and beer, I'll be there. He gives me the date of their next gig and tells me where they're playing. This turns out to be The Charlie Pigdog Club, a room above a pub called The Chippenham, on the corner of Malvern Road and Shirland Road in west London. It's not far from the squat some of the band share in Walterton Road, whose house number they are named after, which is, handily, close enough for them to push their gear to the pub in a pram. There's no sign of Woody when we get there, although the band have already set up their equipment, such as it is, and look like they're getting ready to play without him. Not long before they're due to start, he turns up. He's just been to see Chuck Berry at The Rainbow, and he's buzzing. Within a couple of minutes, he's worked the room – he seems to know everybody – and is plugging in a guitar that looks like it's been pulled out of a skip. He plugs in and there's a squall of feedback, but he counts them in and The 101'ers are off. They open, as they will always seem to open, with rock 'n' roll chestnut 'Bony Moronie', played with untutored ferocity. What follows is crude, loud and technically deficient, I suppose, in many ways. But unforgettable in the ways that matter most. Their set is mainly covers of rock 'n' roll and R&B standards, the staple repertoire of what, back then, is known as pub rock, the prime exponents of which, of course, are Dr Feelgood. I think they're fantastic and after the show they drive me home to south London in a hearse, which seems impossibly cool.

There are lots of other great nights with The 101'ers after this, most of them at The Elgin, a pub just south of the Westway in Ladbroke Grove, where they start a Thursday residency in July that runs until the following January, their epic two-and-a-half hour sets quickly becoming the stuff of local legend, with a small but loyal following gathering around them. It's in the bar of The Elgin in July that I interview them for *Melody Maker*, after months of pleading with the paper's senior editors for some space on the band, and at a time when it's difficult to get written about in *MM* if you aren't some pompous prog-rocker with dry ice for brains. So we sit around a table down there at The Elgin. Mickey Foote, another friend of Woody's from Newport, who does the sound for The 101'ers as he will later do for The Clash (whose first album he ends up producing), is at the bar, arguing with the landlord and another local band, Lipstick. Seems there's been a double booking and they're expecting to play. Mickey's having none of it.

"Look," he says, "what are you doing on Monday? Nothing? Right, you play on fucking Monday, then. Or do you want to take this outside?"

The dispute settled, The 101'ers, by now a four-piece, introduce themselves: on drums, Richard "Snakehips" Dudanski; bass player The Mole; guitarist "Evil" Clive Timperly; and on guitar and vocals... here Woody pauses, not sure what to call himself for his debut in the music press, evidently a significant moment for him. He gets out a scrap of paper with some names, four, maybe five of them, written on it.

"Pick one," he says.

I wish I could remember what the choices were, but I can't, although I'm pretty sure among them is Johnny Caramello, which Joe had briefly called himself. But only one name leaps out from the list, the one Woody's been going by for a while: JOE STRUMMER.

It seems perfect and it's what the world will know him as in the years to come.

"OK," he says. "Done."

For the next six months, The 101'ers play everywhere that will have them: pubs, clubs, benefits, free festivals. But there's negligible record company interest, which is frustrating for everyone, especially Joe, who's starting to think The 101'ers are going nowhere in a hurry.

And then they're thrown a lifeline.

I've just moved into a flat on Riffle Road, Willesden, which would make it March, 1976. That hammering you heard an hour ago? That was Joe, who's turned up hotfoot from wherever, banging on my front door, making an enormous racket, bugles and drums the only things missing from what otherwise sounds like the noisy announcement of an army arriving to lift the siege of a beleaguered garrison. His mood, you could say, is urgent.

"I've got something to play you," he says, following me up the stairs to the mildewed untidiness of the rooms I've recently rented, unpacked boxes everywhere, full of records and books, wallpaper yellow with age, no furniture to speak of.

"Have you got something to play this on?" he asks, producing from a pocket a C60 cassette with a bright orange label. Not much later, we're listening to the familiar wallop of 'Keys to Your Heart', one of the original songs, mostly written by Joe, that have become regular highlights of 101'ers sets. The version we're listening to has been recorded for the fledgling independent label, Chiswick, which, Joe confirms almost unbelievingly, want to put it out as a single. He looks electrified at the very thought, as if he's never had better news to tell anyone. We play the tape nonstop for about an hour, awash with excitement. Later, down the pub, Joe's still lit up. This is a moment of vindication, after all – the pay-off for nigh-on two years of breathtaking slog, The 101'ers perhaps on the verge of something you could call a breakthrough, a chance to be heard by a wider audience than the one that's so far barely sustained them. Back in the Riffle Road flat, 'Keys to Your Heart' playing over and over, this is what Joe talks about, an unwritten future for The 101'ers taking shape in his imagination. Neither of us know then that by the time 'Keys to Your Heart' comes out in May, Joe will have left the band and The 101'ers' story will be almost over.

Things change dramatically for Joe when he sees The Sex Pistols, who support The 101'ers on April 3rd and 23rd at The Nashville Rooms. What looks like a blatantly put-up scrap at the second gig ends up with the Pistols and manager Malcolm McLaren in mid-brawl on the cover of *Melody Maker*, with no mention of The 101'ers. I'm standing at the bar with Joe, Clive Timperley and Dr Feelgood's Lee Brilleaux when the Pistols appear the first night. None of us really get what's happening, apart from Joe, who looks like he's seen something he desperately wants to be part of, which is punk. The next thing you know he's joined The Clash, the band that will turn him into a legend. Joe's loyalty to The 101'ers simply tested by the ferocity of his ambition in a contest that was only going to have one winner.

The next time I see Joe it's July, when we fetch up separately for a gig at the Royal College of Art. Joe, his hair newly blond and reduced to not much more than Aryan stubble, sees me through a crowd of people and hurries out of sight with head-down urgency. There's a bar set up outdoors in a kind of courtyard or garden, which is where I'm standing a little later when Joe, as if he's been beamed down from a passing star-ship, suddenly appears next to me. He seems unusually lost for words.

"It all happened real fast," he says finally, not looking at me and acting like it would be better for both of us not to be seen together.

"I wanted to let you know what was happening," he goes on. "But I was told not to talk to you. I didn't know what to do. Everything's real different now."

I'm wondering who Joe's taking orders from these days when on cue we're rudely interrupted by a pugnacious little dude in a leather jacket and brothel creepers. This is Bernie Rhodes, manager of the fledgling Clash, although it's quickly clear he's missed his true vocation as, I don't know, supreme leader of North Korea or some other dismal outpost of totalitarian oppression we're told must be ruled with what's called an iron fist. I dislike him on sight, but not as he seems to think for luring Joe away from The 101'ers. Things have lately been changing fast, punk's looming if not already here. The 101'ers and the bands they've shared the pub rock circuit with are now apparently out of date, about to be left behind, made redundant by a brutal new noise. The ship Joe's just jumped is in other words already sinking, so good luck to him. What rankles, though, is now being lectured by the windbag Rhodes, who sounds like he's making an accusatory speech in front of a people's tribunal, me in the dock for being a part of Joe's past Bernie demands no further reference to, The 101'ers a crap pub rock band Joe is well rid of, and in Bernie's emerging version was never really part of. Bernie's revisionism seems to have no known limit, the past for him only there to be re-written, with Joe a surprisingly meek witness to Bernie's tantrum, standing with his hands in his trouser pockets, head down, listening to Bernie pour scorn on his former band as he effectively writes them out of Joe's history.

"If I haven't made myself clear," Bernie says, his hot breath in my face, "let me say it again. The 101'ers, they never existed, right? Give it a month and no one will even remember them." He turns to Joe.

"Let's go," he says, stalking off with Joe trotting behind him, like something with four legs and a tail that sooner or later Bernie's going to have to get a license for.

Long after all this and with Strummer five-years dead, I find myself in Ladbroke Grove one night, for the first time in decades. At The Elgin, where in 1975 The 101'ers had their residency. I stand outside for a moment before going in, curious to see how much it's changed since those legendary nights. The old flock wallpaper is long gone, of course, and there are a couple of pool tables where there used to be a small stage. Thanks to some convenient kink in the time-space continuum, I can now see, as if it's really happening, The 101'ers in a typically manic huddle, Dudanski behind a battered old drum kit, Mole on bass, Clive on guitar and Strummer, his leg pumping like something with a life of its own, belting out 'Keys to Your Heart' and blowing the roof off the place as 'Gloria' races to a ferocious climax.

Sitting there with these memories making my head spin, I hear a kind of staticky crackle, something distant but growing louder. It takes me a moment to realise what it is, at which point I have to smile, happy to have been here when the joint was jumping and Joe and The 101'ers were rocking.

It's the sound of London calling from a far-away time.

WAYNE NUTT

Aberdeen, March 1975

The next thing I know, he's twisted my scarf around my neck, lifted me off my feet, hung me over his shoulder and is now threatening to drag me out of the pub and into the street, where he intends to string me up from the nearest lamp post, all for an unflattering review of his album that's appeared the week before in *Melody Maker*, but which I haven't written. I try to tell him this, but the scarf around my neck is choking me and I can't for the moment speak, so just kick my legs, wriggle a bit and make odd guttural noises.

"Son of a *bitch*," he says in a malignant drawl. "Shut th' fuck up and prepare to die like a dog."

"Leave it out, Wayne," someone's telling him now. "Stop fucking about."

This is photographer Tom Sheehan, stepping bravely into the fray, a gallant intervention since Tom and I have only just met.

"He didn't write the fucking review," Tom tells Wayne. "Put him down."

Wayne lets go of the scarf. I drop to the floor, gasping for breath. He looks down at me, prods me with the toe of his boot and spits.

"Y'all were damn near dead and gone to hell," he is keen to let me know, the unforgiving menace in his voice sounding well-practised.

With another painful prod in my side with the toe of his boot, Wayne stalks off, blowing through the pub doors like one of the furies of ancient legend.

"On your feet, Welsh," Sheehan says, holding out a hand. "Bar's over 'ere."

Sheehan goes on to become a legendary rock lensman, working as chief photographer for *Melody Maker* for many colourful years – with a lot of them spent bailing me out of one spot of bother or another. Right now, he's a staff photographer for CBS Records, here to take some press shots of one of the label's new signings, the appropriately-named Wayne Nutt, the fellow who's just tried to throttle me. Wayne's an American oilman, who until becoming a professional country singer and signing recently to CBS was working on the off-shore rigs up here. Now he's got an album out, called *Oil Field Man*.

It's terrible, of course, which is basically all *Melody Maker* has to say about it, clearly riling Wayne as a result. But he seems a colourful sort and when the chance comes up to meet him in Scotland, where he's touring with country veteran Slim Whitman, I grab it and go, flying up to Aberdeen with a contingent from CBS that includes Sheehan and Roseanne Cash, daughter of Johnny and later a country star herself but currently working in some menial capacity as an intern in the CBS press office. When I meet them in the bar of Aberdeen's Imperial Hotel the night after our initial skirmish with Wayne, Sheehan and Roseanne are already drunk and Tom's just convinced her that corgis are the national dish of Scotland, which she's right now trying to order from a waiter whose confusion couldn't be more apparent if his head was on fire.

Not long after this, Wayne appears.

After finally being convinced the previous night that I really hadn't written the *MM* review that had so enraged him, Wayne invites me and Sheehan to his dressing room for a drink, by way of apology. He's got a cask of some ancient whiskey, 200 per cent proof, or something, probably moonshine, I don't know. Whatever, he tells us it's of some priceless vintage, every drop to be savoured, taken neat or not at all. Even as he's telling us this with a nasty little look in his eyes, I can see Sheehan busily pouring Coke into his whiskey and looking for ice to add to it. This doesn't go down well with Wayne, who frankly looks like he's going to shit.

"What th' *fuck*, boy," he asks, horrified, "d'yall think you're doing? Get th' fuck outta here before I shoot you between the legs."

Sheehan retreats to a far corner of the dressing room, muttering something about dark spirits and voodoo. Wayne re-fills my glass and raises his own in a toast.

"Here's to it and from it and to doin' it again and if you get to it to do it and if you don't you'll never get to it to do it again," he says, laughing, me joining in.

"Now *you* say it," he says, but I can't, which makes him laugh even more, a mirthless evil gurgle. "Y'all realise you gotta keep drinkin' till you say it right, yeah?" he asks, pouring another large one, settling in for the night or however long it's going to take me to master the tongue-twisting toast, which I finally do, miraculously without keeling over like a rummy at the wrong end of a three-day bender.

Anyway, here we are in the bar of the Imperial Hotel. Sheehan and Roseanne have scarpered. Wayne's telling me about his life, which turns out to be as colourful as imagined. He was born in 1940, in Comanche, Oklahoma. His father – immortalised on Wayne's album in a song called "The Ballad of Wendell Nutt" – was racing across Oklahoma with Wayne's mother in labour in the back seat of their car, heading for the state line, so that Wayne could be born across the border in Texas.

"He didn't make it," Wayne says. Clearly a bit of a sore point, this. "But it don't mean a damn thing. I'm still a Texan and no one's ever gonna tell me no different. Don't mean a bean wherever the hell I was born, I'm a *Texan.*"

As if somehow to prove this, Wayne is full of anecdotes about bar-room brawls, assaults on total strangers who have unwittingly provoked him, and what he calls "knockdown drag-outs just for the pure hellish fun of it".

This is Wayne on what's so great about fighting:

"A good fight," he says, "is as good as a good drink. Ain't nothing like fighting just for the fun of it. The... the *manly* thing of it. *You* should try it some time," he says, punching me on the arm hard enough to numb it from shoulder to fingertips.

"The worst beating I ever got was in Houston," he goes on, positively misty-eyed at the memory. "The Polka Dot Lounge. Three ol' boys got to mouthing off and I thought, 'Hell, there's only *three* of 'em.' So I jumped 'em and they proceeded to kick the living hell outta me. I was in hospital for four days. But what the hell? It was a good fight."

In Wayne's world, you clearly don't back down and if you go down, you go down fighting.

53

"It's a live-and-let-live world," he opines sagely. "I've got my little corner of it and you've got yours. And I'm not gonna try to get into your corner, and you *damn well* better not try to get into mine."

And now he's telling me how much he hates New York.

"Never seen such a place. The people are *idiots*. Damn Yankee idiots. I had six fights on my first day there and I won 'em all, by God. The people were just rude and intolerant. Don't have time for no one. Don't talk polite at all. Hell, where I come from, you talk to a man like that, he's gonna knock your damn head off. That's what I did. I knocked heads off.

"I stayed at the Barclay Hotel. Rented a suite. I'd just got in from Trinidad with a pocketful of money and looking for a good time. I stayed in New York a day and a half. Fought my way from one end of Manhattan to the other. I've only been back once. Three years ago. And I got into it all again. At the airport. Trying to get some tickets to fly to Nigeria. I knew they were there. I told the guy at the counter who I was and politely asked him for my tickets. He said he didn't have any in my name. He didn't even *look*. And I could *see* the damn tickets. They were there, with *my* name on the envelope.

"I told him he was making a bad mistake. And he said..." Wayne gets very grave at this point. "He said, '*Go away, Texas trash.*' I just looked at him in total surprise for a second. You know what I did then?"

I couldn't possibly imagine, but I'm guessing it didn't end well for the fellow.

"Damn right," Wayne says. "I grabbed his tie, dragged him over the counter and stomped his guts into the ground."

Wayne's still laughing at this a couple of nights later at his house in Dunblane, where he hosts a party for the support bands on the Slim Whitman tour. There's a dog at his feet that looks every bit as mean as he does, a cross-bred Alsatian-Husky thing. Its name is Rebel.

"He might look docile now," Wayne says, although this is not how I would have described the vicious-looking mutt. "But when he's angry even I wouldn't tangle with ol' Reb. If he's after you, then your soul may belong to God, but your *ass* belongs to Reb."

Wayne chuckles heartily at this and knocks back another large one.

"Anyone want to hear a nigra joke?" he asks then, rubbing Reb's big head and looking baffled when the room clears like someone's just lobbed a grenade through the window. Reb is his only audience now.

MICK RONSON

Newcastle, April 1975

A couple of hours ago, the imaginatively-titled Hunter-Ronson band – recently formed from the ashes of Mott The Hoople – played one of the first shows of a British tour, at Newcastle City Hall. Now, back at the Newcastle Holiday Inn, here comes Mick Ronson, stepping out of a cubicle in the hotel's ground floor men's room, just off the bar where the rest of the band, their entourage and a bunch of music journalists who've come up from London for the gig are getting drunk. Zipping up his flies, Mick gives himself a quick once-over in the mirror, and gives me a bit of a laddish, keep-it-to-yourself grin. There's a bit of a commotion then, when a buxom young woman comes out of the stall behind Ronson. I can't begin to imagine what they've been doing in there together, but I will say this: on her way back out to the bar, the buxom young woman pauses at a sink and spits out a gob of something that smacks against the porcelain with a wettish thud. She then gives her mouth a quick rinse, her hair a quick brush and without further ado flounces out the door.

"Right," says Ronson. "You ready to do the interview now?"

I am, and about 15 minutes later we're in Mick's room, me on a chair by the side of the bed, Mick on the bed itself, flat on his back. I'm chatting away breezily about the first time I saw Mick on stage with David Bowie, at the Colston Hall, Bristol, one of the first shows of the Ziggy Stardust tour – "Hello, Bristol! I'm David Bowie. These are The Spiders from Mars. Let's rock!" – when I notice that Mick's gone a bit quiet. Further investigation reveals that he is in fact asleep.

I sit there for a while, wondering what to do. I sit there for a while longer after that. By now, Mick's snoring. I'm flummoxed. What should I do? I'm still contemplating this when Mick suddenly sits bolt upright, scaring both of us.

"I wasn't sleeping," he says, though you could have fooled me. "I was thinking."

About what?

"David," he says, a little huskily. Bowie, of course, had dumped him brutally and without undue explanation after they had worked together so closely on *The Man Who Sold the World*, *Hunky Dory*, *Ziggy* and *Aladdin Sane*, the success of these records being in no small part due to Ronson's talents as a guitarist, band leader and arranger.

What was it about David you were thinking?

"How exciting it was, meeting him for the first time. He was so sharp, so full of ideas. I really dug him."

Did he dig you?

"Don't know," Mick says, more than a tad forlorn. "He never told me. I think he must have, though. Of course, he must have." He goes a bit quiet again now, me wondering what's brought all this brooding on.

"There were times, though," Mick goes on, darkly, "when I hated him and he hated me. There were times, when we were together, when I thought he was such a fuckin' prat. But that would pass and then Dave'd be fine again and I'd think he were a champion lad. You know," he continues, looking for something on the bed he can't find, "even when I couldn't stand him, I were glad we were together. I wish we were together now, in a way…"

His voice trails off, into a glum little silence.

"I just wish Dave would get himself sorted fuckin' out," Ronson says then, a blunt angry edge to his voice that wasn't there before. "He's just totally fuckin' confused, that lad. I know he is. What he really needs is some good friends around him. I'll tell you this, Allan," Mick tells me. "David Bowie doesn't have a friend in the world. Not one good friend.

"He needs someone round him to say, 'Fuck off, Dave, you're fuckin' stupid.' He needs one person at least who won't bow down to him. That's his bloody problem. He believes everybody has to say, 'Yes, sir,' whenever he says something. He doesn't need people like that. If there's no one to tell him he's wrong, he'll just continue to believe he's right all the time. He needs *someone*," Mick says thickly, something catching in his throat. "He needs someone so badly, so very badly. And I really wish he was here right now so that I could tell him that.

"He's such a great kid, and it's such a fuckin' shame he's got so fuckin' messed up. All those people he's got around him now, I think they're all just wankers. Most of 'em have stuck by him, because he's the provider. He's literally paid for all their food, he's paid for their cab fares and their clothes. He's even bought their fuckin' cigarettes. That's been his downfall. And I just wish he could be in this room *right now*, sat here, so I could kick some sense into him."

There's a knock on the door. It's room service with wine we haven't ordered but drink anyway.

"He's an amazing bloke, though, Dave," Mick goes on, no budging him from the subject of Bowie and their squandered relationship. "Even though he could be the biggest prat in the world. You know, he could be your biggest friend one minute, or for two weeks, then suddenly you might be with him in front of 100 people and he'd just put you down. Make you feel such a fuckin' fool. And you'd think, 'I could fuckin' stab you for that.' He's done it to me lots of times. But you can't help but like him, for all that… we should never have stopped playing. We should never have stopped." Mick remembers being told about Bowie's imminent "retirement" – famously announced from the stage of the Hammersmith Odeon – not long before the gig, the splitting up of The Spiders from Mars being explained to him by Bowie and manager Tony DeFries as part of The Master Plan.

"The fuckin' Master Plan," Ronson groans in disbelief. "I never believed in that. It might have seemed great as an idea, but, fuck. Those plans never work.

"I remember the first Ziggy tour, he was so happy then. He loved it all and we were having the time of our lives. And it got knocked on the head. It was such a fuckin' shame. America affected the band so badly. On whatever level you want to talk about. I'm talking about the feeling within the band, about money, and the position of people in the band. It was a bad feeling.

"I'm going to be over there in two weeks," Mick says, suddenly resolute. "And I'm going to see Dave as soon as I get there."

And what will you say to him?

"I'm going," Mick says, "to get hold of him and smack him across the head, right across the earhole, and try to drum a bit of sense into him."

Ronson carries on like this for an hour and longer, finally falling asleep again, exhausted.

When he wakes up, I'm on the train back to London and not long after that Mick's in America with Ian Hunter, The Hunter-Ronson band starting a tour that's cancelled after a few shows because no one turns up to see them. By November, they've split. For a moment, it looks like Mick's career is washed up, talk of another solo album convincing no one it's a good idea. And then, to much speechless astonishment, there's a picture in *Melody Maker* of Ronson on stage in Springfield, Massachusetts. He's kind of lurking in the background, surrounded by some familiar faces. Among them: Roger McGuinn, Joan Baez, Ramblin' Jack Elliott and Bob Dylan. Mick, to the amazement of everyone I know, has somehow ended up playing guitar in Dyan's Rolling Thunder Revue. I've barely recovered from this information when I get a call from former Bowie plugger and mutual friend, Anya Wilson. Mick's in London, she tells me, and would like to meet up for a drink. I'm in a cab in one minute, and heading for West Kensington, where I find Mick in a happy mood, as straight-talking as ever and a pleasure to be with.

We get what happened to The Hunter-Ronson Band out of the way first.

"Basically," he says, "Ian's afraid of doing anything if he thinks he's going to lose money. I'm a bit more of a gambler."

And Bowie? Had Ronson followed up on his promise to seek out Bowie as soon as he got to America and belt him around the head? Did he even get in touch?

"I didn't bother," he says. "I didn't think it was worth it. I didn't really feel like listening to him making a lot of excuses. I didn't see the point."

What I really want to know, of course, is how the former Spider from Mars guitarist ended up as part of the Rolling Thunder tour.

Turns out that after splitting with Hunter, Ronson had started hanging out in Greenwich Village, where he fell in with Dylan consiglieri Bobby Neuwirth and made friends with a lot of local musicians – Rob Stoner, T-Bone Burnett, David Mansfield, Steve Soles – many of whom Dylan would soon recruit for his bicentennial tour. One night, Mick was in the Other End in the Village, where he bumped into Neuwirth, who invited him for a drink.

"He was with this guy," Ronson remembers. "I looked at this bloke he was with and thought, 'Hang on a minute, I *know* you.' And, of course, it was Dylan. We were chatting and he said, 'We're going on the road, why don't you come with us?' I just said, 'Yeah.' I thought it was a joke. I didn't think I'd hear anything more about it. Then Dylan phoned me, said the tour was going to happen. This was a Friday. He said rehearsals were due to start on Sunday and would I be there? I still thought it were a fucking hoax. I really didn't think he was serious."

On the first day of rehearsals, according to a shocked Ronson, Dylan ran the band through 150 songs. The next day, they ran through another 100.

"I was fucking gobsmacked," Mick laughs. "I'd never heard half of these numbers. And, at first, I was completely baffled by all of them. Really baffled and confused. Everyone else was already familiar with these songs and with each other and the way they played. I had a real problem fitting in, and I kept thinking I was terrible. I wasn't comfortable at all. But Dylan, Neuwirth, Stoner and T-Bone, they were all wonderful, really took a bit of time with me. And as we went on, I really grew into the music."

Most of the time, Neuwirth and Stoner ran the rehearsals. So what was Dylan doing?

"He was just… *there*," Mick says. "He'd play what he wanted to play. He'd come in and do his numbers. He did what he had to do and he did it well and quickly. He maybe wouldn't get too involved otherwise. I mean, he wasn't pulling any big star trip. He doesn't have to. He doesn't even have to say anything. With Bob, you just *know*. If there was something he was looking for in a song, you'd try to find it without being told. And that's the thing about Dylan. I'd follow him anywhere, no questions asked. That whole tour was this huge, huge adventure. A real treasure hunt. There was Joan Baez, McGuinn,

Ginsberg – he's a grand lad, is Allen. There was Dylan. And there I was, too. For a lad from Yorkshire like meself, it were truly out of this world."

He gets a bit misty-eyed here for a moment, thinking about it all.

"There'll be nowt like it again," he says then. "Fucking *nowt*."

ALEX HARVEY

Glasgow, September 1975

The last of September's rain sweeps across Glasgow's ruined face, driven by a bitter wind and watched by Alex Harvey from the window of a room on the ninth floor of the Albany Hotel. The city he grew up in is somewhere out there in the drizzle and murk. What's left of it, anyway. Alex stands there for a long time, staring at the growing dark and the slanting rain, putting names to the teeming ghettoes of his youth that are disappearing now, if not already gone.

"The Gorbals. Govan. Anderston. Kinning Park. Castlekilk. Paradise on fucking earth. Fucking fairyland. What the fuck happened here? Where did it all fucking go?"

Alex is still asking the same question the next day when we fetch up in Thistle Street, in the Gorbals – in its time one of the most notorious slums in the world, a place of poverty, unemployment, crime and violence, ruled by gangs. This is where Alex was born and for 17 years lived with his mother, father and brother, Leslie, in a single end, a one-room apartment in a tenement building, thousands like them packed into similar rooms across this grim estate. He's standing now, in the cold Glasgow afternoon, on the site of his former home. Not much of the world Alex used to know is still standing, rather long reduced to rubble, surrendered to the wrecking ball and demolition crews.

"Jesus Christ," he says, looking around him. "Where do you think it's all fucking gone?"

He wanders further down the street, awash with memories.

"There was a woman, lived along here, had a goat," he remembers. "There was a Sunday school on that corner. We used to sing there. *'My cup runneth over.'* Too fucking right. God didn't have much of a

61

fucking chance up here. There were hundreds of people lived in this street. And there were lines of demarcation. If you didn't live here, you weren't welcome. It was *our* territory, and you didnae fuck wi' us. There was a stable here somewhere," he says, moving on. "There was this big hole. We used to drop bread into it, that horrible fucking hole, and the rats would come out for the bread and we'd drop bricks on the little bastards and squash them tae fuck.

"Come over here," he says then. "See this wall?" He's looking for something now. "There used to be a bullet hole... Aye, fuck, it's still fucking there. Will ye look at that?"

Standing there in Thistle Street in the rain, he's suddenly reminded of something else.

"Over there," he says, pointing to some desolate waste ground. "There was a terrible incident. Some kids got two police dogs, cut their heads off and pinned them to a wall with bayonets."

There's a bit more left of Govan near the shipyards on the Clyde, even though entire streets have vanished – or, as Alex says, it's like something has reached down from the sky and ripped them out of the ground. We find a pub on a street corner that looks like someone's front room – a couple of old ladies in headscarves in a corner, two or three men bent over the bar, heads down, one of them with a dog asleep at his feet. The place has the drowsy feel of somewhere days repeat themselves, endlessly and without change. No one even looks at us when we walk in, as if they know we won't be there long and will never come back when we go.

The Sensational Alex Harvey Band, in these mostly grisly pre-punk years, are just about the most exciting band in the country – briefly popular enough for *Melody Maker* to agree after weeks of strident lobbying to send me to Glasgow with Alex to write a profile on him and his home town. This makes for a colourful week. I follow him around many old haunts, meet extraordinary people from his past, listen to astonishing stories and spend a lot of time in pubs like this one in Govan, where Alex, back from the bar with a tray of drinks, is moved to recall the German bombing of Glasgow during the war.

"Clydebank got hammered," he says. "Flattened. Fucking decimated. The great Luftwaffe came down looking for the docks with their bombs. They kept missing the docks and bombed the houses.

I was six. I can remember people in the streets, weeping and crying. You'd start missing people. They just wouldn't be there anymore. A lot of kids got it. If you were in a tenement, you burned. There was no escape."

After a few more drinks, he starts reminiscing about his grandfather, a conscientious objector during the First World War, who was imprisoned along with veteran Labour politician Manny Shinwell and John Kerr, later Provost of Glasgow.

"The military took him," he says. "They smashed his teeth in. During the winter they hosed him down in his cell with cold water, threw him a uniform. If he'd put the uniform on, they would have stopped. When he refused, they just carried on doing what they were doing to him."

When it came time for Alex's own National Service, he refused to go.

"They tried to take me into the army, but I wasnae going to fight any wars for the fucking English. They put me in the booby for a while. I couldn't say I was a conscientious objector. I wouldn't have convinced them or me that I was a fucking pacifist. They put me in front of a tribunal to assess my suitability for the army. They said, 'Imagine you're on the street and a band of armed men come up to you and threaten you. What would you do?' I thought they were fucking joking. *What would I do?* I said, 'Look. I've lived in the fucking Gorbals all my fucking life and I've *seen* armed men threatening people on the fucking streets. I don't have to fucking *imagine* it. And I know what I'd fucking do if they threatened me. But I'm still not going to fight in your fucking army.

"Those cunts were trying to convince me that it would be great to be one of those armed men. To join their gang, their team, and go into someone else's country and fuck up their streets. I'd been brought up in a single end in a tenement. Me and my old man and my mother and brother. And these people come along and say, 'Fight for your country!' In this place I lived, there were rats crawling through the walls. Fight for that? For Christ's sake, what were they talking about? I couldn't have cared less if the fucking Germans had come and taken the Gorbals. They could have taken it any time they liked. They were fucking welcome to it. I mean, I hold no brief for Hitler. He was a monster who should have been smothered at birth. But I wasnae going to fight in the fucking army to protect

63

the fucking Gorbals. This was a place where 100 kids had to use the same shithouse. Where entire families were crammed into one fucking room with a picture of the Queen on the wall where the rats were crawling. It was like an outpost of the fucking Empire. They wanted us to join the army to protect our country. Well, *that* was our fucking country. Rats and tenements. And no fucker was protecting *us* from *that*."

There's a pub in the Gorbals Alex is later keen to visit, a kind of subterranean shebeen, a dark funky place, basically a cellar, low-ceilinged, with a large central space and many scattered alcoves. In one, two of Alex's oldest friends are waiting for us – General Grimes, a swashbuckling character in a rakishly-sported beret who played bass many years ago in Alex's Big Soul Band, a hot ticket in their day, and Joe McCourtney, a former clubland big-shot who now manages the Scottish singer Frankie Miller. Grimes and Alex are soon bantering about old times, McCourtney chipping in with a few usually hair-raising stories of his own. After an uproarious hour or two, we're joined by someone known to Grimes and McCourtney who Alex can't immediately place. They're introduced and Alex smiles. He knows who he is now.

"Ach," he says. "The *Dirty Dozen* man."

The Dirty Dozen man? What's all this about?

Turns out we're talking to a feller named Tom Busby, who in a former life was a Hollywood actor with roles in Steve McQueen's *The War Lover* and, rather more notably, Robert Aldritch's savagely cynical 1967 war movie, *The Dirty Dozen* – as much of a highlight of the Summer of Love for me as *Forever Changes* or *The Piper at the Gates of Dawn*. This all seems somewhat unlikely, if not entirely far-fetched. But here's Busby soon chatting about his *Dirty Dozen* co-stars, Lee Marvin, Ernest Borgnine, Charles Bronson, Telly Savalas and his friend, John Cassavetes, who got Busby the part of Milo Vladek, one of the first of the Dozen to die. So how on earth did Busby end up in Glasgow?

It's a complicated story. In those days, Cassavetes was in reasonable Hollywood demand for his nuanced villainy and tough guy sneer. But his real obsession was directing his own independent films – pioneering stuff like *Shadows, Faces* and *Husbands*. Financing these films was always a problem and Cassavetes – often desperate – recklessly didn't care where the money came from. In the story Busby tells, he was pressed by Cassavetes into acting as go-between in a deal Cassavetes cooked up with some New York Mafia-types who fancied themselves as movie producers and had agreed to bankroll Cassavete's new film. When Cassavetes spent all their money without actually making the film, events took an unpleasant turn, the mobsters making the kind of threats Busby had no reason not to take seriously. He went into hiding, waiting for things to blow over. When they didn't, he went on the run, eventually settling in Glasgow, where he works now as a photographer. Did he think that after all this time the Mafia boys were still looking for him?

"You see *The Godfather?*" he asks, and I suppose he has a point, revenge served cold and all that. Apart from the acting bit, I'm not sure how much of Busby's practised hustle to believe, but anyway here's Joe McCourtney demanding our attention, Joe's meaty hand giving the table a rather huge thump to emphasise some point he's been making to Grimes and Alex about their shared pasts, which I now ask about.

"The things we've seen," he says, nodding first at General Grimes then Alex, "Jesus, you wouldn't want to know," he says, before going on anyway to describe in awful detail what happened to one of the security team at a club he used to run.

"Do you remember the boy, Alex?"

Alex nods gravely. Grimes looks grim. Busby seems to have slipped away. McCourtney describes how, after an incident at Joe's club, the boy in question became a target for a rival gang, team, firm—whatever these psychopaths call themselves. They came to Joe's place one night, looking for the boy, trapped him in a stairwell and set about him with a variety of hammers, knives and hatchets.

"They completely destroyed him. It was the most terrible thing I've ever seen," Joe says, an understandably sombre mood descending as we ponder such violence, a young life brought prematurely to a brutal end in a flurry of hacking and stabbing. A silence prevails between us, broken suddenly by General Grimes.

"I need a fucking drink," he announces. "Alex, is it your fucking round or mine?"

Many drinks later, we're in a mini-cab, driving through the Gorbals. Alex and General Grimes are in the back. Alex is thrashing away drunkenly at a huge banjo. The General's having a few problems with his 12-string acoustic. They're singing some old rebel song and making a lot of noise, when Alex notices where we are.

"There goes fucking Thistle Street," he shouts. "See that corner? I had my hand slashed open there once, by a guy wi' a razor."

Then, suddenly very angry, Alex winds down the window on his side of the cab, sticks out his head and starts screaming into the night.

"Fuck Thistle Street!" he roars. "Fuck the fucking Gorbals! Fuck the fucking lot of youse!"

"Fer Christ's sake, Alex," says General Grimes. "Shut up and play your fucking banjo. What the fuck are ye trying to do? Give the fucking place a bad fucking name, or what?"

GORDON LIGHTFOOT

London, October 1975

He barrels into his suite in London's Westbury hotel like someone looking for trouble – and who won't be happy until he finds it. A surprisingly burly man in a leather flying jacket, with a face that's clearly seen hard times and worse weather.

"Man flies all the way from Frankfurt," he's shouting over his shoulder as he comes through the door, "the least he expects of his record company is that they get him a goddamn beer."

Gordon throws a case across the room and follows it with a shoulder bag flung with some force against a wall.

"Someone," he booms, "get me a *drink*," and you'd have to say straight off that the first impression Gordon makes is that he's a bit of a bully, someone used to having his own way in pretty much every circumstance, and very much in love with the sound of his own voice.

As are, of course, at the time of which I'm writing, many hundreds of thousands of fans around the world. Gordon is the author of mawkish MOR hits like the folkie 'Early Morning Rain' and 'If You Could Read My Mind', songs that have, or will be, covered by Dylan, Cash and Presley, among others. Anyway, today Gordon storms around the room banging doors, ill-tempered. I presume he's looking for the mini-bar, which I have myself only located with some difficulty while searching the premises during a long wait for Gordon, whose flight from Frankfurt has been considerably delayed. I pipe up now, telling him where it is, clearly startling the Canadian songsmith.

"Who the fuck," Gordon wants to know, noticing me for the first time, "are *you*?"

I tell him I'm from *Melody Maker*, and he looks at me suspiciously, like he thinks I might suddenly leap on him and nail his head to the door frame.

"And what are you doing here?"

It's a good question. Why I am here to talk to this grizzled old cur? Even after all these years, I have absolutely no fucking idea. I suspect, however, it has much to do with my nemesis at *Melody Maker*, the quiche-nibbling, cravat-sporting, Chablis-sipping Michael Watts who, with impish regularity, sends me out to interview people he knows I won't get on with, clearly in the hope that at least one of them will end up taking a swing at me. Anyway, back at the Westbury, I'm engaged in what passes for conversation with grumpy Gordon, the morose Canadian telling me now with no great animation about his early career in Canada, where he played the same small club circuit as Joni Mitchell, or Joni Anderson as Gordon knew her back then, when you'd think the mists of time were just parting, the way he tells it.

"This is going way back," he says, like he's remembering the world's first dawn. "We were just callow youths. You were probably kicking the slats out of your cradle."

These days, he only tours maybe once every 18 months, the rest of his time spent sailing on the Great Lakes, he tells me, mistakenly thinking I'm interested.

"There comes a point, though," he adds with a manly shrug, "when a man has to get out and be active. It's my job. A man," he says with suitably masculine sagacity, "needs his work." How we came to be talking about it, I can't remember, but the next thing you know, Gordon's lambasting the young American draft dodgers who made lives for themselves in exile in Canada rather than get shipped off to Vietnam. As far as he's concerned, Canada should have booted them all out, sent 'em packing back to the States or banged 'em up in prison. A man, he says, is nothing without a sense of duty. If he'd been an American, he would have volunteered to fight in Southeast Asia.

"Only Americans know the anguish of that war, but what kind of leniency can you extend to a guy who skips out of his country when 50,000 men get killed in a war?"

I may in some circumstances have let this pass. But during the long wait for Gordon, I have been pecking frequently at a stash of the amphetamine sulphate I can't these days seem to do without, and the speed is making me somewhat cantankerous and not a little addled. I launch into a patently ridiculous speech about America and Vietnam and the peace movement, generally coming on here like a veteran of the Weather Underground or the SLA, a history of random bombings on an FBI rap sheet, guns stashed in every cupboard of a South Compton safe-house, Patty Hearst trussed up in a closet close-by, peeing on the carpet and going out of her mind.

"Why didn't I write about the war?" he says, in answer to that very question. "It was none of my goddamn business," he says. "The United States at that time was a target for every loose tongue around. I didn't think it was my place to say anything. I have," he goes on, "a lot of sympathy for America. I also make a lot of money there. And if you don't mind me saying so, some of the nicest people on earth are Americans and I wish you wouldn't dwell on this particular subject. I suggest we talk about something else."

We do: his songs. In one of them I have come across the following lyric: "*In the name of love she came, this foolish winsome girl/She was all decked out like a rainbow trout...*" I fail to stop myself laughing out loud when I read this to Gordon from my notebook, where I have dutifully jotted it down, alongside words like "sentimental" and "schmaltz".

"*Schmaltz?*" Gordon seethes through grimly gritted teeth, almost coming at me out of his chair. "You're calling my songs sentimental?"

In a word, yes.

Gordon, taking deep breaths, then says: "Well, I guess I've been accused of that before. Just not to my face. But I'd defend myself against an accusation like that. We all know the world isn't exactly in a placid state right now, but I don't think we have to dwell on it."

Your songs, generally, though, are pretty wet, aren't they?

"Wet?"

Like I say, they have a tendency towards sentimentality, weepiness, that sort of thing.

"One or two, maybe," he grudgingly consents. "But people love 'em. So I sing 'em. I'm not going to apologise if you have a problem with that."

It must be embarrassing, though, being lumped in with the kind of tepid troubadours whose serial confessional outpourings are often sentimental to the point of complete banality.

69

"'*Sentimental to the point of complete banality?*'" Gordon splutters. "Whose work are we talking about?"

I reel off a list of singer-songwriters, most of whom it turns out he's friends with, and mention of whom in such a disparaging context is turning his face puce.

"Interview's over, son," he snaps.

I tell him I have one more question, and he leans over the table between us, close enough for me to feel his breath on my face.

"Listen," he says, "beat it now. That's my advice," Gordon sounding like he means business in a big way.

I'm out the door before he unclenches his fist…

BE-BOP DELUXE

Shrewsbury, January 1976

I'm sitting on Stalybridge railway station, watching snow blow down from what I guess are the Pennines. It's getting dark, there's no sign of a train, the valley a haunting emptiness. I'm beginning to feel like the last man on earth.

What am I doing here? Pull up a chair.

I'm supposed to be on the road with Be-Bop Deluxe, who last night played the opening show of a tour that professional music business fantasists believe will turn the band into international superstars, a comical thought that most sane folk I know have received with loud guffaws. However, Be-Bop main man Bill Nelson is being touted in some quarters as a musical visionary, and the editorial bigwigs at *Melody Maker*, fingers as ever on the nation's musical pulse, are intrigued by the band's post-glam prog-rock bluster. I've therefore been dispatched to see what all the fuss is about.

Anyway, back to the beginning. I arrive in Shrewsbury on a freezing night and make my way through oddly empty streets to The Music Hall, where I find Be-Bop in their dressing room. Here's plummy drummer Simon Fox, whose playboy looks give him the slightly dissolute air of James Hunt, the rakish Formula One racing driver. Also in the room: pasty-faced keyboards player Andy Clark, Maori bassist Charlie Tumahai, and Bill Nelson. Bill is remote, intense, with tombstone teeth and a chin you could land a helicopter on. He's wearing a purple suit with lapels as wide as the wingspan of something worshipped by Aztecs, and hugely flared trousers. He looks like the hapless groom in some early comic masterpiece by Mike Leigh, a bleakly droll entertainment about family fallings-out at a wedding

71

where everything goes badly wrong – as, by convenient narrative coincidence, tonight's show does.

As a kind of warm-up for the tour story I'm now supposed to be writing for *MM*, a couple of weeks earlier I travel to Glasgow, where Be-Bop play a somewhat scrappy show at Strathclyde University, and later Bill Nelson, in the bar of the band's rather grubby hotel, tells me not to judge them on tonight's performance but to wait instead until I've witnessed the ambitious production he has planned for their forthcoming tour. Bill's eyes glint as he evokes the promised spectacle, possibly reminiscent of Noah unveiling the ark to Ham, Japheth and the rest of the gang. *This will work*. The plan as Bill lays it out is that the show will open with him in a Perspex tube, standing to attention like a guardsman in a futuristic sentry box. When the stage lights go up, so the Perspex tube, by now filling dramatically with smoke, will also rise, with Bill then stepping forth to dazzle all with his fearsome fretwork, his guitar playing so hot by the show's end that his guitar will appear to spontaneously combust.

This, at least, is the idea. Backstage in Shrewsbury, however, I run into a pair of cheerfully cynical roadies who smirkingly tell me that the hall Be-Bop have been booked in is too small for the hydraulic system designed to lift Bill's tube. They've therefore had to hastily improvise a rather basic hoist and pulley system. Worryingly, this makeshift rig has already displayed an unfortunate tendency to get stuck, which – to my admittedly undisguised glee – is exactly what happens tonight. Anyway, at the start of the show, the lights go up, and on stage there's the band, with Bill centre stage in his tube. From the hall's balcony, I can see the roadies at the side of the stage and the tube shuddering as the roadies pull on the ropes attached to it, the tube filling rather quickly with smoke and Bill already looking a tad uncomfortable. The roadies are really putting their backs into it now, trying to hoist the tube high enough for Bill to be able to step out into the spotlight and save himself the embarrassment of crawling out of the thing on his hands and knees, coughing like a dog in a burning room.

But the tube won't budge. In fact, it seems rather firmly stuck. You can barely see Bill now, there's so much smoke in the tube, although I'm sure that's a hand – presumably one of Bill's – clawing at the Perspex, a face appearing then through the smoke that looks stricken, alarm giving way to terror. The road crew make another manful effort to lift the tube, but the fucking Pyramids went up quicker than this. Bill now appears to be actually choking in the smoke-filled tube, almost to the point, perhaps, of succumbing to fatal smoke inhalation. This adds an even greater urgency to the roadies' labours. The tube is lurching now, the road crew heaving like field hands. And finally, the tube is rising, rising, slowly rising.

And Bill – years before Spinal Tap's Derek Smalls finds himself similarly trapped in a Perspex pod – stumbles, spluttering, into the waiting spotlight. He gathers himself after what's obviously been an unnerving experience, assumes the suitably heroic stance of the legendary rock axeman and strikes what I imagine is intended to be a ringing opening guitar chord, something grand and epic, a clarion call to the Be-Bop faithful. Unfortunately, in the previous mayhem, Bill's guitar has apparently either been switched off or come unplugged. Instead of the intended six string uber-storm, what emerges is a whimpering strum. There are further problems with Bill's many effects pedals, which appear to have a life of their own, more than once giving out random shrieks when Bill is least expecting it, whatever he's playing transformed by malfunctioning circuitry into cacophonous howls and the screams of the mad.

We eventually get to the part of the show where Bill's guitar is meant to spontaneously burst into flames. Bill presses a button on the guitar designed to ignite the pyrotechnics, but nothing happens. There's not even a spark. Bill, somewhat embarrassed, swaps it for a second guitar that a roadie has already set somewhat feebly ablaze. Bill swings the smouldering guitar over his head a couple of times in half-hearted rotation, before handing it back to the roadie who extinguishes with an asbestos blanket what we could exaggeratedly describe as the "flames" that are lightly scorching it. It's not exactly Jimi Hendrix at Monterey, and the mood backstage is predictably grim.

"It's just embarrassing when nothing works," Bill complains testily. "It's like busking."

I'm taken aside now by tour manager Paul Bailey, who explains the group have just been offered a slot on *Top of the Pops* to promote their new single, 'Ships in the Night', a big break they can't turn down, which has occasioned a change in schedule. The band will therefore be leaving almost immediately, driving overnight to London where they will record their *TOTP* appearance before flying to Leeds on a charted plane for tomorrow's show at the university, which Bailey thinks they'll just about have time to get to if everything goes according to plan. Unfortunately, they don't have room in their car to take me with them. I'll have to make my own way from Shrewsbury to Leeds. So the next morning I catch one train, then another, make a connection at Crewe before fetching up here in Stalybridge, where you found me at the top of this story and where the snow is now coming down in flurries as the weather takes a noticeable turn for the worse. I share a desolate station buffet with an elderly woman who I at first understand to be talking to me about The Beatles, the gurning moptops ever-popular it seems, even in such remote outposts. After several baffling minutes, I realise she's actually talking about *beetles*, the insect kind, several of which species – invisible to me – she claims are crawling out of her sandwich, a sad confection she glares at with some contempt, brushing things only she can see from its withered crusts. I make my excuses and step out into the stark chill of the lonely station platform, the last of the day's light being sucked from the glowering sky, feeling rarely more abandoned and cursing the very name Be-Bop Deluxe.

I get to Leeds, eventually, where at the university everyone's waiting for the band and no one's sure where they are. It's been an hour since the support act finished, there's still no sign of Be-Bop Deluxe and the crowd is getting restless. They look like a timid lot, though, and not inclined to riot. So I'm not surprised when they accept the show's eventual cancellation with not much more than a bit of swearing, a few catcalls and the odd beer can lobbed in the direction of the uni's beleaguered social secretary. The entire crowd's probably at home and tucked up in their beds, when the band finally turn up. Turns out their flight from London was diverted because of fog from Yeadon airport, near Leeds, to Manchester, where just before landing, their pilot had announced that one of the plane's engines had failed, alarming news for his passengers, but which yet brings great mirth to me, even as they stand around the empty hall where they were meant to have played, their roadies already packing their gear, someone with a broom sweeping the floor around their feet.

And that's where I leave them, looking quite disconsolate, generally a bit hapless, but perhaps not as downcast as they are when after all their recent efforts 'Ships in the Night' shortly runs aground outside the Top 20, then disappears completely from sight, a bit like I'm about to.

PATTI SMITH

London, May 1976

As for what follows, all I can say in pitiful mitigation of my sorry behaviour is that, at the time, I am not easily embarrassed and usually up for anything. A toxic combination, all told.

Anyway, we're meandering towards the dull end of a *Melody Maker* editorial meeting. Ever-cheerful *MM* features editor Chris Welch shakes the crumbs from some kind of bap, pie or favourite sticky bun from his notebook, opens it up and breezily runs through what's coming up for the next issue. When he's finished, editor Ray Coleman thinks we need one more feature. Chris pipes up immediately, brightly recommending one of those exciting new bands he's forever coming across, whose line-ups always seem mysteriously to include the same former members of musical powerhouses like Humble Pie, Uriah Heep and Blodwyn Pig. I love Chris dearly. He's kindness itself in a chunky-knit turtleneck. But when he starts buntering on like this, I want to nail his hand to a tree and leave him in a forest for wolves. However, another feature on a bunch of old lags who've somehow conned yet one more record company into bankrolling an album no one will buy isn't what Ray's looking for today.

The heavily-fragranced editor is apparently after something a little more 'colourful', possibly even 'off-beat'. Has anyone got any ideas? Cue a rather sinister rustling noise, like bones being wrapped in parchment. It's Mick Watts, vivid this afternoon in a burgandy tank-top and matching cravat. He's coming awake, it seems to me, like some coiled agent of ancient mischief, possibly with an unfolding of scaly wings. Mick makes a steeple of his fingertips, lips pursed, eyes narrowing, a hint of the Fu Manchu of villainous legend in his general wiliness. He makes a murmuring aside to Ray. What's he on about? He certainly has Ray's attention and I don't like the way they're looking at me and smirking, as if they have agreed upon some plan, plot or scheme in which I have been unwittingly cast. What is going on?

Mick now assumes the no-nonsense manner of a spymaster in a black and white British war film, unsentimentally sending one of his people tumbling into enemy territory, perhaps never to return. Plucky chap, off you go. We'll look after your dog. Down, boy, down.

Patti Smith's in town, he now says, all business, in full operational mode. Patti's new album, *Radio Ethiopia* has recently had a mauling in the music papers. She's never been popular with the boys on *MM's* top table, and now also seems to have fallen out of favour with her admirers elsewhere. She's therefore cancelled all scheduled interviews, but under pressure from her record company has reluctantly agreed to turn up at a press conference tomorrow at the Dorchester or the Inn on the Park, one of those places, anyway, where the reincarnation of beat might want to put her feet up, possibly on a table, Patti being such a rad bohemian and all. Such press conferences tend, as a rule, to be largely anodyne affairs – dandruffy Fleet Street bar-jockeys availing themselves of the gratis plonk, music press malcontents nicking all the food, pockets stuffed with canapes and sundry pastries, a half-hearted Q&A with some sulking star and then back to the free drinks and finger food, job done.

Here's Mick's plan, devilish in its cunning simplicity: one of us – and I can't help noticing who he's looking at when he says this – will go along to the press conference, affecting a clearly bogus interest in anything Patti might have to say. Possibly enlivened by a strong drink beforehand, he will proceed to test Patti's patience with questions inane even by the standards of these events, and prod, poke and otherwise cajole her into saying or doing something suitably outrageous, thus guaranteeing lively copy for next week's *MM*. All we need is a volunteer, he says, meaning me. I shake my head, no. He can find another dog to jump through that particular hoop. Unfortunately, I'm still on a short leash, due to recent serial misdemeanours, and I don't have much wriggle room here, so Mick brings me quickly to heel and, the next day, when he whistles into the pasture, as it were, I am obediently at his side in the swanky cocktail bar of a hotel on Park Lane where Patti is shortly due to present herself to the journalistic throng. The cunning Watts now plies me with sundry drinks, four or five whiskey sours, a concoction new to me, a few large brandies and a couple of beer chasers. We then make our way to the suite Arista have booked for the press conference, which, when we get there, is full of milling hacks, knocking back the free booze and nicking the food. Mick gets some more drinks from the bar and we wait for Patti.

She arrives late, looking like she's been dragged by her heels through a hedge, her hand bandaged. Guitarist Lenny Kaye is in tow. The hand injury is the result of an accident the previous evening, she explains, beginning a rather interminable and somewhat confusing story about a gig at a slaughterhouse in Paris, and another show, later, at a smaller venue – a club opened by Arthur Brown, the former King of Hellfire. There'd been a riot at one of the shows, presumably the latter. The electricity had been cut off and she'd ended up playing a drum solo. During said percussive epic she'd cut her hand on a cymbal. By the time she's finished this rambling account, no one can remember what she's talking about, or why. And what's she on about now? Something about the sad absence from the current tour of her regular keyboard player, Richard Sohl, about which she proceeds to get pretty emotional.

"I don't know if you guys are aware of this," she tells the gathered press, "but rock 'n' roll is really hard work. It's worse than being in the army," she goes on, more than a whit preposterously, the absurdity of the remark making me laugh out loud, those whiskey sours starting to take effect. This annoys Patti no end and gets me a thumbs-up from Mick Watts.

"I think you should tell that to the assholes that write for *Melody Maker* and *NME*," she snarls. "*Next question*!"

Someone asks her why she resents the press so much.

"I don't resent the press, man," she says, protesting her innocence of any such charge while trembling with animosity.

"We *invented* the press," says Lenny Kaye, somewhat haughtily.

You *were* the press, I'm moved to remind him.

"Damn *right*!" he shouts back. Patti and I are soon arguing about Blue Oyster Cult, the very mention of whose name has me rolling my eyeballs theatrically and muttering vague obscenities about poodle-haired dwarves loudly enough for her to hear. The brandies are kicking in now, too, on top of those whiskey sours. Cheers, Mick.

"My boyfriend's in Blue Oyster Cult," she says, testily. "So don't start saying bad shit about them or I'll throw my food at you. Physically, except for my boyfriend, they ain't the best-looking band in the world," she concedes, reluctantly. "But they got the most stamina and the most heart and they've lived like dogs."

The next thing you know, she's telling us what a fantastic guitarist she is. This sounds like an exaggeration, I tell her. On the evidence of *Radio Ethiopia*, you might better describe it as pathetic and inept. I don't mention the fact that I haven't at this point actually *heard* the album, but that's all part of the fun that we're having here, if that's what you can call it.

"*Inept?*" she more or less howls. "Doesn't 'inept' mean 'moronic'?"

Sounds about right to me. Another thumbs up from the manipulative Watts.

"*Heyyyyyy!*" she's moved to shout, if not exactly screech, picking up a plate of sandwiches from the table in front of her and throwing it at me with commendable force for someone with only one working hand. I duck and the plate bounces with an audible clang off the head of the chap behind me, stunning him. This sets off the fellow sitting next to me.

"You're ruining this for everyone," he simmers, an indignant little man who clearly doesn't know how far beyond caring I am.

"Whaddaya mean, *inept?*" Patti's yelling at me, an angry barroom moll with her hackles up. "I think the record's great," she says, and it might well be for all I know. "Whaddaya want from me? Ya want me to review the record for you? Tell me the name of your paper. I'll review the record. I think 'Radio Ethiopia' – the cut itself – is a very sensitive and heartful and courageous voyage. It's us improvising alone in a dark studio with a hurricane coming, with the moon shitting on us."

I'm trying to imagine the scene so colourfully described, when the bloke behind me, who caught Patti's flying sandwich plate in the kisser, prods me rather aggressively in the back. He's got a piece of lettuce stuck to his forehead and now he's recovered his senses and is threatening to drag me outside, where he evidently intends to give me a bit of a beating. He looks like he means it, too. But I can't take the indignant blowhard seriously, not with that lettuce stuck to his head like a misplaced fig leaf. So I just give him a cocky you-and-whose-army look that I don't feel any particular confidence in anyway and, much to my relief, it makes him back off. Patti, meanwhile, and for no particular reason that anyone can fathom, starts telling us about her family, who are apparently telepathic. Her brother Todd is a genius, she's keen for us to know.

"He was in the Navy," she elaborates. "He's like Leonardo da Vinci, only in his own stuff. My whole family is full of da Vincis. Todd can do anything. He'd be a great butcher."

She tells us a rather sad story about being stung by four wasps, which I loudly presumed was, hic, why she had a voice like something buzzing in a bell jar. A double-thumbs up from the Machiavellian Watts.

"Yeah," Patti sneers. "That's why I'm not a great singer and why I have bad pitch and sound like I have marbles in my mouth and shit up my ass. You guys think I didn't have any training, but I was actually trained to do opera."

Pull the other one.

"I did Verdi's, uh, *Ill Trovotoree*... uh, *Ill*, uh, *Trovo*... What's the one with the gypsy boy and the prince?" she asks me. "You must know. You're so cultured."

There's a question from the back. What does she think about British punk bands? Since she claims not to have heard any, she hasn't got an opinion although she's sure they're all great and full of, you know, energy and commitment, things like that. These are important to her, as she goes on to explain.

"All I care about is that people who perform have energy and commitment," she says, putting it into something of a nutshell, "not that they take some intellectual pose. If somebody has real heart and believes in what they're doing, it communicates. I'm not specifically into rock 'n' roll. I'm into anything that has pure heart. That's why I like Puccini. That's how I like Stravinsky and them guys. That's why I like Brancusi. It's all the same to me. Nijinsky. Mick Jagger."

And what did she bring to the party that made her unique? Just about everything she's ever been through, it turns out.

"Everything I have inside me, whether it's cosmic or telepathic, or my knowledge about ancient Egyptology or having a baby or being raped or beaten up, everything wonderful or horrible that's ever happened to me. Every experience. The temple of my experience is my body," she says and I can see the sinister puppet-master Watts trying to stifle a hearty guffaw, "and that's what I use on stage."

She then announces she has one more thing to say. She's declaring war, presumably on the music press, or at least the part of it that's recently been so unkind to her, which makes us all sit up.

"That's right," she hollers, bristling. "You can call me Field Marshall if it makes you feel better. I'm the Field Marshall of rock 'n' roll. And I'm fucking declaring war! My guitar is my machine gun!"

And with that, she storms – yes, actually *storms* – out of the conference room, knocking over a table and a couple of chairs, Lenny Kaye and sundry other faithful retainers scampering in her turbulent slipstream. Mick Watts watches them go from the bar, rubbing his hands together and cackling like something in a pointed hat about to unleash a flock of flying monkeys.

"Another whiskey sour?" he asks when I join him.

Oh, why not.

PHIL LYNOTT'S MUM

Manchester, August 1976

Safari-suited assistant editor of *Melody Maker*, Michael Watts, polishes off a last glass of Chablis, dabs at his lips with a pink paper napkin and packs away what's left of his specially prepared gourmet lunch. With an imperial wave, he then beckons me to his desk for what I imagine will be a routine bollocking for what he has recently been provoked to describe as my "unacceptable insolence and comically poor timekeeping".

Oddly, he starts chatting to me somewhat amicably, which as ever means he's up to something. The topic of conversation? Leather-clad Thin Lizzy bass player Phil Lynott. Mick's read somewhere that the hard-rocking Lizzy legend's mother runs what he calls a "showbiz hotel", somewhere in Manchester. I begin to see where this is heading, and a couple of days later I'm on my way north to interview her. I'm also sulking because Mick has deviously arranged this assignment to coincide with Richard Branson's annual summer party in the grounds of The Manor, his palatial recording studio in Oxfordshire, an extravagant affair I am likely to miss unless I nail the interview with Mrs Lynott tonight and get the first train back to London tomorrow morning.

Anyway, it's called The Clifton Grange Hotel and I find it on the corner of Wellington Road in Whalley Range, a huge, ramshackle place. Philomena "Phyllis" Lynott, who has run the hotel with her "feller" Dennis since 1966, meets me at the front door with a brilliant smile and rushes me quickly into her kitchen where she starts cooking me a meal – "You're just a scrap of a thing!" – all the while talking me through a decade of the hotel, which is known throughout Manchester's clubland as "The Showbiz".

"It's a show business hotel, right enough," she says, boiling up some spuds. "We only take show business people. We don't get to bed until eight in the morning when we have people here," she goes on, and I can feel a very late night suddenly looming. "So we never take the normals."

She's busy with a frying pan now, steak sizzling.

"Ah," she says wistfully, "we've seen all sorts come and go. Mostly cabaret people in the early days. Singers, comedians, conjurors, magicians, ventriloquists, jugglers, Maori dancers."

Maori dancers?

"The mess they used to make in the dining room with their grass skirts!" Phyllis laughs. "Dennis was forever sweeping up after them."

Not long after this, Phyllis is giving me a guided tour of The Showbiz, and we fetch up in the bar. There are autographed pictures on the walls of various celebrities who have apparently stayed here, including – what's this? – Sammy Davis Jr and, er, Gregory Peck.

"It's a lark!" Phyllis shrieks. "Dennis and I signed them ourselves. I *love* Gregory Peck, you see. Oh, I do love me little Gregory."

I spot troubled soccer legend George Best in one picture. A mean-looking drunk. Turns out George used to be quite a regular here.

"He was just a poor young thing," Phyllis recalls with maternal affection. "Just a young man who'd never been allowed to enjoy himself and was very confused. He didn't like people bothering him and asking too many questions, which is why he used to lose his temper sometimes. I was interviewed by Michael Parkinson for his book on George," she goes on. "Yes, Parky came up here to speak to me and we had a great old time. I'm quoted extensively on page 121 of the book."

We talk about some of her more memorable guests, which reminds her of the Christmas she took in a Swedish magician.

"He was a strange one," she laughs. "Forever pulling white balls out of his mouth. Strange, but nice with it. Anyway, he stays for three months and then tries to run off owing me the rent. Someone saw him ducking out with his suitcases, though. 'Nils is doing a runner,' they shout. So I runs up the stairs to get the lads, shouting, 'Quick! Everybody up! Nils has buggered off without paying his bloody rent!'

So the whole team of us, people from every room, we all jumps in me car to chase the bugger.

"We found him at the bus stop, and I jumps out of the car and I said, 'You sod, Nils! You stays with us for three months and we've all been very happy and then you end up doing this! You sod!' And I grabbed all his suitcases and said, 'Right, I'm taking these. Off you go!' And he started crying, blabbing like a baby. I just jumped in me car and started to drive off. Then I looked at him in me mirror. He was standing there, all pathetic and crying, weeping away, because I'd taken all his belongings, all his tricks and his bloody white balls, and I just couldn't leave him.

"I just backed the car up, and he was still tearful. 'Nils,' I says, 'stop all this crying. There was no need for you to run out like that. Come back with us and we'll straighten you out.' It happened that he'd been out of work and was a bit lost. I said he could stay with us until we saw him back in work, and then he could pay me what he owed me. He stayed with us for another three weeks and seemed much better.

"One day, he came in here and thanked me and said he would never be able to repay me for all the kindness I'd showed him... and the bugger was right. He said he was just going out for five minutes and we've not seen him since."

Phyllis is now behind the bar, asking me if I'd like a drink. Which I do. A brandy, perhaps.

"A large one?"

If you insist.

"Have the bottle, why don't you?"

The next thing I know, it's four in the morning, I'm down to the last of the brandy and a girl whose name I didn't catch is sitting on my lap with her tongue in my ear. Meanwhile, I'm trying to hold a conversation with Johnny Burns – Manchester Pub Entertainer Of The Year 1974, apparently – and Jacky Richmond, formerly Manchester's answer to Tom Jones, both veterans of the city's rapidly diminishing cabaret scene. Johnny's still doing what's left of the rounds, but Jacky's running his own hotel. Most nights, though, you'll find him here at The Showbiz.

"Like a second home, this place has been to me," he says. "And I've been all over the world – Germany, Turkey, summer seasons on the Isle Of Man."

At around 6.00 am, the bar still full of noise and people who look like they're going to be here for a while longer, Phyllis's feller Dennis says he'll drive me to the station if I'm still determined to get back to London, which I am. Phyllis gives me a worried look when I then fall off my stool and have subsequent problems getting back on my feet, which I eventually do with a helping hand from the saintly Dennis. Phyllis wants me to stay, get some sleep, sober up. But I'm already getting into Dennis's car, and not long after that I'm on the train to London, where I get the first cab I see and head for Notting Hill. With seconds to spare I stagger on to the last coach to The Manor, to cheers from the *Maker* wrecking crew and a stern look from Mick Watts, who's sitting up front, dressed like he's on his way to Henley for the fucking regatta. I then pile into the beers with the boys from *MM*, and off we go. We get loud pretty quickly, me apparently making most of the noise. This inevitably again brings me to the attention of the schoolmasterly Watts, who stiffly reminds me that I'm an ambassador for *Melody Maker*, which makes me hoot somewhat. He tells me he'll have more to say to me on Monday in the office, which makes me laugh even more. The way things are going I'll be lucky to see out the fucking afternoon.

We arrive at The Manor. Wandering into a shadowy room, I come across parrot-voiced Janet Street Porter playing snooker with The Sex Pistols. Before she's even had a chance to break, I'm in an argument with Steve Jones, who calls me a "long-haired hippie cunt", the Neanderthal oaf squaring up to me, fists clenched. A highly-amused Johnny Rotten intervenes.

"We love you, really," he says, guiding me towards the door. "Now fuck off."

Outside, I meet up again with the *Maker* gang, among whom there is great excitement. The wife of our news editor has won a raffle! The prize? A brief trip in one of Richard Branson's hot air balloons, which I can now see tethered yonder. Turns out, she's not keen, so with drunken bravado I grab her ticket, stride over to the balloon and hop in the basket. Next thing you know, I'm being kitted out with a helmet and Branson himself is asking me to sign some forms.

"In case there's an accident," he explains.

An *accident*?

"These things happen," Branson says, and he's not joking.

I'd been under the impression the balloon would merely ascend a few hundred feet while remaining firmly – if distantly – tethered to the ground. Well I've got that all wrong, because we're about to go not only *up* but also *away*, into the wild blue skies above. Rattled now to distraction, I try to get out of the basket. It's too late, of course. The pilot, a toothsome chap, a hearty soul, no doubt a veteran of ascension – no stranger to the skies, the clouds a second home – is firing gas cylinders, and the basket is beginning to buckle and tug. Mick Watts barges through a gathering crowd.

"Where do you think you're going?" he asks.

I jerk a thumb heavenward and flinch as the basket rocks, the pilot getting ready for take-off.

"Get out," Watts says commandingly, adding something inevitably superfluous about me not going anywhere until I've written up the Phyllis Lynott story.

Whatever, here's someone thinking on their feet! It's *MM* reporter Brian Harrigan, the bearded Brummie's hurrying towards us with a six-pack of lager, which he proceeds to lob over the head of the purple-faced Watts. I rip open one of the cans, raise a toast to Mick and with a heart-stopping lurch we're plucked from the ground and given a roughish shake, climbing fast. We are now airborne, moving at speed across a beautiful summer sky. Some miles back, and what I presume to be thousands of feet below us, a convoy of cars and vans roars along country lanes.

"That'll be Richard and the retrieval crew," the pilot says, as if we're astronauts in some stricken capsule, hurtling through space, into Earth's orbit, in danger of burning up on re-entry ("Branson, we have a problem!").

"We're starting our descent," the pilot announces. He then gives me specific instructions about our imminent landing. Contrary to popular misconception, the balloon above us will not slowly deflate, thus gently depositing us in some sun-dappled meadow or welcoming pasture. We will, in fact, be coming down fast, and at a somewhat sharpish angle. At the point of impact, we'll be pitched out of the basket.

"Your natural inclination will be to grab hold of something," the pilot says.

He's right. That's *exactly* what I mean to do.

"Don't," he says. "You'll rip your arm out of its socket."

The field we are rushing towards is coming at us awfully quickly now.

"Here we go!" the pilot shouts.

I'm no expert, but it seems to me we're coming in too fast for anything but a bone-breaking landing. Then there's an enormous jolt and for a moment the whole world's a tumbling blur and I'm flying through the swarming air, after which I land with a thump. Then people are pulling me to my feet, laughing, slapping me on the back, that sort of thing. One of them is Richard Branson.

"Ready to go again?" he asks, beaming. I give him a sick look, spit out a tooth and begin to wonder at exactly what point my day came so completely off its hinges.

"Maybe next year, then," Branson smiles, more teeth than a horse.

Maybe not, I think, limping across the field.

BRYAN FERRY

London, January 1977

"Are you absolutely sure it's actually the finished thing?" Bryan Ferry asks, clearly incredulous, fishing out the copy of David Bowie's just-released *Low* he's spotted in my bag and holding it twixt thumb and forefinger like something odious. "It looks so... *Woolworths*."

What did he mean by that?

"I mean, it looks so... *cheap*," he says, sounding strangely upset. "Rather, you know... *tatty*," he adds, as if mortally offended. "I hope," he goes on, "that it *sounds* better than it *looks*."

I tell him it *sounds* brilliant.

"If you say so," he says, the hint of drift in his voice a subtle indication that he doesn't want to talk any more about David Bowie or *Low*. He has more pressing things preoccupying him, anyway – like finishing off his new solo album, *In Your Mind*, which, with a release date looming ominously, he's still fussing over, his perfectionist inclinations at this late date beginning to worry all and also sundry, a tour having already been booked to coincide with the record's on-sale date.

It's gone midnight here at Air Studios, high above Oxford Street, where, in a bid to meet his deadline, Ferry and his production team have been putting in regular 12–15 hour shifts. We've just been listening to a playback of a song from the forthcoming album. It's called "Night Operator" and now Ferry and co-producer Steve Nye are discussing subtle shifts in the mix—imperceptible sonic adjustments that Ferry clearly thinks are crucial, however long it may take to achieve them. Nye, evidently long-suffering, starts another re-mix of a track he's been working on since I got here some hours ago. Ferry suggests we retire to one of Air's tape playback rooms to listen to some of the album's finished tracks – including 'Tokyo Joe', 'One Kiss', 'Love Me Madly Again' and 'In Your Mind' – after which, as previously agreed, he'll talk about the record and what's currently happening with Roxy Music.

At the time of which I'm writing, Roxy have recently announced that they are on an extended sabbatical, which leaves the individual members free to pursue solo projects. Things have been fractious between them for some time and this seems more like a split than a break from each other, and Ferry, inevitably, has been cast as the villain of the piece. Since ousting Eno from the line-up, he's been regarded by sections of the press, fans and even some of the band – from conversations I've had with them – as a ruthless musical despot, self-centred and obsessed with his own personal ambitions.

"The press love to portray me as this absolute *tyrant*," he says wearily. "But I don't think the reputation is justified."

I think of Steve Nye, slaving over the mixing desk in the studio next door, Eno being given his cards after falling out with Ferry – and also Roxy sax player Andy Mackay who, when I interviewed him the previous August for *Melody Maker*, launched an attack on Ferry that surprised both me and Roxy's management, who thought he wanted to talk to me about his solo plans. The rest of the band, including Ferry, who reacts badly to what he reads, are similarly taken aback by Andy's outburst. Mackay had bristled at the notion of Ferry as the principal architect of the Roxy sound, a singular visionary who had plucked from obscurity the players who would best realise his musical innovations.

"The idea of Bryan as a fisher of men," Andy remarked tartly, "is really rather amusing and totally inaccurate." He further opined that Roxy could get along fine without Ferry ("We could always get another singer"). I ask Ferry now for his reaction to Mackay's outburst.

"You're trying to lure me into an attack on Andy," he says warily. "And I won't get into that," he adds before doing just that, at length. "What can I say? It was unprofessional and it was very embarrassing for the other members of the band, because we get on well. I really don't have the time to get involved in a petty squabble like that. The politics of Andy's argument are simply silly. I'd prefer to forget it.

I just don't need to listen to all that from Andy and, really, that's why I have no positive plans for Roxy at the moment. It's not as if I in any way *need* Roxy Music, and Andy should know that. I'm in a situation with this album where I can work with people who in turn like playing with me. With Roxy, there's a set of people I like working with sometimes, but who are often incredibly resentful about me and what I do. It's weird."

Andy's attack, I suggest to Ferry, seemed to coincide with a view that probably took root around the time of Eno's sacking – that Ferry is someone growing increasingly remote and authoritarian, dictatorial and aloof, seduced by the glamour of a social scene far removed from his modest Tyneside upbringing. At the time, he's beginning to get a lot of stick for his new-found airs and fashionable graces, which will only get worse over the years to come.

"It's just jealousy, really, that motivates people to attack the way I live, what they think I'm like," he says firmly. "They've built up an image of me as a pompous, arrogant, totally horrible character. That's unreasonable, I think. People who know me realise it's untrue. Perhaps I've provoked it to a certain extent, because I'm afraid I'm simply not really interested in propping up the bar of whichever musician's hang-out may be fashionable at any particular time, spilling beer over everyone and being generally raucous.

"The music business," he goes on, "is as redneck as it gets and has certain conventions that aren't supposed to be broken. And Roxy and I broke them all – we made so few concessions and we never denied our ambition and that did a lot of people's heads in, I think. They were very suspicious of us. I used to be very sensitive about it, but I simply don't care anymore.

"People will say, 'Oh, Bryan Ferry – he's not a man of the street anymore.' But I was *never* that and never pretended I was. It would be utterly false for me to walk about in hobnail boots with a cloth cap on my head. It would be quite ridiculous. I wouldn't for a moment deny my background – I don't think I could. But that doesn't mean I have to go around looking like a Jarrow miner," he says, evidently appalled by the image. "I think that's unnecessary, really, and I feel," he adds, somewhat huffily, "no such obligation."

THE BYRDS

London, April 1977

Roger McGuinn, Chris Hillman and Gene Clark, three of the original Byrds, are due in London for dates that will mark the first time they've toured here together since the original line-up came over for their only UK visit, back in 1965. I put in a few calls and set up interviews for *Melody Maker*.

They fly in separately, since they all now have individual solo careers, and will be playing their own sets on the forthcoming shows, only coming together at the end for a handful of Byrds classics – which, on the night I see them at the Hammersmith Odeon, includes, I seem to remember, a quite transcendental 'Eight Miles High'.

Chris Hillman arrives first, and I meet him in his manager's suite at the Mayfair Hotel. He's brusque, business-like, a little ill-tempered. I get the impression he thinks he's been poorly-rewarded for the major parts he's played in bands as wholly influential as The Byrds and Flying Burrito Brothers, a repressed bitterness coming nicely to the boil when I mention that less than a year earlier I'd gone on the road with a version of the Burritos put together by original members Sneaky Pete Kleinow and Chris Ethridge, augmented by another former Byrd, Gene Parsons, fiddle player Gib Gilbeau and burly vocalist Joel Scott Hill, a thoroughly obnoxious specimen.

"I really wish you hadn't brought this up," Hillman says flintily. "The fact that Sneaky Pete took the name wouldn't have made me quite so mad if that band hadn't been quite so terrible. But they were just awful. They made me so angry I wanted to punch 'em out.

"Sneaky was in the original group, I can't deny that. But he did *not* write the songs. Neither did Ethridge. Chris actually quit just after they reformed and apologised to me for being part of all that crap. Those guys just took the name and milked the reputation of the original band. And Joel Scott Hill was damned awful. Could not sing in tune. The man was a buffoon. I shouldn't say these things, but they've been on my mind for some time."

A couple of days later, I'm in another room at the same hotel, with Roger McGuinn who, after telling me he's in a "confessional mood", lays down on his bed as if he's on a psychiatrist's couch, me on a chair beside him, and starts talking about the general wretchedness his career had recently become.

"I went through a slump," he says, determined, as if on professional advice, to be thoroughly candid. "It happens. I got lazy and bored and apathetic, which is something I hate about myself. I'm sorry for it now. I've paid dearly for it. My career has not been the most illustrious in rock 'n' roll these last few years.

"I know I've contributed to history with The Byrds, but I certainly could have managed myself better financially. I look around and I see all these rock 'n' roll millionaires, and I wonder where all *my* money went. I just squandered it all, like I've squandered a lot of things.

"But one thing I've learned," he says, oozing humility and hardwon knowledge, like he's a guest on Oprah or a show like it, coming clean in public, "is that money doesn't make you happy." He pauses, like someone waiting for a round of applause. "Making people happy makes me happy," he goes on, his voice fairly throttled by sincerity. "It makes me almost cry sometimes to think of the people I've made happy. I mean, millions of people have been made happy by the things I've done. I feel wonderful about that.

"After the initial success I had with The Byrds, though, I became very blasé. By 1968, we'd been through folk rock, jazz rock, space rock, raga rock. I was bored, complacent. So when Gram Parsons came along and suggested we do a country album, I was ready for that. We went down to Nashville, did *Sweetheart of the Rodeo* and lost our entire fucking audience. The hippies thought we were rednecks and the rednecks thought we were lousy hippies. So no one liked us, we alienated our entire fucking audience. Now the album's regarded as a classic and everybody loves it. That shows you the stupidity of the public, how fucking *dumb* they can be. After that I became very disenchanted for a long time, until Dylan picked me up again for the Rolling Thunder tour. I spent three or four years in a very low, strange place," he says by way of whispered conclusion, sitting up on the bed now, facing me, and, I notice, holding my hand.

I meet Gene Clark in a record company office. At least that's where I am. Where Gene is, I couldn't possibly say. The profound psychological problems that led to his early departure from The Byrds have been well-documented, and his ongoing battle with alcohol and drugs is well-known, and both no doubt contribute to his apparent absence from the here, and also now, of things.

I have a hard time getting through to him, and he becomes notably disturbed when I ask him about *No Other*, one of the greatest records of its time. When it comes out in the autumn of 1974, it seems like an album everybody should hear, nothing short of a masterpiece. I beg for enough space to review it at appropriate length in *Melody Maker*, to a wholly unsympathetic response, people regarding me as someone who's taken leave of their senses and should be approached with caution and a very big stick. I'm told to stop my infernal whining and write 100 words on the album, which I do sulkily, most of them superlatives.

The extravagant claims I make on its behalf maybe inspires a few people to actually go out and buy the thing. But many more simply ignore the album altogether and it quickly sinks without trace, barely a copy sold. It has been thus for Clark since he quit The Byrds in 1966, his solo career to date not much more than a catalogue of commercial failure, great music on albums like *Gene Clark With The Godsin Brothers*, *The Fantastic Expedition of Dillard & Clark*, *Through The Morning, Through The Night*, *White Light* and *Roadmaster* all routinely overlooked, leaving Clark often disheartened, with solace found increasingly in hard liquor and drugs.

No Other was meant to be the album that returned him to former glories, and was lavishly financed by David Geffen's Asylum Records; to the tune, some said, of $100,000. This is a lot of money for only eight completed tracks and an album that could only have sold more poorly if it had remained unreleased. When Clark announces to an appalled Geffen that for a follow-up he intends to record an album of "cosmic Motown", he's introduced to the wooden thing in the wall otherwise known as the door. Three years later, he's on another label with a new album, just out, called *Two Sides to Every Story*.

Clark's departure from The Byrds is blamed on his chronic fear of flying, which compromised the band's touring and promotional schedules. Even the most naïve of fans, however, suspects there's something more seriously askew, which eventually turns out to be Gene's increasingly debilitating dependency on alcohol and narcotics, both of which he partakes in to the point of damaging excess. It's certainly a shock meeting him, not least because my memory of him in The Byrds, as their impeccably cool and imperious front-man, is still so vivid. He cuts a shambling figure now as we are left in a room so full of furniture it might otherwise be used as a storeroom, somewhere things are dumped and possibly forgotten. There's something worryingly astray about him, a puddled fretfulness, an inclination towards drift and vacancy. He seems like someone with a fragile sense of himself.

He's a big man still, heavily-bearded, with the lumbering momentum of a slow-moving tug on a sluggish current, a bulky craft with a possibly rusty hull. Unmentioned habits have clearly taken their toll, as well as the thudding blows of serial disappointment at the dismal turns his solo career have taken. When he speaks, haltingly, his voice seems to come from a far away space I'm concerned may be somewhere he these days spends too much time, with only his worried self for muttering company.

He seems trim of neither body nor mind, and I'm genuinely sorry when I push him for a response to the colossal public indifference to *No Other* – which he truly believed was his ticket back to the big time, as he so describes it. He becomes agitated, struggles for the right words, can't find them and so simply shrugs, waves a hand, stares out the window, increasingly estranged from the moment.

"After that I didn't want to do *anything*," he says eventually, with the drowsy diction of someone on heavy medication, senses somewhat dulled against a hurtful world, his voice drifting slowly off in yonder direction.

You can tell, though, that he's trying, whatever obscuring fog he's peering through, to tell me something, although I'm not sure what.

"It's eventually all about," he says, the words coming slowly, "the pursuit of an essential goal. And that's the essential part of any art: the pursuit of a goal that continues to be indefinable, with the result that the pursuit of that goal remains unpredictable when you attempt to express its nature…" He pauses, and then continues, picking his words as one might pick one's way across inhospitable terrain. "What I'm saying," he says, "is that the goal is understood more easily in the pursuit of it, even though its definition remains elusive. That's the best way I can think to put it."

In the distant hum of office life, a telephone is ringing and going unanswered. It continues to ring and is still unanswered.

"Do you think that's for me?" he finally asks.

I tell him I have no idea.

"Neither do I," he says, rising to go and then actually going, the interview, such as it has been, evidently over.

ANGIE BOWIE

Somerset, April 1977

The directions I've been given are vague, at best. But the cab driver seems to know where we need to go and drives me the six miles from Weston-Super-Mare to the Loxton Valley where, on this blustery Sunday night with the weather closing in and storm clouds gathering overhead, we find the Webbington Hotel & Country Club, self-proclaimed NITESPOT OF THE WEST!

This is obviously no idle joke. Here in the imposing lobby of the Webbington, there are posters advertising forthcoming attractions. These include such international favourites as JESS CONRAD ("Pop star and entertainer, one of the recording successes of recent years!"), IAN KENT ("the lad to set you laughing!"), LYNN SHARON ("Vocal charm and talent!") and NORMA LEON ("a songstress with style!"). Look closer at this colourful display, at the poster for tonight's show, and you'll see a man and woman locked in a curious embrace. She's got a leg cocked over his shoulder. He's fondling her foot. He's naked from the waist up, with a face that looks like it's been moulded out of something grim and synthetic, possibly brewed in a vat in an underground laboratory. She's fashionably androgynous, with the look of a hard-boiled glam rock moll. His name is Roy Martin. She's Angie Bowie, wife of David. This is what the poster has to say about her: "Following her West End theatre success, the sensational wife of international star David Bowie brings the Soul House Company to the Webbington Country Club for their first appearance in the provinces. An appearance not to be missed!"

So that's why we're here. Now on with the show.

Webbington regulars The Colin Peters Set are on stage, limping rather forlornly through a feeble jazz-tinged arrangement of "Fool on the Hill". The meagre audience in the hotel's cavernously draughty ballroom stifle yawns of gasping indifference. "Fool on the Hill" dribbles to a weary, washed-out conclusion. The Colin Peters Set chat among themselves, three old pros who've seen it all before. The audience sits in morose silence. A prancing little man who turns out to be resident compere Tony Graham now appears and tells us how much pleasure it is for him to be able to announce "a very talented vocalist and wonderful person - Miss Joanne Bennette!"

Joanne bounds on to the stage to applause only she can hear. The audience stares at her balefully. Joanne, however, is a trouper, not easily put off by their staggering indifference. "Are you sure you're not drinking cement?" she shouts brashly at an old couple in the front row who appear to have fallen asleep. Tony Graham is now back in the spotlight, grinning madly, like someone who's recently lost their mind. There'll be a short intermission, he tells us and then we'll have "the sensational Angie Bowie and that'll be REALLY something!"

And it is. The lights dim. The Colin Peters Set have been joined by a large, shambling man with a beard and funny hat who turns out to be none other than Andy "Thunderclap" Newman, of "Something in the Air" fame. He's followed on to the stage by two scantily-clad women, one of whom I am amazed to realise I actually *know*. It's Gladys Shock, former star of a spectacular all-nude review that had briefly featured a stripper named Candy Box, with whom, only a couple of years ago, I shared a flat in Earl's Court. What Gladys is doing here, I have no idea. And by the look of it neither does Gladys, who's wearing a bemused look and not much else. Roy Martin, meanwhile, the dead-eyed android cavorting with Angie in the poster in the lobby, has made an appearance, shouting something above the music. He's introducing ANGIE! And here she comes, here she comes, fairly naked herself, apart from a fur stole draped over her bony shoulders.

"IT'S SHOWTIME!" Roy screeches, voice going off like a fire alarm, the very shrillness of which has some of the more enfeebled pensioners in the crowd clutching their chests, mass cardiac arrests just an interrupted heartbeat away. Angie and Gladys and the other semi-naked nubile, whose name is Charlotte, break into a sexy little vamp called "Give Your Soul to Man". The noise they make sounds like it belongs in an abattoir, a cacophony of high-pitched whinnies, whines and indiscriminate yelping. Mercifully, they are soon scampering into the wings and Roy is introducing an acoustic interlude by Bob Willum, a folk singer. This turns out to be a truly pathetic parody of Bob Dylan. Since me and this Willum character are probably the only people in the entire place who've even heard of Bob Dylan, this is hardly a show-stopping routine.

Off goes Bob. Back on come Angie, Gladys and Charlotte, this time dressed as belly dancers with skimpy little scarves tied around their chests. They start on the old music hall number, "The Old Bazaar in Cairo", while a chap decked out as an Arab does a sand-dance. Gladys gets a bit carried away at this point and jumps off the stage, wiggling her naked belly in the face of a conspicuously corpulent old codger in the front row. He turns a worrying shade of purple. The girls retire. Roy races on stage, waving a pistol. "THIS IS A STICK-UP!" he screams. "More like a COCK-UP!" comes the inevitable reply from the Colin Peters Set.

Roy and Charlotte, who is now wearing a skin-tight green dress, attempt a Sonny and Cher-style duet on "I Want to Give You Love" and then Andy Newman performs a solo version of "Frankie And Johnny", sounding like a drunk at closing time. He returns eventually to the piano, where he's joined by Angie, now dressed like something from the pages of a sticky little S&M magazine. What at first sounds like a parrot being disembowelled turns out to be Angie, singing. And so it goes on and on, with Gladys Shock increasingly hogging the limelight with a rather lurid bump and grind routine, during which she sheds what few clothes she's still wearing and whacks her ample tits in the face of the old feller in the front row she'd earlier terrorised with her belly dancing. He almost dies of fright. Angie and Charlotte join La Shock for a light-hearted episode called "Maybe it's Because We're Soho Hookers", set to the tune of "Maybe it's Because I'm a Londoner". The entire Soul House Company – all six of them – line up for the grand finale, a high-kicking "We'll Meet Again", after which they slink off. Tony Graham tries to whip up some applause from the audience, but all they can muster is some half-hearted clapping. Angie returns to receive their adoration by blowing kisses into the darkness. She seems to be expecting someone to rush the stage with a basket of roses. Most of the audience, however, is already drifting towards the bar.

Which is where, a little later, I bump into Angie. She's positively gushing when I introduce myself. Yes, darling, she had been terribly, terribly nervous. Petrified, in fact. First night nerves, and all that, and there had been one or two little goofs, but, darling, no one really noticed, did they? Oh, but it had been so swell to be back on the boards! When she was working with David, she let her own career slide, didn't she, darling? But David was always encouraging her to pick up the pieces, wasn't he, darling?

Had she been expecting David to turn up tonight, for a show of support, that kind of thing?

"No, darling," she says. "He's busy with his own things in Berlin. And he's looking after Zowie."

He was also looking after Iggy, apparently.

"Yes!" she trills. "And *he's* even more trouble than Zowie!"

And with a theatrical toss of her head, she's off.

Colin Peters watches her go, a blackish mood descending on the surly old pro.

"Terrible," he says, when I ask him what he thought of the show. "Fucking terrible. I felt like an idiot. It wasn't the fault of my lads. Angie Bowie turns up with this fellow Thunderclap as her MD, and he can't even read music. It's irresponsible.

"I don't blame Angie," he goes on, a fount of sympathy. "If she'd just come down here on her own and played with my lads, we could have put something decent together. It wouldn't have been *brilliant*, but it would have been better than this. She's a lovely girl, but she's got all these people around her trying to convince her she's got talent and she's a star. But would you have come down here if she wasn't David Bowie's wife? No, of course not.

"Trouble is," Colin whispers, conspiratorially, "she can't carry a show on her own. Not like Jayne Mansfield. Oh, yes. We worked with her. One of the best. A great entertainer. Now *she* could carry a show. A real professional. Not," he says darkly, "like *this* lot. Care for another?"

I did.

99

LOU REED

London | Stockholm, April 1977

There is a black cloud in the corner of the room with something scowling inside it, and it turns out to be Lou Reed, who is clearly not having one of his better days. He stares at me through aviator shades tinted gun-metal grey for what seems an uncomfortably long time, lights a Marlboro, speaks.

"What locker room did *Melody Maker* find *you* in, faggot?" he asks, his voice a low rumble ominously pitched somewhere near the bottom end of the conversational frequency and sounding like thunder in a bucket.

"How *old* are you? You look about *eight*," he says, possibly aggrieved that *Melody Maker* has whimsically sent a mere waif to interview him, some child who might be more usefully employed as a raw-kneed chimney sweep or nimble bookie's runner. "And your head's too big for your body," he adds. His nastiness seems well-practised. I give him a smile, putting a lot into it. There is more of his bile to come.

"It's been a long time since I spoke to any journalists," he says, but not before knocking back a large glass of whiskey. There are two bottles of Johnnie Walker Red on the table in front of him, one of them already half empty. "This afternoon, I've been interviewed twice. Now I remember why I gave up speaking to journalists. They are a species of foul vermin. I wouldn't hire people like you to guard my sewer. Journalists are morons. They're idiots. They're ignorant and stupid."

It seems fair to say that this Lou Reed, who I meet in April, 1977 while he's on a brief visit to London to promote his new album, *Rock and Roll Heart*, is, so far, the Lou Reed I always imagined Lou Reed would be if I ever actually met him. So I'm reasonably braced for such rants as the one he now delivers – a toxic tirade, mostly directed at the journalists he so loathes, that, when I play back the tape of the interview, runs uninterrupted for 27 minutes. It's an astonishing performance and when it's over I'm laughing out loud and feel like giving him a round of applause. Instead, I ask if he feels obliged to put on such a show because he's Lou Reed and it's expected of him. He surprises me by giving this some thought, his reply, when it comes, prefaced by a chuckle that sounds like bark being torn from a tree.

"Sometimes I need to be reminded who I am," he says, somewhat disarmingly. "Sometimes performing as Lou Reed and *being* Lou Reed are so close as to make one think they are one and the same person. I've hidden behind the *myth* of Lou Reed for years. I can blame anything outrageous on *him*. I make believe sometimes that I'm Lou Reed. I'm so easily seduced by the public image of Lou Reed that I'm in love with Lou Reed myself. I think he's wonderful. No, it's not something I do to disguise my vulnerability or insecurity. Sometimes I just like being Lou Reed better than I like being anyone else."

There's a pause, just a heartbeat.

"Have a drink," he says then, offering a bottle of the whiskey that will soon be the hysterical ruin of our afternoon. And unless I'm mistaken, he's stopped being one Lou Reed and become another, this one much less like all the evil in the world coming to the boil at once. "What's your next question?"

What indeed? This is the man who in dark alliance with John Cale in The Velvet Underground overthrew existing notions of what rock music could be, nearly everything worth listening to since influenced by the noise they made. Richard Williams put it best. "They are not the reason rock 'n' roll exists," he wrote of the Velvets. "But you could call them the reason it sounds the way it does and not get laughed at."

I have a lot of questions.

I've been taken aside, however, before meeting Lou and been discouraged from asking him about any number of things, starting with The VU and including David Bowie, the much-lambasted *Berlin* and just about anything else of predictable interest. This is so absurd I decide to ignore such advice and see what happens if I ask him what he thought were the highlights of The Velvet Underground's brief but spectacular career. To my relief, truculence gives way to palpably fond reminiscence.

"They're too numerous to mention," he says, voice audibly softening. "I love what we did and I'm proud of it. We stood for everything that kids liked and adults hated. We were loud, you couldn't understand the lyrics. We were vulgar. We sang about dope, sex, violence—you name it. If I wasn't me, I would have idolized myself in The Velvet Underground."

We talk a while about people's attitudes towards him, the resentment of some that he didn't die when his reputation was intact, indisputable, untarnished.

"I know half the people turn up at concerts to see if I'm going to drop dead on stage," he says. "And they're *so* disappointed that I'm still around and writing and capable of performing without falling down. But I haven't OD'd. And I know that a whole mess of those people would have been just *ecstatic* if, say, five years ago I had. The legend for them would have been complete.

"But I didn't want to do that. And they were appalled. 'Lou,' they said, 'You write all these songs and say all these things and then you don't go out and finally *do it!* You've let us down.' Come on. Have a heart. They never even offered me the dope to do it with. They expected me to do it with *my own dope*. My dear, they must have been *joking*. And even when I was approached, it was invariably with the wrong dope. Someone comes staggering up to you and you wonder just what the fuck they're on. Like, they're turning *green* and vomiting and they say, 'Here's some stuff, Lou.' And you throw your hands in the air and say, 'My *dear*, no!'

"I couldn't possibly turn green and go out like that. I'm too fastidious. Anyway, I'm not into dope. That's true. Why are you laughing? I don't smoke grass and I don't like things that everyone sniffs off a table. That's tawdry. It's so *common*. I like to play with my own system, alone. I'm into drug masturbation. Hey, that's really good," he laughs. "I've just given you the headline for your article. 'LOU REED – DRUG MASTURBATION EXCLUSIVE!' It doesn't mean anything, but it's like Jim Morrison, who was a fool, but he was interviewed once and came up with that line about being an 'erotic politician'. It didn't mean a thing, but sounded fantastic and he got so much press out of it. Drug masturbation must be good for at least two columns...

"And you know if he was around today," he says of Morrison, "they'd be saying the same things about him as they're saying about me. You know, 'Why doesn't he stop before he desecrates his best works totally and completely? He's taking away the admiration of us, his closest friends. Why doesn't he stop before it's too late? Why doesn't he leave part of it untouched?' Well, having met the ingrate, you know that I'm not to be taken seriously. I lie. I cheat. I hate. I'm going to take it all down with me when I go."

Mention is passingly made of 1974 album *Sally Can't Dance*.

"I hate that album," he says. "I just *can't* write songs you can dance to. I make an effort and *Sally Can't Dance* was an effort. But I despise that record."

What about "Ennui" a stand-out cut, as chilling in its way as anything on *Berlin*?

"That's not bad," he says quickly. "You notice how I change my opinion of the album with the mention of that song? It's the track most people skip on the album, I suspect. It must be. It's the one I like. David was there when we mixed it," he goes on, "and he had a fit. 'I can't hear the words,' he kept screaming. I could hear the words. But he kept screaming, 'I can't hear the fucking words. Don't you realise that's one of the reasons people listen to you? I can't hear the words.' I just said, 'So?' I can't really be bothered."

And what of the album Bowie produced, *Transformer*?

"That album had nothing to do with anything," he says. "It did get me a hit single, which was cause for much subsequent dismay in many circles, including mine. So David, if you read this, I hope you feel real proud of yourself. I really don't have any memories of making that album. I was in pathetic shape. I had a nervous eye twitch and David thought I was drunk all the time, which I wasn't."

Much reviled at the time, *Berlin* is now acknowledged as a classic. The critical mauling it received on release in 1973 is still painful, his tone when talking about it sombre, full of raw hurt.

"The way that album was overlooked was probably the biggest disappointment I ever faced," he says, almost whispering. "From that point on there was nothing that anybody could do that would affect me. I pulled the blinds *shut* at that point. And they've remained closed. There's really no talking to me now. You think I'm kidding, don't you? I don't care what people write about me anymore. I have no respect whatsoever for their opinions. I may never hit that peak again. Like *Metal Machine Music*, it's the kind of album you only do once."

We talk late into the afternoon, not much left in either bottle of Johnnie Walker Red when we're done. As I'm leaving, he asks me what I'll be doing the following week, which of course depends on my fickle paymasters at *Melody Maker*.

"Fuck *them*," he says. "You're coming to Sweden with me," he seems suddenly to decide.

To my great astonishment, he seems to have taken a shine to me and is even now commanding a passing flunky to take care of the relevant travel arrangements. I'm pretty speechless.

"I'll see you next week," he says. And he does.

When I roll up to the plush Stockholm hotel where he's staying, he's actually waiting for me in the lobby. We're soon being driven through oddly-deserted streets to an address Lou has scrawled on a piece of paper. It turns out to be the pad of a high-end dealer and it looks like the lair of a minor Bond villain. By the time we leave, we're both fearsomely high on something or other, and not long after this we're in Lou's hotel room. Rachel, the glamorous transvestite who's Lou's lover at the time and the inspiration for 'Coney Island Baby', is standing at the window, following the flight of a helicopter buzzing over rooftops. 'Sister Morphine' is playing on Lou's Uher tape recorder which he takes with him everywhere, slung over his shoulder like a rocket launcher. His arrival anywhere is invariably predicted by the strains of Abba's 'Dancing Queen' a current favourite, and the only other track he seems to be currently listening to.

Lou's sitting across the room from me, tuning a guitar and talking non-stop about anything that occurs to him. I've never met anyone so relentlessly funny and Rachel and I are still laughing the next night at dinner after a phenomenal show at Stockholm's handsome Concert House when Lou entertains us with an account of trying to get ice for his drink that morning.

"We're in Sweden, right, and they can't get me some *ice*. Good Christ! Sweden's almost in the goddamn *Arctic Circle* and they can't get me some miserable fucking *ice*. There must be ice *everywhere*.

I told this guy to get his wife or whoever to fill her mouth with water. Then I told him to send her out into the street with her mouth open, wait for the water to freeze and then come up to my room and spit in my fucking drink."

Lou's next show is in Gothenberg, after which the local promoter invites everyone out for a drink. Lou's band perk-up at this, but Lou orders them back to the hotel for an early night. He says he's up for a drink, though, and takes me with him, even as the band troop off, somewhat downcast. We fetch up, many cocktails and whatnot later, at a swanky fish restaurant where we're seated at tables around a large circular pool. The waitress gives us small remote control devices, which makes us wonder what the fuck's going on. It turns out our food will be served on large dinner plates placed on model boats. Using our remote control devices, we will guide the boats with our food on them to docking berths adjacent to our tables. What unbelievable fucking fun! Lou is soon laughing like a madman, sailing his boat around the pool in a manner that can only be described as reckless, with said boat careening wildly and capsizing the boats of other diners.

"I wish they had some fucking *submarines*," Lou cackles, the pool now awash with sinking boats, food bobbing on its surface like flotsam. A large schooner drifts by. "Sink that fucker, Jones," Lou commands with a certain nautical swagger. I reach out and plunge it under the water, three large seafood platters going down with it. A group of blustery businessmen at a table opposite is now screaming at us. One of them stands up, purple-faced and ranting. Lou throws a knife at him. The businessman ducks the knife, but loses his balance and ends up in the pool. He starts wading towards us, the furious little man. "Time to go, Jones," Lou says, laughing hysterically as we pile into the back of a car and roar off. Much, much later, we are in Lou's hotel room, drunk, squabbling over the last bottle of schnapps while Rachel gives us a fearsome ticking off. Lou passes out on the bed, me next to him, vaguely aware of Rachel calling Lou's tour manager who soon arrives, slings me over his shoulder and carries me to my room, where I wake up the next morning feeling like I've been attacked by dogs.

Olivia Newton-John

Lake Tahoe, Nevada, April 1977

We get an early flight out of San Francisco, flying through American sunlight to Reno with barely enough time for a couple of cocktails and a packet of peanuts before we land, the stewardess trying to wrestle the drink out of my hand even as the plane hits the runway, with me trying to bat her off with the in-flight magazine.

At the airport, we hire a car – a flame-red Monarch, very swish – for an afternoon drive to Lake Tahoe that takes us through the Washoe Valley. Our passage is flanked by the formidable passing beauty of the Toiyabe National Forest and overlooked by the snow-capped peaks of the Sierra Nevada mountains. We're about 20 miles out of Reno, driving along Nevada State Highway 395, when the first in a succession of massive billboards looms into view, advertising the current season of shows by Olivia Newton-John at Del Webb's Sahara Hotel in Tahoe – where Frank Sinatra once partied hard and dreamed of building a gambling and entertainment empire to rival Vegas or Atlantic City.

The billboards are a timely reminder of the dulcet-voiced Australian songbird's immense popularity in the United States where, since 1974 (according to the press pack I'm looking at), she's sold millions of records and won no less than 39 industry awards, including three Grammys. My companions are duly impressed – unsurprisingly, perhaps, since one of them works for Olivia's record company and the other's a journalist from a woman's magazine who appears to be a fan and is genuinely excited to be on her way to interview the antipodean warbler. Me? I haven't got a fucking clue what I'm doing here, though as always I suspect it has quite a bit to do with *Melody*

Maker assistant editor Michael Watts who, apparently for his own amusement, keeps sending me off on unlikely assignments. When he tells me, for instance, that he's sending me to America to interview Olivia Newton-John, I can't quite believe it. It's 1977, for God's sake! Somewhere across London, Joe Strummer is barking out "*No Beatles, Elvis or The Rolling Stones...*" I'm sure if I can get a call in to him, he'd cheerfully add Olivia's name to the list, rectifying at a stroke a pretty serious oversight. Mick's having none of it. Be gone, he says. And I am.

Following a 15-hour flight to California and on our arrival in San Francisco, my companions sensibly retire early to their rooms while I head out on the town. This means they're utterly refreshed today whereas I'm slumped in the back seat of the car, grumpy, exhausted and hung-over. Not far outside Carson City, I suggest it might be time to stop for a drink – a couple of beers at least. So we pull into the parking lot of a place called Scotty's Diner and walk in. Heads turn as we do, a surly bunch of coves at a table in the corner hunched over their drinks, apparently unable to take their eyes off me, muttering something about the length of my hair, what I'm wearing, whatever, that I don't quite catch but which sounds more than vaguely menacing. They're a classic gang of rough-house unpleasants, sporting more tattoos between them than the Sixth Fleet, and I can tell in a moment they're looking forward to trouble.

We take a table and order a round of beers. I head for the gent's – the washroom, bathroom, men's room, whatever they call it – and wash up, a face full of cold water bringing me around a bit. Back out in the bar, the boys continue to glare. One of them, eyes too close together for my liking, gets up, goes into the men's room. He's not in there long, and he comes out smirking, an evil little look on his face, the promise of unqualified nastiness to come. At which point, I realise I've left my watch on a shelf above the sink in the men's room just vacated by the yahoo yonder. I push back my chair and wander in. There's a message scrawled on the wall that wasn't there five minutes ago.

It says this: "LONGHAIRS ARE LIVING PROOF THAT NIGGERS FUCK WITH DOGS."

Well, this spooks me more than somewhat.

I'd like to say at this point I swagger back into the bar and kick some serious cracker ass. I don't. What I do is sidle over to the table where my travelling companions are sitting and suggest that an early exit is probably advisable. A few hours after that, we're in South Lake Tahoe, where we are booked into individual suites at Del Webb's Sahara Hotel, each as big as a housing estate, and proceed to live it up on room service for the next couple of days, with everything free.

The second night we're there, we go to see Olivia's show as guests of the hotel, thoroughly pampered. We get a big table, the best seats in the house, it looks like. We get champagne, and the most expensive wine. I order something called a Neptune Salad and end up with Kew Gardens on a plate the size of an ice-rink. I'm just about to start hacking away at the undergrowth in front of me when one of Olivia's underlings appears and says she'll be available for an interview during the interlude between her two evening concerts.

Come the break, I'm escorted backstage, where she has quarters as sumptuous as anything known to the Ottoman Empire. I find her tiny and perched on a sofa big enough to seat a coach party. We make a little small talk, she tells a couple of fluffy anecdotes that sound like she's reading from an autocue and I'm just about to ask her something about the dark narrative sub-text of 'Take Me Home, Country Roads' when she announces that meeting me has been "t'riffic" and she's really enjoyed the interview. And with that, she just kind of wafts out of the room, like something lifted up by a light breeze and blown away. We've been talking for about six minutes. I sit there for a moment, quietly stunned.

Is that it?

"Don't knock it," her stage manager says. "Lotta people don't even get that close. She really opened up with you there."

I laugh all the way back to the bar where I order everything twice, on the house.

THE SEX PISTOLS

London, May 1977

A few weeks before "God Saves The Queen" goes, unlisted, to number one, Johnny Rotten is standing on a street corner in Notting Hill, being frisked by a policeman – PC B510 who, after giving Johnny a beady look, tells him to be on his way. Sid Vicious starts to walk off with Johnny, down Westbourne Grove towards the Virgin Records HQ on Portobello Road, where shortly I'm supposed to be interviewing The Sex Pistols for *Melody Maker*.

"Not so fast," PC B510 tells Sid, getting out his notebook. "What's *your* name?"

"Sid Vicious."

"That would be V-I-C-I-O-U-S?"

" 'Spose so."

"Address?"

"Here and there."

"Date of birth?"

"How the fuck should I know?"

Johnny Rotten stares at this absurd spectacle with bristling disgust.

"This is called living in England in 1977," he says to me. "We look different and it frightens them."

A guy from Malcolm McLaren's office now turns up and asks the policeman what the problem is.

"Turn out your pockets," the officer replies, somewhat to our collective disbelief.

What's *he* done? This gets me a look from the copper.

"I'd like you to turn out your pockets as well, sir," PC B510 tells me.

"Arrest them both," Sid thoughtfully suggests to our friend from the local constabulary. "They're Nazis."

"And you're a big mouth," the copper tells Sid, looking at him like he's some kind of pond life. "Now, move along or I'll book the lot of you."

"Happens all the time," Johnny Rotten says not much later, as he, Sid, Paul Cook and Steve Jones barge into a small office in the Virgin HQ in Vernon's Yard. "All the time. Wherever I go. If it ain't a copper, it's some big, fat ignorant turd."

This bright Tuesday afternoon is the first time all four members of the Pistols have visited their new record company, with whom they signed three weeks ago after being dropped first by EMI and then A&M. They seem determined to make an impression.

"Where's that cunt Branson?" Sid Vicious, a loose-limbed pile of rags and leather and skin with the sheen of mildew, suddenly wants to know. "And where can I get something to eat?" he asks, a needy little wretch.

"More to the point," Rotten now remarks, "is where we can get a fuckin' drink?"

"I'm so fuckin' ill, I'm going to puke," Sid says.

"You've just gorra big *spot* on the end of your fuckin' nose," grumbles Steve Jones, apparently fresh off a building site with biceps to match, giving Sid a charmless slap.

"Where's the fuckin' *drink*?" Johnny wants to know now, whining impatiently, making a noise like something you'd put down rat poison for if you heard it under your floorboards.

Dapper Virgin press supremo Al Clark, who is more used to dealing with the woolly-hatted likes of Gong and musical cereberalists like Henry Cow, now arrives with a crate of Foster's and The Sex Pistols fall on it like something out of a wildlife documentary.

"That's fuckin' better," Rotten says, belching, then launching into a tirade that takes up most of what's left of the afternoon.

"The Sex Pistols," he begins, "are the only honest band that's hit this planet in about two thousand million years. People hate us because we tell the truth. But we don't care. We won't change. We'll always tell people to fuck off if they try to tell us what to do. It doesn't matter what anybody thinks about us. It doesn't matter what *you* think of us. You could go away and slag us off. I don't care. I don't expect anything from anyone.

"We set our own direction, and we don't follow anyone. Not like the rest of those fuckin' bands, like The Clash and The Damned and The Stranglers. They're all bollocks. They're just doing what every other band has done. It's the same big fat hippie trip. They make me cringe.

"I think it's vile when I see a band that's obviously imitating us. I think that's absolutely disgusting. That shows a complete lack of intelligence. It shows they have no reason for being on stage. You have to do your own thing. You have to be yourself, otherwise you've got nothing to offer. And if you've got nothing to offer, you're in the wrong place and you should just fuck off and die. You have to be honest. You have to believe in yourself. Whatever anyone says or whatever happens. That's another reason people hate us. We don't conform to their stupid standards. Like at press conferences, you know? They try to get us to be nice and polite to what they call the 'right' people. That's dreadful. If someone says to me, 'Watch that person, they're in a position to really slag you off, keep away from them,' then I just go up to them and say, 'You cunt. I hate you.' Why should I be fuckin' polite to some cunt that fuckin' hates us?"

"Someone described us the other day as a fuckin' 'kamikaze band'," Steve Jones says. "But we just play music. We don't crash fuckin' planes."

He seems pretty clear about this, but – look out – Rotten's off again.

"Music should be *fun*," he says. "It's meant to be a relief from working 9 to 5 in a factory. It shouldn't be about some cunt on stage yapping about how terrible it is to be on the dole. When I was on the dole, it was *not* terrible. I was being paid for not working. Marvellous! I don't understand why people complain about it. I was getting paid a tenner a week. More than I'm getting now."

Someone mentions the new Chelsea single, "Right to Work", and Rotten grins maliciously.

"Gene October screaming about wanting the right to work is fuckin' hysterical," he says. "He's *got* a fuckin' job. He's in a *fuckin' group*. How ridiculous."

111

More ridiculous still for Rotten are past-it pop legends, who now come into his line of fire.

"I hate those cunts," he says. "They're full of lies. Always contradicting themselves. Like, I was reading a thing about Pete Townshend talking about punk. And I thought, '*Who are you*? How *dare* you presume to have the right to tell us what it's all about?' He half admits he doesn't understand what's happening. I don't think he ever did."

"It's that other cunt, I hate," Steve Jones says. "Roger Daltrey."

"I'd like to give him a good fuckin' kickin'," Sid adds, although you would not fancy his chances against a bruiser like Daltrey.

"I don't give a fuck for any of 'em," Rotten goes on. "I never even liked the Stones. Jagger was always too distant. You could never imagine talking to Mick Jagger. If you saw him in the street, you probably wouldn't be able to get anywhere fuckin' near him for fuckin' bodyguards. I don't see why he has to have fuckin' *bodyguards* carting him all over the place."

"He came down to Sex one afternoon," Sid says. "Stood outside for three hours because he was too terrified to come in. And then just as he was about to come in, John slammed the door in his face. He's a fuckin' comedian."

"Ian Hunter's a cunt, too," Steve Jones says. "All that talk of coming from the street. Fuck off."

"I know we frighten these people," Rotten says. "Like Robert Plant came down the Roxy, surrounded by millions of bodyguards. One of them came up to me and said, 'Robert Plant wants to talk to you. You aren't going to start anything, are you?' And all these heavies are standing there, waiting for me to have a go at him. And he's twice my fuckin' size. What am I going to do? I just looked at him and he's a real ignorant old northerner and I felt really sorry for him. The geezer looked so shy. How can you respect someone like *that*?"

Could he see a future for The Sex Pistols as part of the rock establishment they now evidently despise? These things happen, after all.

"*Never*" he says without hesitation. "We're still the only band that doesn't hold press conferences every two weeks and pay for some far-out binges for the social elite and grovel around and fly every other reporter in the music press over to New York on a private plane. Fuck that. But we're going to be around for a while. We've got a record out now and we're going to finish the album and we'll find somewhere to play. They won't stop us.

"They can shut us out," he says. "But they'll never shut us up."

ELVIS COSTELLO

London, June 1977

They put us in a small room on the top floor of 32 Alexander Street where, on the ground floor and in the building's ratty basement, Stiff Records have their HQ. It's noisy this afternoon with various comings and frequent goings and volatile Stiff supremo Jake Riviera giving raucous voice to his typical impatience with just about everything.

A couple of weeks earlier, the scrappy 23-year old sitting opposite me had made his live debut at the Nashville Rooms in West Kensington as Elvis Costello, a name by all accounts attributable to Jake.

By then Elvis had released two great singles on Stiff – "Less Than Zero" and "Alison", the latter, unusually for the time, a ballad. At the Nashville, he plays most of his still-unreleased debut album, *My Aim Is True*, which means songs like "Mystery Dance", "Miracle Man", "I'm Not Angry", "Welcome to The Working Week" and "(The Angels Wanna Wear) My Red Shoes". He leaves to the sound of jaws dropping. I meet him briefly afterwards, and arrange an interview he initially has to cancel because he can't get time off from work at the Elizabeth Arden cosmetic works (the "vanity factory" of "I'm Not Angry"). When we eventually meet, he stroppily refuses to answer questions about his background and swears a lot.

"I don't want to talk about it," he says bluntly about his past. "Nobody showed any interest in me then, so I'm not going to get into it now. If you weren't there, you missed it."

We do establish early on, however, that he's a prolific songwriter.

"I've written hundreds of songs," he says. "They're not *all* classics, though," he adds, no hint of modesty, just a pragmatic assessment of his own songbook, which to his ire has already been compared to people he doesn't like, Bruce Springsteen among them.

"Springsteen's always romanticising 'The Street'," he says contemptuously. "I'm bored with people who romanticise the fucking 'Street'. 'The Street' isn't fucking attractive, there's nothing romantic about it. I mean, I live in fucking *Hounslow*. It's a very boring area, a terrible place, awful. It would be fucking ridiculous of me to try to romanticise fucking *Hounslow*."

How did he end up on Stiff?

"Well, it wasn't for the fucking money they offered me, that's for sure. There was no phenomenal advance," he laughs. "They've bought me an amp and a tape recorder and I'm glad they're not subsidising me to any great extent beyond that. I don't want to end up in debt to a fucking record company and I don't want fucking charity. I went to a lot of record companies before I came to Stiff, major labels. And I never went looking for charity. I didn't want any *favours*. I didn't go in and say, 'Look, I've got these songs and, well, with a bit of polishing up and a good producer I might make a good record if you'd just be kind enough to sign me to your wonderful label.' I went in and said, 'I've got some great fucking songs, why don't you get off your fucking arse and put them out?'

"I went around for nearly a year with demo tapes before I came to Stiff and it was always the same response," he goes on, building up a formidable head of steam now. "'We can't hear the words.' 'It isn't commercial enough.' 'There aren't any singles.' They were just idiots, all of them, those people. And I'd just like them to know I haven't forgotten them.

"I felt like I was bashing my head against a brick wall. It's a terrible position to be in. You start thinking you're mad. You listen to the radio and you watch the TV and all you hear is a lot of fucking rubbish. And all the time you know you're capable of producing something infinitely better."

Did he feel embittered by the experience?

"No, it didn't *make* me bitter," he snorts derisively. "I was *already* bitter."

There's a pause, a rare thing in his conversation, now and for years to come.

"I knew what it would be like," he says then. "I had no illusions about the music business. It was no sudden shock to be confronted by

115

these idiots. I didn't ever think that I was going to walk into a record company and meet some fat guy with a cigar who'd say something like, 'Stick with me son. I'll make you a STAR.'

"I'm not starry-eyed in the fucking slightest. You can tell what these people are like instinctively. You just have to look at them to know they're fucking idiots. But I don't want to come off sounding like I'm obsessed with the music business."

God forbid!

"Seriously," he says. "I couldn't give a shit about the music business. They don't know anything, those people. They're irrelevant. I don't give any thought at all to them. They're not worth my time."

He'd been backed on *My Aim Is True* by American country-rockers Clover and was now putting a band together, a very specific sound in mind.

"I want to get away from the conventional group sound," he says. "I certainly don't want it to be a *rock* band. I hate rock bands. I hate anything with fucking extended solos or bands that are concerned with any kind of musical virtuosity. The songs are the most important thing. I like and write short songs. It's a discipline. There's no disguise. You can't cover up the weaknesses in songs like that by dragging in banks of fucking synthesisers and choirs of fucking angels. They have to stand up on their own, with none of that nonsense. Songs are just so fucking effective. People seem to have forgotten that.

"People used to live their lives by songs. They were like calendars or diaries. And they were *pop* songs. Not elaborate fucking pieces of music. You wouldn't say, 'Yeah, that's the time I went out with Janet, we went to see the LS-fucking-O playing Mozart.' You'd remember you went out with Janet because they were playing The Lovin Spoonful's "Summer in The City" on the radio."

We talk a little about the vagaries of fame.

"If ability had anything to do with success then there would be a whole lot of obscure people who would be famous," he says, "and there would be a whole lot of famous people who'd be lingering in extremely well-justified fucking obscurity."

And was there anyone he'd like to see becoming famous?

"Yeah," he says, not missing a beat. "Me."

THE SEX PISTOLS

London, June 1977

I get a call from Al Clark, head of press at Virgin Records. He wants to know what I'm planning for the Queen's Silver Jubilee. I tell him I'm seriously thinking about climbing to the top of the tallest nearby building and raking street parties with hostile gunfire. He's kind enough to laugh at this, but I can tell he's pretty stressed-out.

And no wonder. Virgin have recently signed The Sex Pistols, and they're proving quite a handful for Al – Fleet Street constantly on the phone, digging for dirt – after several years dealing with more typical Virgin acts like Gong and Hatfield and The North, in whom even the music press have long-since lost interest. Things are hotting up even more for Al right now, following the release on May 27th of the Pistols' "God Save The Queen", at which point, of course, all hell breaks loose. Fleet Street's glare these past couple of weeks has been blinding, like nothing Al has ever known – Henry Cow and Wigwam never coming in for this kind of treatment.

Anyway, what he's telling me now is something I'm not supposed to mention to anyone else – as if! – but the gist of it is that, in a gloriously calculated act of defiance, the Pistols will be sailing down the Thames on a boat they've hired and on which they intend to play a short set as they cruise past the Houses of Parliament, some time during the late evening of Monday, June 7th: Jubilee Day itself, the 25th anniversary of the Queen's accession. Do I want to be there? I don't even have to think about it.

I arrive with my girlfriend at Charing Cross Pier in the early afternoon. It's a grim old day, overcast, the sky dull and gloomy, a nipping wind coming off the river. Down on the pier, it's bedlam. Word about the trip has got out, obviously, and there's a teeming horde of punks trying to get on the boat, which my girlfriend now points out is called The Queen Elizabeth. Someone with a clipboard and a guest-list is trying to maintain order, but it's a losing battle, and he starts shouting for the boat to pull away from the pier.

It's touch and go at this point whether we're going to make it onto the boat before it – what? – casts off, I guess is the nautical phrase I'm looking for. A bit of pushing and a fearless amount of barging, however, and we're at the bottom of the gang-plank and then we're on the boat. Behind us on the pier, it's more chaotic than ever. Furious punks, angry at being excluded from the Pistols' party, are screaming, spitting and cursing. Some of them leap from the pier, cling to the side of the boat and scramble onto the deck. There's a splash or two as the boat chugs down the river, out of their reach. Packs of them now begin to race along the Embankment, trying to keep up with us as we steam out into the middle of the Thames, heading towards Greenwich. On one of the bridges ahead of us, we can see a gang of punks dismantling a road sign. As the boat goes under the bridge, they lob the road sign – this huge metal sheet – over the side of the bridge and onto the deck of the boat, which it hits with an enormous clang, luckily killing no one.

The mood on The Queen Elizabeth is oddly sour, tense and vaguely unpleasant. There's not much sense of this being any kind of celebration. The atmosphere's too fraught. Every other person you bump into is speeding off their tits, everyone hitting the sulphate early and washing it down with can-after-can of lager, beer, whatever. We're going back up river now, towards Chelsea Bridge, and tempers are fraying badly. There's a scuffle towards the back of the boat, a photographer getting kicked about by someone we're told is Jah Wobble.

It's getting dark now, as we turn around and start back towards Charing Cross Pier and the Houses of Parliament. Which is when we first see the police launches, keeping at a fair distance, but just close enough to let us know they're there.

The Sex Pistols have set up their gear on the top deck of The Queen Elizabeth and at around 9:30pm, Rotten, Jones, Cook and Sid Vicious get ready to play. There are squeals of feedback, horrendously loud in this cramped space, as Jones plugs in his guitar.

Cook smacks a couple of drums. Sid is – who knows? – somewhere else. And Rotten? Rotten looks ready for war. And suddenly – when did this happen? – they're screaming into "Anarchy in the UK", and the whole deck takes on a life of its own. The crowd is a heaving mass, delirious, lost in the sheer electricity of the moment. I'm about four feet in front of Rotten, whose eyes look like something from the final seconds of Rosemary's Baby, burning from the ghost his face has become. They play "No Feelings" and "Pretty Vacant" ("And we don't caaaaaare!!!!!!"). The police launches are closer now, we're alongside the Houses of Parliament and the Pistols are playing "No Fun". The police launches have searchlights on and they're circling us, and on one of the launches there's someone in a uniform and he's shouting something through a megaphone that we can't quite hear but take to be instructions to get the boat back to the pier.

And there's the pier up ahead, and on the pier there are the police, lined up under more searchlights, rank-upon-rank of them, looking mean and menacing, metropolitan storm troopers. Now the power on the boat's been cut off. You can't hear Jones anymore, and I don't think Sid's been plugged in at all. Cook hammers the drums. Rotten's screaming, "No Fun! No Fun!" Now we're alongside the pier and you can see how pissed-off the police are. They've been on duty all day, smiling the good cop smile for the Silver Jubilee crowds. They're tired, irritable. Any excuse and they'll be among us, busting heads. Whoever's in charge comes aboard. He tells Pistols' manager Malcolm McLaren and Virgin supremo Richard Branson that he wants the boat cleared, sharpish.

McLaren throws a fit. Branson says he's hired the boat until midnight, has a contract to prove it, and won't be moved. He waves a bit of paper, a dramatic little flourish that brings supportive cheers. The copper's not impressed, and repeats his demand for the boat to be cleared. McLaren wants to know what will happen if we refuse. Then it's made clear the police will come aboard and with as much force as is required will remove us. This makes everyone twitchy. Branson suggests that anyone who wants to leave should leave now because things look like they're getting ugly in a hurry.

The police thunder up the gangplanks, angry men in leather and serge. It gets rough pretty quickly, people being man-handled onto the

119

pier in headlocks, others with their arms twisted behind their backs, some simply dragged by the hair, arms, the occasional leg. There's a lot of shoving, punching and kicking from the boys in blue as we're herded up the steps to the Embankment, police on either side of us. McLaren goes down in front of me. A couple of us scoop him up before he's trampled. This is all turning very nasty. We stumble into the street and McLaren – I can't believe this – raises a clenched fist and in the direction of the nearest police and screams: "You fucking fascist bastards!" He's then dragged behind a souvenir kiosk, beaten up and arrested – one of 11 people from the boat trip who ended up in jail that night.

I stand there on the Embankment, police vans screaming off into the darkness, Jubilee bunting strewn across the road, blood on the wall behind me, sirens in the distance. The sound of England at war with itself.

STIFF RECORDS

London, July 1977

The roof's there, so Jake Riviera hits it – the Stiff supremo, who marches into rock legend as the highly-combustible manager of Elvis Costello, now giving a typically fearful ear-bashing to some unfortunate underling.

"No," Jake is shouting, a noise like a chainsaw howling through teak, "it *won't* be too late, not if you do it *now*. It *will* be too late if you don't get *off* the phone and *on* the fucking *case*. Good. Let's start *shaking*. Speak to you later. Groovy."

It's 10:30, on an overcast Tuesday morning, and it's turning into another typical day in the life of 32 Alexander Street. I've been nagging Jake for weeks about spending a day here for a story I want to write for *Melody Maker*. For just as long, Jake's been stalling. Last night, however, he'd called me, told me if I still wanted to write the story to be at Stiff this morning, early.

"If you're not here by nine," he yells at me, "we'll start without you."

What's become clear as the morning goes on is that whatever Jake's been plotting is going to involve CBS – who's annual international sales conference is being held this week in London, at the Hilton Hotel – and Elvis Costello, who's just arrived at Alexander Street, with his guitar, a Vox practise amp and the recently-formed Attractions, who will later tonight be making their London debut at Dingwalls in Camden Lock. The Attractions soon head for the pub next door.

"Get some *cabs*, somebody," Jake is now screaming. "We need *wheels*, and we need them now."

The cabs arrive. Jake bundles Costello into the street, storms the line of taxis, yanking open doors, pushing people inside. He races into the pub, re-emerging with The Attractions and a bottle of cider. The Attractions take off in a transit, followed by a cab with Elvis in the back, clutching his guitar and practise amp, the cab's boot door flapping open. Jake tears after it, screaming, slams the boot shut as the cab takes the corner of Alexander Street, accelerating into Sunderland Terrace and onto the Porchester Road. This is what the final minutes of life on Earth will be like, I remember thinking. There will be this same sense of sheer panic and inarticulate frenzy, and Jake Riviera swigging cider from a bottle and shouting at everyone at the top of his voice.

Anyway, the rest of us now pile into a taxi with Jake and speed off in the direction of the Hilton.

Costello had famously been turned down by every major record company before signing to Stiff, who'd happily given him a home. Jake had quickly recognised, however, that if Elvis was going to make the kind of international commercial impact he was capable of, sooner rather than later he was going to have to get him signed to one of the labels that had previously rejected him. CBS, for instance. The most immediate way Jake can think of to bring Elvis to the attention of the label's powerbrokers is to have him busk outside their convention, so that when they break for lunch or a little afternoon shopping, they'll be confronted by Costello, armed with a guitar, a horn-rimmed angry musical ambush. The bastards had ignored him before. Jake would dare them to ignore him now.

Elvis straps the Vox practise amp over his shoulder, plugs in his Fender Jazzmaster, assumes the determined stance of a man you wouldn't want to fuck with. The Stiff crowd have formed a loose circle around him. There's a moment's hesitation, then he's thrashing away at his guitar, playing "Welcome to the Working Week" astonishingly loud.

"*Go to it*," Jakes yells, by way of unnecessary encouragement, adrenalin pumping, eyes shining like flares. "That's my *boy*!"

Elvis is now hollering "Waiting for the End of the World", with as much attention to the tune as he can decently afford in the circumstances. A gaggle of Japanese tourists stops to watch, weighed down with cameras and souvenirs, puzzled beyond description. They applaud politely as Costello finishes "Waiting for the End of the World" and launches straight into "Less Than Zero". A group of CBS conventioneers wanders out of the Hilton, clutching little paper tuck bags that bear the legend: "A BIG FAT THANK YOU FROM TED NUGENT". They stand there, gaping at Costello. Jake is swigging cider and cackling gleefully. The crowd begins to swell as more tourists and convention guests pile onto the pavement.

"All right. Who's in charge here?"

This is a security officer from the Hilton, unpleasantly aggressive.

"Who's in *charge*?" Jake screams in his face. "Who's in CHARGE? NO ONE'S IN CHARGE! It's a free fucking country and we can do what we *like*. Who are YOU anyway? From the hotel? You must be American. Did you know that some parts of America go back to 1934? Well? Did you? You're an American, aren't you? Uh?"

The fellow reels back, stunned.

"I – I'm not American," he splutters. "I'm from *Hampshire*."

By the time Elvis roars into "Mystery Dance", it looks like most of the CBS convention is on the street outside the Hilton. Here, for instance, is Matthew King Kaufman, head of San Francisco's Berserkley label, home of The Modern Lovers, and over there Herb Cohen, Frank Zappa's manager. Even Walter Yetnikoff, president of the entire CBS empire, has been drawn into the action. Everyone's clapping along quite merrily. Then the law arrives.

A spotty-faced young copper clears his throat nervously and tells Jake that Elvis will have to move along.

"WHY?" Jakes snarls, in his element.

"Because he's. . . er. . . *busking*," the PC says, floundering.

"He's not BUSKING, man," Jake retaliates, terrifying in his excitement. "He's just SINGING IN THE STREET! You can't stop people SINGING IN THE STREET!!!"

"Get down Elvis!" Matthew King Kaufman calls to Costello.

The copper's now on his field radio, calling for reinforcements, a crowd of punk rockers, he's telling someone, is rioting outside the Hilton. Within minutes, three squad cars and a police van are screeching to a halt on Park Lane and a full inspector is marching up to Jake, demanding the dispersal of this unruly mob.

Jake's having none of it. "These people are ENJOYING themselves, man," he shouts. "Look at them! They're clapping. They're singing…"

The inspector is unmoved and advances on Costello.

"Move along, son," he says.

Costello takes a step to his left and continues singing. He's lost somewhere in the murky depths of "Miracle Man".

"RIGHT!" the inspector snaps, unamused by Costello's flippancy. "You're *nicked*."

With a splendidly melodramatic flourish, the inspector grabs Elvis by the collar and frog-marches him to the waiting police van, Costello's feet barely touching the ground as he's hauled along. The crowd, disappointed, begins to boo the police.

"COLSON!" Jake roars, calling to PR Glen Colson, another maverick member of the Stiff team who's quickly off in pursuit of the police van, which by now is turning into Hyde Park Corner with Elvis in the back.

"They'll probably take him to Vine Street nick," Jake calls after Colson. "Whatever you do, *spring him*," Jake adds. "He's got a sound check at four."

It's now maybe 20 minutes later and the crash you just heard is Jake bursting into the Stiff office, hot foot from the Hilton, an entire posse of us galloping after him. Within what seems like seconds, Jake is on two phones at once, talking to David Gentle, Stiff's solicitor, on one and to Glen Colson, calling from Vine Street with the police charges against Elvis, on the other.

"David? Jake. Look, the police have nicked Elvis. I've got Glen Colson at Vine Street. He says they've booked him for unlawful obstruction. Can you spring him? You CAN! Great. Colson? Gentle thinks we'll get him off with a fine. He doesn't think they'll keep him in overnight. As soon as they let him out, *bring him straight back here*. Have you got that? Good. Just don't start winding anyone up, Colson, got it? Groovy. See you later."

Riviera puts down the phones, takes a breather.

"Fuck me," he says then. "I think I probably need a drink."

So probably do we all, at which point we head for the pub next door, where Nick Lowe is at the bar with the legendary Dr Feelgood, whose new album Nick is supposed to be producing. The Feelgoods look like they're settling in for the afternoon.

"They've already been here for hours," Nick complains to Jake. "I can't shift them."

"It's your own fault," Jake growls. "The pub's the last place you should have brought them. You'll never get them out before closing time. You know what they're like."

"What am I going to *do*?" Nick moans.

"Be *firm*," Jake advises him sagely, ordering a pint of cider.

Feelgood's vocalist Lee Brilleaux, meanwhile, is at the bar discussing the procreative activities of jellyfish with Kosmo Vinyl, the Stiff roadie who goes on to become a kind of public cheerleader for first Ian Dury and then The Clash.

"No, Kos, you're wrong," Lee is telling Kosmo, surprisingly up to speed about the sexual activities of marine coelenterates. "Jellyfish don't *fuck*. They sort of *split up*. Like worms. Fascinating, really."

"Another drink, Lee?" Kosmo asks.

"Why not?" Lee grins. "We're only supposed to be recording an album, after all."

There's a dull thud as Nick Lowe's head hits the bar.

Some time later, the Feelgoods have been dragged out of the pub, The Attractions are on their way to Dingwalls and Jake is back in the Stiff office shouting at people. Ian Dury drops by with a test pressing of his new single, a song he tells me is called "Sex & Drugs & Rock & Roll." He sings me a bit. I tell him it sounds great, and it does. And now here's fabled former Led Zep and T Rex PR, BP Fallon.

How are you, Beep? "I'm effervescent, man," he says, disappearing.

Costello arrives with Colson. He's got a court appearance in the morning, where he expects to be fined £5. The police, he reports, had been surprisingly courteous.

"They only picked you up for *busking*," Jake smirks. "I didn't think they'd hang you up by the thumbs."

Costello wants copies of his album, *My Aim is True*, which has just come out after a potentially damaging delay caused by a tiff between Stiff and their distributor, Island Records.

"If they want the record," Jake insists, "they can pay for it like everyone else."

Costello's show that night at Dingwalls is sensational. He plays most of *My Aim Is True*, and nearly all of its follow-up, *This Year's Model* – giving public airings for the first time to "Lipstick Vogue", "Lip Service", "Radio Radio", "Night Rally" and "Watching the Detectives", The Attractions playing with a white-knuckle intensity that's astonishing.

The audience pushes forward, clamouring for more. But it's already all over. The Attractions are leaving the stage and Costello is shouting angrily into the microphone, clearly furious. He's berating the crowd at the back of the club, where they have been eating, drinking and talking throughout his set. He threatens never to play Dingwalls again, and then quits the stage in a huff and a flurry of expletives.

Jake, meanwhile, is at the bar. He's angry, too. The target of his immediate wrath is John Knowles, who works for Island. Knowles is known to his friends as "Knocker". Jake is about to find out why.

The dispute mentioned earlier that had delayed the release of *My Aim Is True* had inflicted severe financial pressure on Stiff, and Jake is now taking out his frustration on Knowles, or "Knocker" as we should properly call him. Jake's sort of frothing at the mouth, screaming in Knocker's face, poking him in the chest. Knocker looks like a man who will be pushed only so far. Jake is taking him to the limit.

I'm standing there with Glen Colson and Matthew King Kaufman. I don't see Knocker throw the first punch. Neither does Jake. Knocker has moved with a destructive panache that seems well-practised. He flattens Jake with a cross to the chin that would have dropped a mule and catches the hapless Riviera with another brain-scrambling wallop as he heads for the deck.

Former Pink Fairy guitarist Larry Wallis and Stiff general manager Paul Conroy pile on top of Knocker, preventing him from inflicting any more damage on Riviera, who's been sent sprawling in a tangle of disconnected limbs. With incredible presence of mind, Matthew King Kaufman attempts to cause a diversion by unzipping his flies and pissing on the bar.

Colson and I bend over Jake, who's still horizontal. Jake's mouth is puffing up, his lip is split and there's a gash on his nose. The side of his face is already badly swollen and one eye is shut. He looks like he's been hit with a house brick.

He tries to speak, his voice a ghastly croak.

"Is... my... nose... did he break my nose?" he asks, obviously in some distress.

"No, no. Your *nose* is fine," Colson reassures him cheerfully. "But I think he's knocked out most of your *teeth*."

Jake groans, closes his eyes. For the first time all day, words seem to fail him.

THE MONT DE MARSAN PUNK FESTIVAL

Southern France, August 1977

I'm arguing loudly with a baffled French security guard when a passing Joe Strummer taps me on the shoulder and asks if I fancy a line of speed, as if he thinks this is going to somehow calm me down. The weekend has long since come off the rails, so why not?

The nonsense that follows starts, not for the first time, with a telephone call. This one's from a friend named Rick Rodgers. Rick goes on to manage The Specials, but at the time has a small PR company called Trigger Publicity. Rick tells me he's doing the press for a punk festival being held in a bullring in a place called Mont de Marsan, in the far south of France, near the Spanish border. Rick asks me if I want to cover it for *Melody Maker*. He promises a flight, a decent hotel, free beer and enough drugs to stun an army. I sign up for the jaunt without a second thought.

The day before we're supposed to fly out, Rick calls again. The festival headliners – The Clash, Dr Feelgood, The Damned and The Jam – will be flying out as planned, but the rest of us – journalist, support bands, photographers – will now be going by coach, which Rick tries to laugh off as a bit of an adventure, something we'll still be talking about years down the line. He's right about the last bit, at least.

We meet the next morning for an early start, at an address that turns out somewhat ominously to be opposite the London Dungeon. When I get there, I can't believe the rusting hulk the coach company's laid on for us. It doesn't look like it will get us to the end of the street, let alone the south of France. There are a lot of people milling around in various states of grumpiness. Among them, I am surprised to find veteran guitarist Andy Summers, who I've known for a few years as a member of a great little band fronted by radical singer-songwriter Kevin Coyne. What's he doing here? And what's he done to his hair, which is dyed blond and looks like it's been cut by the local council? Turns out he's joined a punk band called The Police, which is why most of his former muso chums are no longer talking to him.

We get on the coach and he introduces me to one of his new band-mates, a bass player named Sting, who sits down next to me and on the way to Dover tells me all about himself. Seems he gave up his job as a teacher in somewhere called Cramlington, a small mining village outside Newcastle, to move with his wife and young son to London, to join The Police. He's wondering now whether he's made the right decision and frets, basically, all the way to Paris while the rest of us abandon ourselves to the beer and sulphate that seems in generous and ample supply.

When we get to Paris, we find we've been booked overnight into a decrepit slum of a hotel where we're expected to sleep 16 to a room. A bunch of us decide there's no realistic chance that we're going to get what we most need, which is rest, and instead head for the near-est noisy club, where we drink until just before dawn, at which point we're thrown out, the place finally closing. We make a terrible racket when we get back to the hotel, which gets us a dreadful telling off from Sting, who rather conspicuously fails to the see the funny side of our by now quite insensible behaviour. "Will you just, please, you know, *shut up!*" he shouts at us, but we can't hear him because we're singing, which annoys him even more.

Of course, a couple of hours later, Sting's the first one on the coach. The rest of us aren't quite so perky, until someone digs out a bag of speed. The next thing you know, people are screeching like monkeys, and Brian, the Teddy Boy coach driver who's never had speed before but has taken to it with some gusto, has whipped off his shirt and is now driving the coach *standing up* and whooping like an Apache.

"I really do think someone should have a word with that driver," Sting says, the coach veering across several lanes of traffic. "If he car-ries on like this, there's going to be an accident."

It's gone midnight when we finally roll into Mont de Marsan, where we find there are no rooms for us in the town's main hotel, The Sablat. We've been re-housed a couple of kilometres down the road in what at first glance seems to be some kind of tree house. Sting says this will be good enough for him and settles in for the night with a book. More than a few of us decide the night is still young and hike back into town.

We're looking for somewhere to get a drink when we run into Jake Riviera, here as manager of The Damned. From what he has to tell us, we've missed quite a bit of fun already, most of it starting at Heathrow. The Clash were late for the flight, but The Jam and Damned made it on time and immediately got into a drinking contest at the airport bar, according to what Jake tells us. The drinking continued on the flight. Both bands arrive in Mont de Marsan absolutely legless. It's blisteringly hot when they get here, so The Jam decide to cool off by stripping naked and jumping into the fountain in the town square. They're immediately arrested by local gendarmes.

Rat Scabies, meanwhile, has thrown up in the hotel lobby before the band have even booked into their rooms, evacuating his stomach in spectacular fashion. The Damned are banned on the spot and forced to seek alternative accommodation. Later, Rat is out drinking with The Damned's new guitarist, Lu, when they provoke a bit of a fracas with a dozen or so French paratroopers and have to leg it, pursued by the homicidal squaddies.

"Chased them around town," Jake tells us. "Despicable lack of bottle on Rat's part, I thought. Any punk worth his salt would've taken on 12 French paratroopers without thinking twice about it."

We troop into a bar where we find various members of The Damned and The Clash, including Strummer, Mick Jones, Dave Vanian, Brian James and Captain Sensible. Some hours later, the sun already up, we're staggering back to our hotel, Captain Sensible trailing loopily behind us. There's a blood-curdling scream just about now. I turn in time to see the Captain running full-tilt at a clump of shrubbery, howling as he goes. He proceeds to chain-whip the shrubbery to leafy pieces. He stands there then, glaring at the former bush, breathing hard.

What did he do *that* for?

"It was taking the *piss* out of me," Sensible replies, as if this explains everything, before passing out under a bench, where he apparently spends what's left of the night.

Day two of the festival begins with a drink in either hand and a couple more lined up on the bar.

"Comin' through," announces Dr Feelgood tour manager, Fred "Borneo" Munt, a man for whom life is there to be lived at full speed, at all times.

Fred sets a tray of breakfast brandies on the table in front of us, hands a glass to Feelgood's singer Lee Brilleaux, who knocks back a large one with seasoned aplomb and a bit of a grimace.

"If that stays down," he says, "I might go so far as havin' another one."

We're sitting in the fierce morning heat, outside the Sablat hotel in Mont de Marsan's picturesque town square. There's Lee, Feelgood's bassist Sparko and the band's manager, Chris "Whitey" Fenwick, Jake Riviera, Rat Scabies, grumpy pub rock veteran Sean Tyla and various members of Les Press Anglais.

"The thing about your French," Lee's telling us, "is that they're not what you or I would describe as gentlemen. I'd go so far," he goes on, getting into his stride, "as calling them rude. Ill-mannered, certainly. And I can't imagine *what* God was playing at when he created France. They should turn it into a golf course and have done with it.

"Nothing personal," Lee says to the lone Frenchman at our table, "but I hold the French more or less directly responsible for the unfortunate death of my Uncle Ernie. Fucking died for you lot, he did. On the railways. Bomb fell on him. Dreadful business. If you lot had sorted out the Germans on your own, he could be here now, enjoying himself, having a drink with us. But where were you when the skies were black with Dorniers?"

Meanwhile, as Brilleaux chatters on, manfully trying to talk himself out of his hangover, chaos reigns supreme down at the bullring, where the festival was meant to have kicked off at noon, the day's bill scheduled to include appearances from The Clash and The Damned, supported by The Police, The Maniacs, The Boys and a raft of French punk bands, many of whom we sadly never hear from again after today. It's around four in the afternoon now and the festival hasn't even started yet. At the Sablat, Rat Scabies is furious when someone tells him the bullring stage is dominated by The Clash's White Riot backdrop.

"If that's up when we go on," he tells Mick Jones, "I'll burn the fucking thing down."

"Do what you fucking like, mate," Mick says, not bothered.

Les Press Anglais are now in the bullring, where an all-girl group called The Lous are playing to about eight people. They're followed by a band called Asphalt Jungle, who play a version of "London's Burning" that has people laughing out loud at them, like they're village idiots, or something. Next on are The Maniacs, one of the bands we've travelled over with on the coach. They're barely half way through their set when the bass speakers blow out. In a fit of anger, their bass payer, Robert, a fearsome German with a Mohican, flings down his guitar and lashes at the recalcitrant amplifiers with a length of electrical cable. The band look on, not a little embarrassed. Someone in what suspiciously looks like it's becoming an audience shouts something at Robert. He's clearly unamused by what had seemed from this distance an impishly jocular remark and jumps off the stage, leaping over a metal barrier and into the slowly growing crowd, bearing down intimidatingly on the heckler, a scrap ensuing.

Making their first appearance with Andy Summers on guitar, The Police are on now. As you know, Sting hasn't been having anything approaching a good time on this particular jaunt into the hinterlands of the highly absurd. He's been appalled by the juvenile antics of the more unruly members of the coach party from London, and continued to worry himself to the point of total distraction about his future with the group he's re-written his life to join. Has it been worth it, all this upheaval? On the strength of their performance this evening at Mont de Marsan, perhaps not. You would not, in fact, put money on them still being together six months from now. They're pretty fucking dire.

Some time later, The Damned end a set scuppered by a malfunctioning PA by destroying everything they can lay their nasty little hands on. By the time they're finished, the stage looks like a war zone, Rat chucking the remains of his drum kit into the crowd and Captain Sensible running amok in splendidly unhinged fashion.

Sensible is back in action when The Clash play. The daft tosser slinks onstage during one ranting Clash number and lets off some overwhelmingly aromatic stink bombs, much to the fury of a supremely indignant Joe Strummer, who gives the Captain a right ticking off. Joe's not alone in finding the Captain's behaviour somewhat to the far side of reprehensible. A couple of security guards grab the unfortunate Captain and throw him off the side of the stage. His fall is painfully broken when he lands, legs apart, on a length of scaffolding, his testicles at that moment, as he will later report, suddenly relocated somewhere in the vicinity of his throat.

He's on the deck, writhing in understandable agony, when he's set upon by a squadron of French Red Cross medical attendants, who drag him on to a stretcher. They almost have him in the back of an ambulance when he freaks out completely, leaps off the stretcher, bolts out of the ambulance and, doubled over in pain, scuttles crab-like into the night. He's later discovered hiding on the roof of an equipment truck by another irate security man who thinks he's trying to hijack the vehicle and proceeds, therefore, to beat him up. Thus ends what's turned out to be quite an eventful weekend for the Captain.

That night, after The Clash have finished and the crowd's gone home, I'm walking through the narrow Mont de Marsan streets with Jake, Fenwick, Fred Munt, Rat Scabies and a few other cheerfully pissed-up malcontents. We keep seeing, always just ahead of us like some kind of apparition, a blond-haired figure, alone, haunting these streets beneath a waning moon, a book tucked under his arm, lost in thought.

It's Sting and it looks like he's still agonising about giving up so much to join The Police, a decision which must seem to him more reckless than previously thought, after their performance that afternoon ended with them being heartily barracked by the meagre crowd. This turns out to be the case as I find out when we board the bus for the long drive back to London on Sunday morning. I'm not really in much of a mood for it, I just want to curl up, really, in a miserable little ball, but I have to listen to him dither aloud over his future, which is something he's beginning to think he doesn't have. "Should I just give up?" he asks finally. I look at him, blearily, and tell him that if he's that unhappy then, yes, he should walk away from all this, put such foolishness behind him, knock it on the head, call the whole thing off, pack it in, go back to Newcastle with the wife and kid. He could be back in the classroom by Christmas, leather patches on a tweed jacket, a much-needed new teacher at an overcrowded comprehensive. He thanks me for my advice, says he'll think it over.

The next time I see him, of course, he's a millionaire and The Police are on their way to becoming one of the biggest bands in the world.

DAVID BOWIE

London, September 1977

It's Thursday afternoon and I'm off to a hotel on Park Lane to interview David Bowie. When I get there, beady-eyed flunkies look me over with tutting disapproval, and at reception I'm kept waiting for a very long time before the sallow-faced cow behind the desk deigns to acknowledge my meagre existence long enough to reluctantly give me Bowie's room number.

Anyway, not long after this, I'm in a lift that rises like air – effortlessly, silently, luxuriously – to what I imagine is one of the hotel's exclusive penthouse suites. There's a discreet ping as we reach the appropriate floor and the elevator doors open with a sexy little whoosh. I step into a long silent corridor, awash with gentle muted light, and start checking room numbers. I am, I have to confess, very nervous. Bowie is one of my musical idols, has been for years. I still shiver with excitement at the memory of seeing him at Bristol's Colston Hall on one of the first dates of the Ziggy Stardust tour – when "Sufragette City" seemed the most impossibly exciting thing I'd ever heard. Most recently, in May 1976, I'd been at Wembley Arena for all six of his London concerts on the *Station to Station* tour, which remain probably the most exciting rock shows I've ever seen. This year's *Low* and *Heroes* albums are, meanwhile, among the best records I've ever heard, the sound of the future now.

So I'm sitting in a small ante-room, one of a number of journalists who've been invited here this afternoon to meet the Thin White Duke. There's fruit in baskets, soft drinks, tea, coffee. It's like the waiting room in a private hospital. We speak in whispers, like someone's dying next door. One by one, we will be ushered into Bowie's presence. The afternoon drags by and I'm on my second pack of Marlboro when I realise someone's calling my name, discreetly, like they're trying to wake me from some uncommon trance.

Now I'm walking through the doors into the main suite which, when I get there, is empty. No trace anywhere of Bowie. I look around and notice the windows to the balcony are open and that the lace curtains are billowing into the room, sunlight streaming through them. And then, surrounded by a glowing halo of light that can only be described as celestial, David Bowie is standing in the doorway to the balcony and all that's missing from the scene is a choir of angels and their booming blissful harmonies. I'm momentarily dazzled, rooted to the spot like a slack-jawed hillbilly. And now I realise he's talking to me.

"Allan," he is in fact saying, "so very pleased to meet you at last. Brian's told me so much about you." He's talking about Brian Eno, who I've interviewed a couple of times. This is the D-Day – *the Omaha Beach* – of charm offences, and I have to say I'm pretty bowled over.

"Sit," he says with a vague wave. "Sit."

Hoping the sofa's where I think it is, I fall backwards, knees coming up to my chin as I sink into its cushiony embrace. And it's from this somewhat less-than-dignified position that I get my first real look at Bowie, who seems in pink-cheeked good health and is dressed in a flannel lumberjack shirt and jeans. Later, I mention how ghastly and ill he'd looked on the cover of 1974's *David Live* and he laughs.

"*David Live* was the final death of Ziggy," he says. "God, that album. I've never played it. The tension it must contain! And that photo of me on the cover. My God, it looks like I've just stepped out of the grave. Which is actually how I felt. That record should have been called *David Bowie Is Alive and Well and Living Only in Theory*."

Famously, the album preceded a great deal of cocaine-inspired weirdness in Bowie's life. He's keen at first to play down the strangeness and excess of his Bel Air adventures, which we now know nearly killed him. He moved back to Europe, he says, simply because he had grown stale and restless in America – where, as he puts it, he had been merely *staying*, not *living*, for two years.

"The conditions were thus," he says, reaching for a packet of Gitanes. "I realised I was tired of the country. I wanted, generally, to

134

re-evaluate what I was doing. There was no longer any enjoyment in the working process – although I'd exclude from that *Station to Station*. That was fairly exciting because it was like a plea to come back to Europe for me. It was one of those self-chat things that one has with oneself from time to time..."

At this, he suddenly throws down the pack of Gitanes, apparently annoyed with himself over something.

"Christ, no... what am I *talking* about? A LOT OF *Station to Station* and *Young Americans* was damn depressing. It was a *terribly* traumatic time. I was in a terrible state. I was absolutely infuriated that I was still in rock 'n' roll. And not only *in it*, but had been sucked into the centre of it. I *had* to move out. I'd never intended to become so *involved* in rock 'n' roll, and there I was in Los Angeles, right in the middle of it. There I was, living in the middle of this crazy and filthy rock 'n' roll circus. And it really was no more than a circus. And I should not have been in it. I should not have become such a major part of it."

It had always seemed otherwise to me, that being a major part of it was always your ambition, no point bleating about it now.

"But you wouldn't believe how much if it was entirely *unwitting*," he protests. "I think I did play *outside* the boundaries of what is considered the general area of rock 'n' roll. Some of it was just pure petulance, some of it was arrogance, some of it was unwitting, but, inevitably, I kept moving ahead.

"Ziggy, particularly, was created out of a certain arrogance. But remember, at that time I was young and full of life, and that seemed like a very positive artistic statement. I thought that was a beautiful piece of art. Then for years that fucker wouldn't leave me alone. That was when it all started to go sour. And it soured so quickly, you wouldn't believe it. And it took me an awful long time to level out. My whole personality was affected. Again, I brought that upon myself.

"I can't say I'm sorry when I look back, because it provoked such an extraordinary set of circumstances in my life. I thought I might as well take Ziggy out to be interviewed as well. Why leave him on stage? Why not complete the canvas? Looking back, it was completely absurd.

"It became very dangerous, too. I really did have doubts about my sanity. I can't deny the experience affected me in a very exaggerated and marked manner. I think I put myself very dangerously near the line. Not in a physical sense, but definitely in a mental sense. I played mental games with myself to such an extent that I'm now very relieved to be back in Europe and feeling very well... But then you see," he says with a smile so charming there should be laws against it, "I was always the lucky one."

DR FEELGOOD

Leicester, September 1977

When they finally close the bar at the Holiday Inn we have difficulty standing, and according to their manager, Chris 'Whitey' Fenwick, Dr Feelgood have spent the entire profits of their UK tour on its opening night.

"What're the implications, as it were, of that, exactly?" Feelgood's singer Lee Brilleaux asks Fenwick.

We're staggering towards the lifts, which seem an incredible distance from the bar – much further than they were three or four hours ago when we arrived back at the hotel from the De Montfort Hall, where the tour's opening show had gone well enough to put the band in the mood for an epic jolly-up that's apparently set them back a few bob.

"What are the *implications*?" Fenwick says. "The fucking *implications*? The fucking implications couldn't be fucking clearer," he goes on. "We're fucking *bankrupt*."

"How did that 'appen?" Lee wants to know.

"Without going into too much detail," Fenwick tells Lee, "it might have had something to do with trying to drink this place dry."

"Out of interest," asks Feelgood's bassist Sparko, "how did we do on that front?"

"Splendidly," Fenwick tells him. "No problem there. The place is well and fucking truly fucking dry."

"Fucking excellent," Sparko says. "Now for the mini-bars."

I don't remember getting into the lift, let alone getting out of it, but we now appear to be in someone's room – me, Lee, Chris, Sparko and the band's tour manager, Fred "Borneo" Munt. Right now, Fred is unwrapping a large block of cocaine, only slightly smaller than a house brick, specially bought in for the tour. Fred chops out some lines, one of them roughly the size of a baby's leg that he snorts in one go.

"Fuck me," he says with a wince. "That hit the spot."

"Don't mind if I do," Lee says, taking a rolled-up note from Fred. "Just to be sociable."

Sparko, meanwhile, is flicking through the pages of a Bible he's found in a draw.

"Don't believe a word of it," he announces with a defiant flourish, ripping out half the Old Testament.

"I should be very careful if I was you," Fenwick warns him gravely.

"*Why?*" Sparko wants to know.

"Because God's got your room number," Fenwick tells him a bit creepily, Sparko looking over his shoulder and no doubt remembering something about the Lord moving in mysterious ways and not wanting to be taken entirely by surprise by any unexpected manifestation of heavenly intervention.

Some time after this, I'm making my way somewhat unsteadily to my room, horrified by what looks like daylight outside, when I find Sparko flat on his back in the corridor, eyes wide open, staring at the ceiling. I doubt he's been smote from on-high by the hand of God but is more likely to be currently incapable of speech, thought or movement. So I step over him and unlock the door to my room, which I don't remember tilting at quite this angle when I was last in it. I make it to the bed, kicking off shoes and various items of clothing as I go, I lay down. The room is moving at some speed around me, a unique feature of the Holiday Inn I hadn't noticed earlier. I'm just starting to calm down a bit when the telephone starts ringing like it's feeding time in Bedlam, making me first jump and then wonder who could be calling me in what surely must still be the middle of the night. Unbelievably, it's Fred Munt, last seen what seems like only minutes ago crouched atop a wardrobe and muttering to himself in a language of indeterminate origin. He's now down in the hotel lobby, where he expects me in five minutes, which is when – whether I'm there or not – he and the band are driving off to Bradford for tonight's show. I make it to the group's van with seconds to spare. Everybody looks remarkably chipper, including Sparko. Me? I feel like Dresden after a night of Allied bombing.

"I don't know about anybody else," Lee says, about 30 minutes outside of Leicester, "but I've got a terrible thirst. Anyone fancy a drink?"

Apparently, everyone does.

"Pass the book, Whitey," Lee says, and Fenwick passes Brilleaux a directory of the country's best pubs that they've compiled on their many travels. Lee flicks through it.

"Right, where are we?" he says. "OK. Got it. Little place off the motorway, just south of Nottingham. Home-made grub and a decent pint. Couldn't ask for more."

We get there just after the pub opens and stay until they chuck us out. Everyone else tucks rather heartily into the scoff, but all I can manage is a couple of pints and a few large Bloody Marys. Then we are back in the van, somewhat revived.

"Right," Lee says. "Anyone care for a spot of beak lunch?" He starts chopping out some lines of coke. "Just a sharpener," he says, taking a hit, "to see us through the afternoon."

There's another great show that night at Bradford's St George's Hall, and much merriment after that, followed by a long drive the next day to Edinburgh, where the band have a night off. We're motoring through sun-dappled countryside when Fred, at the wheel, starts telling us how he once had a job as a sheep scatterer and developed a whistle that had the wee creatures running for cover at some speed. Sparko doesn't believe a word of this, so Fred pulls over, gets out of the van and strides over to a field full of dozing sheep. He takes a deep breath and then delivers a screeching whistle. The sheep duly scatter, quite dementedly, racing in all directions.

"Fucking amazing," Sparko says. "Does it work with cows?"

"Don't be fucking stupid, Sparko," Fred says, scornfully. "Nothing works with cows."

"Why's that?"

"Because cows," Fred says, walking back to the van, "is fucking deaf."

Sparko looks at me. "I never knew that about cows," he says, contemplating this sad bovine affliction.

The band's night off in Edinburgh turns out to be somewhat eventful. Someone decides we should go to a club called Tiffany's, where on arrival we're soon aghast at the garish decor. The place is done up like a South Seas holiday resort, nets and palm trees and suchlike hanging from the rafters, umbrellas in cocktails, waitresses in grass skirts, that sort of thing. This plunges Lee into a foul mood, a festering obsession now developing with what the men in the crowd are wearing – mostly flares, big-collared shirts and, to Lee's growing horror, *kipper ties*. Even when he comes off stage looking like he's just been put through a car-wash, there is always something of the dandy about Lee, and such sartorial naffness as flares and *kipper ties* is simply too much for him.

"It's bang out of fucking order," he seethes, gripping the bar hard enough to put a crack in it, white-knuckled and offended by the ubiquity of paisley wherever he looks.

"Oi," he says, demanding the attention of a hapless bystander. "What the *fuck* are you wearing around your fucking *neck?* Call that a *tie?* A *tie*, mate, shouldn't be thicker than your finger. And it should never – I mean, *fucking never* – be tucked in your bleedin' trousers."

The allure of Tiffany's is fleeting and we are soon on our way back to the hotel, Fred at the wheel of the band's van, Lee in the seat beside him, still smouldering. I'm in the back with Sparko, drummer Big Figure, guitarist Gypie Mayo, Chris Fenwick and Peter Clark, who does the band's light show. We've just stopped at some traffic lights when Lee spots a couple on a concrete forecourt outside a club that looks like it's just closing. They're having an argument, the guy now pushing the woman he's having words with, a bit of a tussle ensuing, with the guy then slapping the woman. Lee is immediately in gallant action.

"I'm not havin' any of *that*," he fumes, ripping open the van door and leaping out, brandishing a jack handle, and sprinting across the forecourt.

"We'd better go after him," Fred decides. "The mood he's in, he'll fucking kill someone."

Peter Clark goes after Fred. I look at Sparko and wonder if we should also pitch in.

"No fucking chance," Sparko says. "Let's just sit 'ere and see what happens."

Lee closes in on the squabbling pair. The guy is clearly startled by Lee's intervention and the clout on the shoulder Lee gives him with the jack handle.

140

"LEAVE HER ALONE!" Lee yells at the fellow. "You touch her again and I'll take *this*," he shouts, brandishing the car jack, "to your fucking *head*."

This prompts the woman to pipe up, just as Peter and Fred arrive on the scene.

"Who the fuck," she screams, "are all youse bastids to poke your noses in where they're nae fucking wanted?"

This is a turn of events I didn't see coming.

"Oh, fuck," Sparko says then. "Here comes trouble."

There are about eight... nine... oh dear, maybe a dozen rather rough-looking types now emerging from the club. Sparko's quickly identified them as pals of the warring pair. They size up what's happening, may even have seen Lee whacking the guy with the car jack, and decide to get stuck into Lee, Fred and Peter. Lee looks ready to stand his ground, the woman still screaming at him, the guy now finding his voice, too, and getting in Lee's face. Fred reacts by punching the guy on the side of the head, putting him down in an untidy heap, grabbing Lee and pulling him back to the van. Lee, Fred and Peter are moving quickly back towards us, with the blokes from the club in hot pursuit. Fred gets behind the wheel of the van, its engine thankfully still running, ready to go. Peter flings himself through the open side door of the van. Lee snatches open the door on his side of the van, Fred and everybody else yelling at him to get in. He pauses before he does, flings the jack at the advancing mob, braining one of them, then leaps into the van with a frantic laugh.

"Not exactly *Culloden*," Lee hoots as we roar off, a manic edge to his voice. "But lively enough."

NICK LOWE

Glasgow, October 1977

About a week after announcing to anyone who's listening that I'm just popping out for a couple of hours to interview Nick Lowe in west London, I call the *Melody Maker* office from a hotel in Glasgow. Suavely-coiffeured assistant editor Michael Watts is soon on the line.

"Where are you?" he asks, feigning a vague nonchalance about my current whereabouts. I'm not fooled, though. I can tell he's furious, even at this distance.

Scotland, I tell him.

"You'd better be fucking joking," he splutters, blowing whatever a gasket is. There's a ghastly silence now, and I can't think of anything to say, the conversational void a dreadful unoccupied tundra between us. Mick, however, has plenty to say, and I get a typically windy lecture on trust, responsibility, professionalism and other such virtues that I apparently lack in some abundance. I start to drift off.

"Are you even listening to me?" he suddenly barks, and I can imagine the sniggers in the office as he works himself up into a conspicuous fury.

"And exactly what," he asks, "are you doing in Scotland?"

I'm with Nick Lowe and the Five Live Stiffs Tour, I tell him.

Another grim silence ensues. I can too clearly imagine Mick, white-knuckled, trying to regain what's left of his composure – a tattered thing by now, his patience with me apparently fully expired. My head is something, I'm given to understand, he'd like to see on a stick.

Speaking with the measured diction of someone addressing a sadly impaired person with profound learning difficulties, Mick now reminds me that my pursuit of Nick for the feature I have promised him started on the opening night of the Stiff tour, in Hemel Hempstead, a show from which I returned with a thunderous hangover after Nick suggested we do the interview in a nearby pub. Our chat was accompanied by an endless succession of beers and much laughter as Nick went through an extraordinary repertoire of anecdotes, all of them hilarious but few of them wholly pertinent to the piece I'm supposed to be writing. Which is why I arranged another chat and headed off to Stiff's Alexander Street HQ, telling Mick, among others, that I would be out of the office for only as long as it takes to get across London to spend an hour with Nick before hot-tailing it as quickly as possible back to *MM*, whose offices at the time are in a bleak complex of huts in Waterloo that resemble a German POW camp, with only searchlights, low swirling mist and snarling guard dogs missing from the mix. Anyway, that was the plan.

"What went wrong?" Mick wants to know.

I tell him that things started to go awry not long after I arrived at Stiff, when the first thing Nick suggested was a drink in a pub he knows.

"Why was that a problem?" Mick asks, genuinely puzzled.

The pub Nick had in mind was in Liverpool.

"Let me get this straight," Mick says, struggling to keep a lid on his temper. "You went to Liverpool for a drink?"

Well, a couple, actually.

"That's really not very funny," Mick tells me sternly, breathing a bit heavily. I hope he's not going to work himself up until something vital bursts, blood flooding into internal cavities, his entire system on the verge of haemorrhage and collapse, paramedics leaning over him the last thing he sees before waking up in intensive care, tubes in every orifice and loved ones sobbing at his bedside.

"Are you still there?" Mick asks now, his voice shrill. I am, but I've been thinking of the night I spent with Nick in the British Rail bar on Lime Street station, Nick wanting to get away from the rowdy scenes backstage at the Liverpool Empire, where the Stiff tour was playing that night. By then, Nick was happy to go on before everyone else on the bill – which famously include Ian Dury & The Blockheads, Wreckless Eric, former Pink Fairy Larry Wallis and Elvis Costello And

The Attractions – for reasons not much more complicated than having more time that way to spend in the pub.

Anyway, in a corner of the Lime Street bar Nick knocks back vodka after vodka and eventually makes himself quite maudlin.

"What do I want to do with my life?" he at one point slurringly muses, although this isn't something I've asked him. "I dunno," he says. "Sometimes I think I have no real talent, and absolutely nothing to offer as a producer or songwriter. I mean, what have I done? Fuck all, when you think about it. Produced a couple of albums by The Damned and Elvis Costello, released a couple of singles and an EP. It's not a lot, and I don't think it's terribly distinguished.

"What I'd really love to do is write a Eurovision Song Contest winner," he says then, visibly brightening at the thought. "Otherwise, I'd settle for being Abba."

"So you've actually got an interview?" Mick says, breaking into my flashback, relieved that I won't be returning empty-handed from my recent excursions.

Of sorts, I tell him, adding that not long after he got maudlin, Nick decided that he wasn't really in the mood for talking about himself after all, and instead launched into a very long and very funny anecdote about Rockpile touring America with Bad Company.

"So when," Mick asks wearily, like someone who's life has become too miserable to endure, "do you think you'll actually speak to him?"

Confidently, I tell Mick that I'll be meeting Nick shortly and I'll definitely nail the interview today and be back in London not long after that.

"If you're not, you won't have a job to come back to," Mick says coldly, ending our conversation on an unpleasantly terse note.

A little later, on the Stiff tour coach that's going to take us to the Glasgow Apollo for this afternoon's soundcheck, Larry Wallis collapses into the seat next to me, looking haggard.

How are you feeling, Larry?

"Like I've just been nutted by reality," he sighs, blinking wearily behind his aviator shades. And now here's Nick, looking chipper. I ask him if we can finally finish the interview we'd started in Hemel Hempstead.

"No problem, AJ," Nick fairly beams. "Tell you what," he goes on. "I know this lovely little pub. We can have a quiet pint, maybe a bit of nosh and a good chat. It'll be great."

Er, where's the pub, Nick?

"Sheffield," he says with a big grin. In the distance, I am sure I can hear Mick Watts' head hitting his desk with a dullish thud.

GREGG ALLMAN AND CHER

London, November 1977

I'm shown into their suite at the Inn On The Park, a vast interconnection of rooms with a spectacular view of Hyde Park. There's no immediate sign of Cher, although I can hear a great deal of banging and muttering from somewhere that I presume is the sound of her looking for something she can't find. Drawers are being dragged open and slammed shut, coat hangers are rattled with impatient urgency, a temper is beginning to flare.

Across the room from where I'm standing, what appears to be Gregg Allman is slouched low on a couch, seemingly comatose. His head is sunk between his shoulders, the rest of him hair, buckskin and denim. I'm not sure if he's awake. Hell, I'm not sure if he's even alive. We are introduced, however, and Gregg, who I am now beginning to think must at the very least be on some kind of medication that keeps him, for his own good, in a kind of pole-axed stupor, barely registers my presence.

At the time of which I'm writing, Gregg and Cher have just released the grisly *Allman and Woman: Two the Hard Way* and are two years into a spectacularly stormy marriage that ends abruptly in 1979. Gregg has spent the last year painfully trying to kick multiple addictions – principally to heroin, cocaine and anything you can pour out of a bottle into a glass.

Anyway, here comes Cher, who stalks into the room having found – without Gregg's help – whatever she has been ransacking the other room for. She looks like something you might find carved on the prow of a pirate ship, imperious and menacing. She gives Gregg a slap on the shoulder and he heaves himself over on the couch to make room for her beside him.

I attempt to engage the unlikely pair in conversation about *Allman and Woman* and ask Gregg why it had taken a year to make, a question that's followed by a long silence and much staring on Gregg's part at something no one else can see.

"Gregg," Cher says then, "answer the question, why dontcha?"

About now there's a rumble in the room. Something unspecific but seismic, the kind of noise that in some parts of the world would be indicative of an earthquake or something similar, involving tremors, collapsing buildings, giant waves to follow.

It's Gregg, talking.

"Me and… uh… Cher… we… uh… split up maybe two or three, uh, maybe four times durin' the time we were… uh… recordin' the album," he says. His voice is deep and furry, muffled, like someone trapped in a car, talking to rescue workers through an air bag.

"Also," he goes on, but not in a rush, apparently, "during, uh, that time, my alcohol and drug problem got so, uh, damn heavy I just had to say, 'Whoa. Stop. End. Finish.' I was four years on, uh, heroin and booze. Got into heroin in, uh, '72. This was just after my brother, uh, died. I couldn't cope with, uh, anything. It was an easy way out, and a hard way back in. I can truthfully tell y'all that comin' off of drugs and booze was th' hardest damn thing I ever had to, uh, do in my life."

It must've been tough for Cher, too, I offer gallantly, getting a plucky little smile from her.

"No, it wasn't," says Gregg, surprisingly sharply. "I don't think it was as painful for her as it was for me. No sir."

Was it Cher's idea for you to get treatment for your addictions?

"No… uh-uh," Gregg says, fumbling for a Marlboro.

"Yes, actually," Cher says snappily. "It was." She sounds pretty clear about this. Gregg heaves, as they say, a somewhat heavy sigh.

"In the beginning, maybe," Gregg says, sucking so hard on his cigarette his head disappears in a cloud of smoke.

"I prefer him when he's not on drugs," Cher adds. "He's a different person."

"We have to go through this now?" Gregg says, getting cranky.

"I was just saying…" Cher says, sounding stern.

"Well, don't," Gregg says, making Cher fume.

There are darks clouds gathering here, a domestic squall blowing up on yon horizon, a brooding tension, the inevitability of a kick ass row in the making that I don't want to be witness to. As soon as I'm gone I can imagine everything in this room that's not nailed down or too heavy to lift being at some point thrown or broken. I decide to beat a retreat, Gregg and Cher squaring up as I go. I don't think they even notice me leaving.

NICK LOWE

Finland, February 1978

Nick Lowe is standing in the lobby of a Helsinki hotel with the understandably baffled air of someone who's just been struck on the head by lightning. *Wh-what was that?* It's the morning after the kind of night before that makes you sorry there's such a thing as tomorrow. Nick looks washed-out and wobbly, clearly in the grip of the sort of hangover that leaves you less in desperate need of the proverbial hair of the dog than the canine itself, the whole of it, the entire tail-wagging beast, paws, teeth, ears, the lot. He pats himself down, searching for a fag in the pockets of clothes he looks like he's slept in. When he finds a bent old Senior Service, a dog-end basically, he's shaking so badly I have to light it for him. What do you want to do, Nick?

"Find a bar, obviously," Nick says, "and have a drink."

It's not far from the hotel to the nearest bar, but by the time we get there we're frozen, chilled to the fucking bone, teeth chattering like castanets. Last night's blizzard has blown itself out and for the moment it's an unnervingly bright day. It's also unbelievably cold – 20 degrees below freezing, or something. The five minute walk leaves me feeling like I'm in the latter stages of cryogenic preservation, on my way to becoming a pale ghost, frozen in time, an ice zombie. Nick, meanwhile, has actually turned a bit blue. He's shivering uncontrollably, but with a heroic effort manages to get a large vodka close enough to his lips to drink it without spilling a drop, a notable feat for someone in his parlous state.

"That's better," he says, knocking back the vodka, ordering another. "I thought for a moment when I woke up this morning that the game was finally up. There was a turkey on my back, the biggest fucking

149

turkey you could possibly imagine. I thought, 'This bird's got my number. I've *had* it. I'm fucking *dead*.' Then it flew away. I thought, 'Thank Christ. I'm saved.' Then it flew back. With a *twig* in its fucking beak. The fucking thing started building a *nest*. I thought, 'I'm done for now.'"

Nick, feeling perkier by the minute, orders another round of drinks. "Just to be on the safe side," he says, polishing off his third large vodka in about 20 minutes.

It's started to snow again, light flurries at first but getting heavier in a hurry, and by now we're in a battered old van, on our way to somewhere called Rauma, about 300 miles northwest of Helsinki, on the Gulf of Bothnia, virtually in the Arctic Circle as far as we're concerned, where it's even colder and there's even more snow. What are we doing here? Let's ask Nick.

"To be honest, AJ," he says, trying to pour vodka into a plastic cup, a test of his hand and eye coordination that he dismally fails as most of the vodka ends up in his lap, "with the album coming out, I just wanted to get out of England for a couple of weeks."

He's talking about *Jesus Of Cool*, his much-hyped first solo album. Nick's been releasing albums for years with pub rock veterans Brinsley Schwarz, only a dwindling following of die-hard fans taking much notice. Since palling up with Jake Riviera, however, he's become Stiff's unofficial house producer, crafting some great records on startlingly limited budgets, including his own "So It Goes", The Damned's "New Rose" and their *Damned Damned Damned* album, Wreckless Eric's "Whole Wide World" and Elvis Costello's *My Aim Is True*. He now has a reputation as a pop Svengali, a bit of a magician. There's suddenly a lot to live up to.

"I'm a bit self-conscious about the whole thing, frankly," he goes on. "I mean, a *solo* album? I never really wanted to do one. It always seemed such a wanky idea. I had this image of some singer-songwriter type standing by a babbling brook, staring into the sunset with his poetic eyebrows twitching in the breeze. It didn't sound much like me, really. Also," he adds, a little sheepishly, "with a title like *Jesus of Cool*, I didn't want to be seen staggering about, from pub to pub, completely pissed, ranting and raving. It would have been damned undignified."

So Nick, along with Jake Riviera, Rockpile drummer Terry Williams and Rumour guitarist Martin Belmont, has been on an eccentric little tour of Europe, fetching up in Helsinki, were they've been recording with local hot-shot guitarist, Albert Järvinen who, as a member of popular Finnish R&B band The Hurriganes, was briefly considered as a replacement for Wilko Johnson in Dr Feelgood. Albert's got his own band now, the Royals, who have a couple of gigs this weekend in Raumo and then 100 miles even further north, in Siikainen. Nick's going to be supporting Albert and the Royals at the shows and I've flown out with Global Riviera trouble-shooter Glen Colson to join the party. It seemed like a good idea at the time, anyway.

We're a couple of hours outside Helsinki now, moaning like fish-wives. There's a big hole in the floor of the van, covered by sheets of cardboard that barely keep out the jets of freezing ice, slush, snow, whatever, that blow regularly through the fucking hole and into the van, soaking us. Martin Belmont pours himself a very large brandy. Terry Williams sinks deeper into a chunky knit cardigan. Jake is nois-ily rude about virtually everyone he's ever met and a few he hasn't. Nick guzzles more vodka. It's snowing again and it's cold enough to make you weep. We stop briefly on what looks like the shore of an immense lake, frozen over and vast, where we meet up with Albert and the Royals and the photographer who's riding with them. The Finnish lensman wants to take some pictures here. I presume this is his idea of a joke. So does Martin Belmont, who has to be dragged out of the van into the eerie, sub-zero silence. Nick waddles out onto the lake, a Senior Service dangling from his lips. He lines up alongside Albert, Martin and Terry against a backdrop that seems to stretch to infinity, maybe a bit further. And what's this, now? It's a solitary fig-ure, a lone skier, making his way across the lake, just a speck in the far distance.

"Hurry up," Jake barks. "Someone's coming."

"Anyone we know?" Martin Belmont asks.

"Someone just off to the shops, I imagine," Nick says.

Not much later, the mood in the van on the way to Raumo is deso-late. Everyone's miserable. It's snowing heavily again and a freez-ing murk prevails, the light fading quickly – not so much drained as sucked from the sky. The cardboard sheets over the hole in the floor of the van have long since been reduced to sodden pulp and we're regu-larly drenched by geysers of wet muck. Ice is forming on the inside of the van. I think I can hear Martin Belmont sobbing quietly, probably thinking of the loved ones he may never see again. It's scarily cold.

"Just think," says Glen Colson. "If we'd come in the summer, we'd have missed all this."

The venue in Raumo when we finally get there turns out to be at some local youth club, which isn't quite what anyone had been expecting. Albert and the Royals are already in the dressing room, sipping tea and eating the sandwiches they appear to have brought with them in a triumph for forward planning. Nick, who's been drinking since breakfast, crashes through the dressing room door with a whoop and much hysterical laughter. Albert is visibly shocked.

"You..." he says, aghast. "You... are... *drunk*?"

"Pissed as a parrot, old boy," Nick beams, trying to light a cigarette and almost setting fire to his hair.

Needless to say, the show that follows is an absolute shambles.

The next night's gig in Siikainen is even more bizarre. It's in a little shack on the side of a lake, which you can't see much of because there's another blizzard blowing this way. I'm standing with Jake on this sort of pier just outside the shack, the light fading fast around us, when we make out these strange shapes advancing through the treeline. People are approaching us in the strange twilight, wrapped like Eskimos in layers of fur, lumbering towards us across fields of ice and snow. It's tonight's audience, a cheery lot, who form an orderly queue to check in their snowshoes, skis, animal pelts and suchlike at the door. Nick's reasonably sober tonight and manages to get through the show without serious mishap, and after he plays we get in the van as quick as we can for the 10-hour drive back to Helsinki, which no one's looking forward to. It's colder than ever, the night a thing swarming around us as we drive through it, huddled and disconsolate. A freezing wind whistles through every hole, crack and fissure in the van's ancient superstructure. Misery prevails. We sink into a shivering silence, broken suddenly by Nick.

"Anyone fancy a *singsong*?" he now cheerily suggests.

We all look at him like he's lost his fucking mind.

"A *singsong*," Jake shouts at him. "A fucking *singsong*? We're not on fucking *holiday*. A fucking *singsong*? Fucking shut up and suffer in silence like the rest of us."

Nick's quiet for a while, then says he needs to take a pee, which starts everyone moaning again. We pull over and Nick stumbles out of the van. I go with him. We're having a piss against the side of the van and I'm saying something to Nick that he probably can't hear over the banshee wail of the wind. I turn to say something else, and he's not there. He's fallen backwards into a mountainous snowdrift, all but vanished and sinking fast.

"Help... me," he croaks.

Martin Belmont leaps out of the van to lend a hand. We try to haul Nick out of the snowdrift, with Martin then slipping and falling head-first into the snow himself, taking me with him. Somehow, we get Nick to his feet and crawl back into the van, soaked to the skin, shedding snow, getting everyone else as wet as we are. Jake is furious, not a pretty sight. He's got a lot invested in Nick, but at this moment looks angry enough to take a hammer to Nick's head.

"I'm so... so sorry," Nick whimpers, looking for more vodka and becoming utterly bereft when he realises his last bottle has rolled out of the van during the chaos at the piss-stop.

"Just shut it," Jake says, seething. "One more word out of you, *one more fucking word*, and we'll fucking leave you out here by the side of the fucking road."

And then we're lost in the dark maw of the Arctic night, Helsinki 300 miles down the road, with 40 years of dining out on all this ahead of us.

Tony Iommi

Glasgow, March 1978

When the karma wagon pulls up to the steps of Glasgow's Excelsior Hotel, out there near the airport, I'm so distracted I don't see it coming until it's too late. By which time, of course, I'm out in the hotel car park, under a faltering moon, bleeding heavily and panting like a leaf-blower.

Anyway, this all starts with a phone call from bearded Brummie, Brian Harrigan, a former news editor on *Melody Maker* now working in the press office at Phonogram. Brian asks if I want to go to Glasgow for one of the opening shows of Black Sabbath's 10th anniversary world tour. He's got to be kidding! Frankly, I'd rather have my eyes gouged out with spoons and tell Harrigan as much, in rather more colourful language. Brian knows this is bluster on my part and the real reason I am reluctant to entertain the thought of going anywhere near Black Sabbath has a lot to do with threats made against me by Sabbath's famously belligerent guitarist Tony Iommi. It may be recalled that not long after joining *Melody Maker*, I was dispatched to interview Tony at his country pile in the Midlands, an amusing encounter I'd written up in somewhat waspish fashion, playing to the gallery for easy laughs. Tony, however, had been singularly unamused by my description of our afternoon together, which he apparently considered snide and piss-taking, and deserving of severe retribution. He has, in fact, made it known via various intermediaries that there's a space on his mantelpiece that, given the opportunity, he would happily fill with my head, preferably severed from the rest of my body and with the nose and ears cut off.

Harrigan's aware of all this and is immediately reassuring. We'll fly to Glasgow, book into the Excelsior, have a few drinks, see the show, be back at the hotel before the encores and spend the rest of the night – and most of Phonogram's money – in the bar. He'll make sure I don't have to venture anywhere near the group, who won't even know I'm anywhere in the vicinity. This is when, foolishly, I agree to the fateful trip.

On the day we're meant to fly to Glasgow, however, Harrigan calls to say he won't be able to make it because his wife's having a baby, and I'll have to go on my own. He tells me that, by way of compensation, he's given the hotel his credit card number for me to charge what he hopes will be a modest drinks bill. He also adds that due to circumstances beyond his control, the band are now staying at the same hotel and I'll have to travel with them back to the hotel after the show. Which is why I now find myself backstage in Sabbath's dressing room at the Glasgow Apollo, lurking at the back of a ruck of simpering record company-types and assorted back-slapping journalists, hoping not to be noticed by Iommi. I realise I'm standing next to Sabbath bassist Geezer Butler, who's changing out of his garish stage duds – a ridiculous, brightly-coloured satin cat-suit with a scoop neck and bell sleeves, complete with fringes, scrotum-hugging bell-bottomed pants and platform boots, if memory serves. Geezer opens the suitcase on the stand in front of him and rummages around in it for what I presume will be something more sensible to wear. I laugh out loud when he unpacks *exactly* the same outfit and struggles into it, like a diver getting into a wet suit.

Ozzy Osbourne, meanwhile, is also close by and having difficulty opening a bottle of brandy. I offer to help him out, give the top a bit of a twist and hand it back to him for what turns out to be a hefty swig followed by a very wet belch. It's like taking a thorn out of a lion's paw. We're friends for life now. I'm a bit alarmed, however, because the dressing room's clearing out, people drifting to the band's coach for the trip back to the hotel. Ozzy, it turns out, is making his own way back to the Excelsior and – thank you, God! – asks if I want to go with him. Which I do. I'm expecting Ozzy to have his own driver. But when we get to his car, it quickly becomes clear he's driving himself, a proposition that suddenly becomes worrying. He gets behind the wheel, pressing buttons that set off the windshield wipers and the car horn before the car's headlights come on like something you might have seen lighting the skies over London during the Blitz.

"'Ang on!" Ozzy shouts, clutching the bottle of brandy between his knees as we roar off at some speed into the night. "Which way now?" he asks, but I don't have a clue and of course neither does Ozzy. We drive around for a bit, Ozzy guzzling the brandy and swearing like a docker, until we spot a sign pointing us in the general direction of the airport and the adjacent Excelsior. I'm standing at the reception desk waiting for my room key when Sabbath's tour bus pulls up outside and the band get off.

The next thing I know, someone has my arm in what seems like an industrial vice. Through the unexpected and totally excruciating pain, I'm vaguely aware that whoever's inflicting this agony is also talking to me.

"Yew'r Allin Jownz, intcher?" is what he's saying to me. "I've gorra bone ter pick with yew." With a certain amount of dread seeping into every bone in my body I turn around to face – who else? – a clearly irate Tony Iommi who then proceeds to drag me across the hotel lobby, out the hotel doors and into the hotel car park, a couple of burly members of the Black Sabbath road crew following us into the night, where Tony is working himself into a rare old strop.

"Yew remember what yew wrote about me?" he asks. I tell him I do, and I laugh. A dreadful mistake.

"Yew won't be laughing in a minute," he says then, whiskers bristling. He's right about that. I notice him slipping off a chunky wrist watch, a Rolex, or something, with a metal wrist band that he now wraps around his fist like a knuckle-duster. What I don't see coming is the punch in the mouth that follows, a bone-breaking left hook that comes out of nowhere and feels like it's taken my head clean off my shoulders and simultaneously forced all my teeth down the back of my throat. For a moment, I don't know who or where I am and I just stand there covered in blood, like Sissy Spacek at the end of *Carrie*. My top lip, I can now feel, is appallingly split and hanging in two bleeding flaps from my face, the teeth behind it worryingly loose.

"Put 'em up," Tony then demands, fists raised in front of him like something from a Victorian boxing poster.

I spit out a great glob of blood and flesh, which hits the steps in front of Tony like a haddock being slapped on a boat deck, and tell him through a mouthful of gristle and mush that if he wants to hit me again, he's going to have to chase me to Edinburgh first. Tony takes a step towards me. I realise I'm in no shape to run anywhere, let alone Edinburgh. So I close my eyes and stand there, swaying, blood still pouring from what's left of my face, and wait for a pummelling that, thank Christ, never comes. One of Tony's roadies steps in, like he's trying to separate a couple of prize-fighters, and tells Tony in no uncertain terms to "leave it". I open my eyes to see the pugnacious axeman and his surly henchman disappearing into the hotel. I'm not quite sure what to do next, so I head for the hotel bar, where I order everything apart from the carpet and the light fittings and charge the lot to Brian Harrigan's credit card.

About a week after Iommi clobbers me in Glasgow, there's a Stiff outing to see Ian Dury & The Blockheads in High Wycombe. I arrive at Alexander Street, where I run into Alex Harvey, who takes one look at my battered face and starts to howl.

"This is what that fuck Tony-fucking-Iommi did to you?" he seethes, taking my head in his hands like he's going to unscrew it. I kind of nod, hoping my head won't fall off. Alex continues to fume. "He did this to you in Glasgow. My fucking city," he says, breathing hard. "I'll no be having that. Do you remember General Grimes?" he now asks.

I do, vividly.

"Say the fucking word," Alex says, "and he'll have Tony-fucking-Iommi *disappeared*."

If at Black Sabbath's next gig, Iommi fell off stage and broke a leg I'd probably unkindly hoot with laughter. Giving the word to have him, as Alex puts it, "disappeared", strikes me, however, as possibly taking things a bit too far, although even as I tell Alex this I have to admit it's a tempting fucking offer.

ELVIS COSTELLO

Belfast, March 1978

What happens next follows a show Elvis Costello and The Attractions play at Belfast's Ulster Hall, a week after the release of *This Year's Model*. I'm part of a press junket that flies in to see them. The show that night is pretty lively, The Attractions blistering. They play something like 18 songs in what seems as many minutes. It's like listening to machine gun fire – frenzied stuff, barely a gap between numbers.

It's over too soon for the audience, who want more but don't get it. They're a bit stunned when Elvis rips out his guitar lead and runs off stage, like he's got a bus to catch. The crowd take a while to disperse, their cheers turning to boos as the houselights go up. By the time they've cleared the hall, some us are already back at the band's hotel, where a function room's been put aside for a post-gig get-together. It's good to see The Attractions, especially drummer Pete Thomas who I've known since he was in pub rock stalwarts Chilli Willi & The Red Hot Peppers. There's no sign for the moment of Elvis or his pugnacious manager, Jake Riviera, so the mood in the room is pretty relaxed.

This changes when Costello arrives with Riviera, a couple of cocky wise-guys looking for balls to break. Elvis seems to be in an especially inclement strop over something you couldn't put a name to, shooting his cuffs like someone walking into a bar who won't be happy until he finds the trouble he's clearly looking for. Jake, if it's possible, is in an even uglier mood. Let me say here that Jake's got the worst temper of anyone I've ever met, Lou Reed included. If there's one thing I know about him it's that his bite is definitely worse than his bark, which itself is unnerving. This is especially true of Jake when he's been drinking or doing too much speed, or – more often these days, now that there's money coming in and he can afford it – the cocaine that made fools of a lot of us in those bygone days. He scans the room for a likely target or two, someone to lay into with one of his fabled tongue-lashings – verbal onslaughts you would not wish to be on the end of. Pete Thomas recognises the look immediately.

"Let's just step out of the line of fire," he says, steering me to a corner, where we put our backs to the wall. "We should be OK here," he says, "unless we get hit by a ricochet when things go off."

It's not long before the games begin. There's an American journalist here, a decent enough fellow in my opinion, from a New York magazine I enjoy mostly because of his writing. He's a big fan of Elvis and Nick Lowe and his magazine's been very supportive of both. He was in London for other reasons when he was invited on the junket that's brought him fatefully here. Jake now gets hostile in a hurry, letting the room know what he thinks about America and Americans and their many and varied deficiencies, with particular and provocative regard to American music magazines and the people who write for them, for whom it would appear he feels nothing but unhindered scorn and searing contempt. These sentiments Jake now communicates to our American friend in colourfully uncompromising terms.

"Ouch," whispers Pete Thomas, a veteran witness of many such humiliations, adding that, if he's not mistaken (and he's not), Elvis will have a pop next. He does, too, and it's like watching him audition for the principal role in a remake of *Don't Look Back*, Jake a bellicose Bobby Neuwirth to Costello's scowling Dylan, a toxic mix of cruelty and cool. I can't hear what he says now to the hapless American in our midst, but it provokes an indignant response on the American's part.

"Hey, man," he says, on the point of spluttering. "I gave your record a good review."

"Big fucking deal," Jake says, sharply, biting down on the words like a shark on a leg. "What do you want, a Pulitzer-fucking-Prize?"

The American journalist looks for a moment like he's going to make more of this than he actually does. He starts to say something, then seems to realise that whatever he says will just give Jake an excuse to push him further, to that point perhaps where people run out of words, when shouting won't do so chairs start flying. Jake looks like that's exactly where he wants things to go, and the opportunity to wade in and slap someone around.

"Just because someone gives me a good review doesn't mean that I'm going to fall at their feet," Elvis announces then, although no one to my knowledge has suggested this particular course of action, even as a joke.

"I don't need you or you or you, or him, or anyone," he says, accounting with a single sweeping glare for the people in the room who aren't on his pay-roll, "to tell me that I'm good. I know how good I am, thanks. I didn't need anyone to tell me that *This Year's Model* is a great album. It's my fucking record, I made the fucking thing, wrote the fucking songs and *you're* telling *me* how good it is? What's the matter with you people? I know exactly how good it is. You don't need to tell me that. Show some fucking imagination when you write about me or don't bother writing about me at all. Do you even understand what I'm saying?"

No one answers, probably assuming that if they do they'll be throwing themselves in as bait, to be quickly chewed up. An uneasy silence prevails. Then a fellow from the London *Evening Standard*, their pop writer, an affable toff with the languid air of the bass player in a band with connections to the Canterbury Scene, asks Costello if he's flattered when people compare him to Bob Dylan.

"I don't give a shit about Bob Dylan" Costello snaps. "I've already forgotten who he was."

This isn't true, of course. It's just an example of the kind of contemptuous comment of which Costello, in the months ahead, becomes well-practised, as if it's a contractual obligation. He gets away with it here. But 12 months hence when he offers an even more outrageous opinion about Ray Charles in an infamous row in America with Bonnie Bramlett and Stephen Stills on the Armed Forces tour, his world comes crashing down around him.

LOU REED

Philadelphia | New York, May 1978

"Jesus God! It's the faggot dwarf! We thought you were dead. You look well. What happened? Did you get religion? Last time we saw you, you looked worse than anybody I've ever seen, except myself. Are you still working for *Melody Maker* trying to influence the diseased minds of cretins?"

As greetings go, I've been more formally received. But this is Lou Reed, so no one's expecting curtsies when we walk into his dressing room, backstage at Philadelphia's Tower Theatre. He's just played a blinding show, his new album, *Street Hassle*, is getting deservedly great reviews and he's clearly on a high, prowling the dressing room like something feral under a howling moon, fuelled by something you might use to launch a rocket. He's bug-eyed and raving, talking so fast you can hardly see his lips move. Sweat is coming off him in a fine spray, a series of tics keeping one side of his face in constant motion, the veins in his neck standing out like ropes. The incurable old narcissist is wearing one of his own tour T-shirts and bright yellow braces over that, hitching up tan leather trousers that flare unexpectedly at the ankles and are laced up with thongs at the crotch. If he wasn't Lou Reed, he'd look a bit absurd.

"Say hi to the band," he says, introducing me to people I already know. "Weren't we great tonight? Weren't we the best rock 'n' roll band you saw in your life? God above, we're a fucking orchestra. Did you ever hear anyone play guitar like I did tonight? Wasn't I just great? No—save your superlatives for the article."

I'm relieved he's lost none of his overwhelming modesty since we last met.

161

"Oh, I still know I'm the best," he says, laughing, handing me a beer. "Who else is there? Kansas? Mel Torme? Come *on*. I'm Dante with a beat. I'm like Bach, Bartok and Little Richard. I'm so hot at the moment I burn myself whenever I touch a guitar. What did you think of "Street Hassle" tonight? Great, uh? That gets spooky. That's me on the line out there. Like Dante. If they put me in purgatory, I'd be the fucking landlord."

Lou can keep these raps going for as long as there's anyone around to listen to his manic babble. Longer, probably, even without an audience, whose opinion he would anyway ignore. "I know what those people are like," he says at one point. "I can do without them. I only need my own applause."

Now he wants to know what's happening in England, and someone mentions what Johnny Rotten's currently up to, which makes Lou laugh, a scary noise.

"Johnny Rotten," he says, "should stick a safety pin in the end of his prick and shove it through his nose."

Mention is made of current rumours about former Sex Pistols Steve Jones and Paul Cook forming a band with Johnny Thunders. Lou cackles again.

"Johnny Thunders?" he says. "Don't make me laugh. There's only one Lou Reed."

He starts talking about his band again. Yes, we agree, they were great.

"I'm going to call them New York," he announces. "What do you think."

Sounds a bit precious, frankly.

"Oh... *oh!*" Lou squeals. "The dwarf thinks it's precious. OK, faggot, we'll call the band *Mutton*. How does that sound?"

I change the subject, Lou getting a bit riled here. Has he seen David Bowie recently?

"Well," he says, "I looked in the mirror this morning and he looked fine. Ah! But why are we talking about *me* when we could be talking about ME?"

Sunday morning, a couple of days later in New York, I'm waiting for Lou in the bar of The Essex House, the hotel on Central Park where we've been staying. Lou turns up an hour late, hungover and in need of a drink. We belly up to the bar and Lou orders an Irish coffee.

"Sure," the barman wisecracks, "I'll just send out for an Irishman to make it."

Lou rolls his eyes, not a good sign.

"Listen," he tells the barman, enough edge in his voice to make you flinch. "If I'd have wanted a fucking comedian, I'd have called room service. Just fix the fucking drink. Make it a double."

"Whaddya want? *Two* Irish coffees?"

"No. I want a double shot. And don't miss the fucking glass. I don't want to have to lick my drink off the bar."

The barman makes the drink and puts it in front of Lou, who's now deep into a foul mood that continues when we go up to the urban wasteland he's turned his room into. When we get there, I can't believe what I'm looking at. The room looks like it's been bombed, like something you might see in newsreels of war zones, refugees huddled in a corner, gaunt-eyed under a single lightbulb, surrounded by the rubble their lives have become. Lou walks in and, indifferent to the clutter, slumps in a chair, surrounded by amplifiers, guitars, flight cases, synthesisers, video games, stacks of cassettes, trailing miles of wires and cables. There are clothes everywhere, glass underfoot. Trays of drinks are stacked on the floor next to the door, a pyramid of empties, testimony, perhaps, to long nights here, fuelled by alcohol and whatever else it is that Lou currently has a taste for. I shift a half ton of debris off a chair and sit down. Lou, meanwhile, is keen to show off his new Roland Guitar Synthesiser, which he now switches on and starts strumming.

"This is the greatest guitar ever built by human people," he starts to babble. "It makes every other guitar look tragic. It's the invention of the age." He presses a button on the guitar and out comes a squall of noise. "Isn't that impressive? Am I not the King of Flash? No? Then fuck you."

Lou now begins to play the intro to The Velvet Underground's "Sweet Jane" and presses something else on the guitar that makes the riff repeat itself. Now, of course, it won't stop, which makes Lou mad. He starts flicking switches, pushing buttons, swearing under his breath. He gives the guitar a smack with the flat of his hand and it starts howling, making both of us jump. Now, he's looking for the mains to turn the infernal thing off at, but can't find a plug. He grabs the Medusan tangle of wires and leads at his feet, tugs hard, pulling a lamp off a table on the other side of the room.

163

"*Motherfucker*," he snarls, giving the recalcitrant contraption a fearful glare and leaning it on the wall behind him, where over the next couple of hours it repeats the same chords over and over and over. Room service arrives about now, with two bottles of Johnnie Walker Red. Lou finds some glasses under the bed, pours extremely large measures of the whiskey into the glasses and knocks one of them back in a hurry, like he hasn't had a drink since Christmas.

"I am of a mood these days," he's telling me now, but don't ask me why, "that tells me that I'm a right-wing fascist liberal. I cover all bases. I'm very legitimate on a number of levels. That's why I'm still here. That's why I still matter. People think I'm vicious and conniving and this and that, someone who doesn't do the right things, who's self-destructive, who can't be trusted. The thing is, it was always, like, LOU REED. I'm the only honest commodity around. I always was. I mean, even if I was an asshole, I was an asshole on my own terms. It's not like I'm dumb and don't know when I'm being an asshole. But even when I was an asshole, I was a literate lunatic. Even my bullshit was head and shoulders above everyone else's bullshit. It's always been honest and personal, you know. When you buy a Lou Reed record, you gotta expect LOU REED. *Metal Machine Music* took care of that."

So when in your career were you the biggest asshole?

"Don't push it."

I'm only using your own words.

"Yeah, well, use your *own* fucking words," he says, sharply, and I don't know where any of this is going. "The thing is," he says then, "I was *never* an asshole. I think an asshole is someone who wastes time. It's not a question of good or bad. There was a period when I didn't care about anything. I just stopped. I was having a little dialogue with myself, about life, my vocation, what I wanted to do. No. I wasn't looking for an identity. I had an identity. I was a lot of people. I'm a pretty expansive creature. I can be one thing and then another. No one of them is any more me than the other. They're all parts that I play. I'm good at 'em all. I mean, it's not that hard. In novels, no one would think twice about it. It's just that rock 'n' roll is such a mutant, idiot-child medium. But *that*," he says splashing another four fingers of whiskey into his glass, "made it easier for anyone with even half a brain to walk in and just dominate that end of it."

We seem to be talking, in some way that's clearer to Lou than me, about fuck knows what, and now he's off again.

"The work I've done over the last four or five years, whatever anyone thinks of it, is by definition the best I could have done at the time. I achieved as much as I could have, by definition. I did the best I could. Because I always do. If someone doesn't like it or thinks I could have done better, fuck 'em. I don't need some simple-minded savage telling me when I'm good or bad. I know when I'm good or bad and I'm *never* bad. Sometimes I just didn't bother, but that's because for a while I just didn't care. Even then, I always assumed I was great. I never doubted it. Other people's opinions of me don't matter. I know my opinion is the one that's right. It took me a long time to learn that. The only mistake I made over the years was listening to other people. 'Hey, Lou,' I finally said, 'can't you understand that *you're* right, that you've always been right?' That's when I stopped listening to other people."

What makes you so convinced you're always right?

"Because I can do it right in front of you, just like *that*," he says, snapping his fingers for emphasis and almost falling off his chair. "It's not very hard for me. Even now, I don't think there's anyone in rock 'n' roll who's writing lyrics that mean anything, other than me. You can listen to me and actually hear a voice. These other people are morons. They really are. I mean," he says, working the top off the second bottle of Johnnie Walker Red, "I've only ever known a few people I thought were that good. Delmore Schwarz. Andy. One thing that Andy taught me was that if you start something, *finish* it. And I started something with The Velvet Underground and we put out "Heroin". Then I left it for two years. But I knew I hadn't finished what we'd started. So, lo and behold, I returned. I decided to come back. What else was I going to do? Walk away and leave it? Uh-uh. I didn't want to have all the people who'd put their faith in me thinking I'd turned out to be a total sham, like everybody else they ever believed in."

By now, we seem to have been here for a very long time, Lou talking non-stop and me trying to make sense of his sometimes tidal incoherence, both of us smoking so much the room looks like it's been tear-gassed, a curtain of smoke hanging in the air between us, thick enough to choke a dog. At some point, we end up discussing "Kill

Your Sons", a song from *Sally Can't Dance*, about the electric shock therapy his parents, horrified by his homosexuality, surrendered him to as a teenager in Long Island. This, he now seems to be saying, is the root of his fiercely oppositional character – his parents, in his pathological demonology, synonymous with society's authoritarian determination to stifle the libertarian impulse to be at all costs oneself, unbound by timid convention. At least that's what I think he's talking about.

"It's like war, right from the top," he says. "The moment you wake up in *their* world and you tune into the fact that you've got to get out, it's war. And they'll do anything to stop you. They're poisoning us from the start and that means we don't stand a chance. I really believe there's a war and that we're on one side and they're on the other. And I think that rock 'n' roll is terribly, terribly political and subversive and that they're absolutely right to be afraid of it. Right across the board, there are lots of albums with words like mine. But I'm more of a threat because of what I represent. I am an enticement to their children. I'm still banned on the radio, not because of what I look like, but because I represent certain ideas. I mean, I don't have long hair. I don't wear earrings or glitter. Maybe they don't like Jewish faggots. How seriously can you take it? So they don't play me on the radio? What's the radio? Who's the radio run by? Who is it played for? They should take me very seriously. They do. They want to keep me locked away. I'm dangerous. They're afraid of that. And they really should be afraid, because a lot of us aren't kidding and we just keep going. And they can't stop us."

KENNY EVERETT

London, July 1978

Whenever I ask him a question, Kenny Everett, as small and dapper as a ventriloquist's dummy, crosses and uncrosses his legs like someone in desperate need of a lavatory, cups an elbow in one hand and his chin in the other, rolls his eyes, purses his lips as if waiting to be kissed, and makes a high-pitched whistling noise reminiscent of a kettle coming to the boil. This behaviour is hugely irritating and thoroughly annoying, and this has been going on for longer than I'm comfortable with. By now I'm looking around for something to hit him with.

I can only surmise that Kenny finds this amusing in ways I find unimaginable, and I wonder how easily the chair I'm sitting on will break over the head of the bearded little fuck. We are sitting in a control room at Thames TV's Teddington studios, where this morning the third instalment of the recently launched *Kenny Everett Video Show* is being filmed. The show's director, an ebulliently demonstrative man named David Mallett, who goes on to an award-winning career as a maker of pop videos (including David Bowie's "Ashes To Ashes" and Queen's "Radio Ga Ga"), is behind and above us, at the centre of a bulky console, barking instructions to the floor manager in the studio below us where Nick Lowe – here by sheer coincidence – is being fussed over by a crew of technicians after an aborted run through of "So It Goes".

"Sorry about that, Nick," Mallett apologises. "Absolutely our fault," he gushes. "So sorry."

Nick blinks wearily in the studio lights as the technicians move him about the set like an ornamental bookend.

167

"One more time, Nick, please, thank you. That's lovely, Nick," Mallett goes on, a geyser of apology and encouragement. "Right, let's try it again." Nick mimes another take of "So It Goes", to Mallett's evident satisfaction.

"That's an absolute giggle. Lovely, lovely. Thank you everyone," Mallett announces. "Let's go down and have a look at it with Nick," he adds. And so we troop down some catwalks and onto the studio floor, where Mallet stands with his arms magisterially folded across his chest and stares intently at a playback of Nick's performance. "What do you think, Nick? Not bad, is it?" the director enthuses.

"Terrific. Wonderful," Nick replies, clearly wondering what time the bar will be open. "Marvellous stuff," Mallett chortles, and signals a break as we climb back up to the control room, where I again attempt to get some sense out of the giggling Everett, whose lack of interest in any aspect of the show that doesn't include him is painfully apparent.

I'm here, of course, on behalf of *Melody Maker*, to talk to Everett about his big break into television – about which the only good thing I can say is that at least it will keep him off the radio. Everett, you'll remember, first became known as a DJ on pirate radio, before being recruited for the starting line-up at Radio One, where, among other things, he gained a reputation for larkish controversy that would be better described as grim inanity. Whatever, some off-colour remarks saw him sacked from the station in 1970 and reinstated in 1972, shortly before he defected to Capital Radio, where he does little to endear himself to me by playing Queen's "Bohemian Rhapsody" 14 times on the day it comes out.

By the time of which I'm writing, Everett's radio shows have increasingly become a vehicle for his supposedly wacky humour, surreal comic inventions, comedy characters, endless spoof jingles and the much farting about that his fans regard as evidence of a rare broadcasting genius now ripe for an overdue transfer to television.

Everett, fidgeting constantly and making odd and worrying noises, is now telling me, I think, that after a couple of ill-fated earlier TV shows – including Granada's *Nice Time*, which he co-presented with Germaine Greer, and three forgettable series for London Weekend Television that he now refuses to even talk about – he was

'He's got a job at the time digging graves for the council…' Joe Strummer in an earlier incarnation as Woody Mellor at an art school party. Newport, South wales, late 1972

'I wonder who I was when I wrote that?' Leonard Cohen, the Sloane Square Hotel, London. June, 1974

'A lot of people think I'm on completely the wrong track these days...' Ray Davies on the snooker table at Konk Studios, North London. September, 1974

'Branson, we have a problem...' Preparing for take off in one of Richard Branson's hot air balloons. The Manor, Oxfordshire. August, 1976

© Barry Plummer

'The press love to portray me as this absolute tyrant…' Bryan Ferry, AIR Studios, Oxford Street, London. January, 1977

'This is called living in England in 1977. We look different and it frightens them...' Johnny Rotten and Sid Vicious, Notting Hill, London. May, 1977

'We never came to destroy...' Paul Simonon and Joe Strummer outside the Metropole cafe, Edgware Road, London. November, 1978

'Jesus God! It's the faggot dwarf!' Lou Reed, backstage at the Tower Theatre, Philadelphia. May, 1978

'In the end, it was rock'n'roll that killed us...' The Pretenders at the video shoot for 'Kid', Gerrards Cross, Buckinghamshire. July, 1979

'A third of the world's population is out there...'
Sting and Andy Summers calculate the sale of
Police T-shirts at the Taj Mahal Intercontinental
Hotel, Bombay. May, 1980

'Open the doors and let Cairo
in...' Sting at the Great Pyramid of
Cheops, Cairo. May, 1980

'When you piss on the Alamo,
you piss on the state of
Texas...' Ozzy Osbourne, San
Antonio, Texas. March, 1982

'Right from the beginning, we knew it was going to be brilliant...' Johnny Marr and Morrissey, backstage at Reading University. February, 1984

'Let me be as weird as I fuckin' like...' Eddie Vedder, backstage at the Paramount Theatre, New York. April, 1994

initially reluctant to follow-up Thames' idea for *The Kenny Everett Video Show*.

"Then they found my weak spot," he gurgles.

And what would that be?

"Money," he says, and it's the first what you might call straight answer he's given me. "Lots of it," he goes on, briefly animated. "They started waving huge cheques under my nose. So I said I'd do it." He then resumes a kind of percolating silence, making more bothersome noises but otherwise not saying much of consequence.

"Let's get one thing straight about what we're doing," it's left for Mallet to elaborate. "This is showbiz! It's not another television rock show. It's not – thank God – *The Old Grey Whistle Test* and Kenny's not Bob Harris. I'm not knocking the *Whistle Test* or Bob," Mallett goes on, making it clear that he has very little time for either, "but this isn't a laid-back rock show. It's meant to be big, brash and colourful. Like rock music itself."

Everett, at this, makes the kind of noise that might put you in mind of someone in a shallow grave, having dirt shovelled in their face. I really do want to give him a clout. Given Everett's apparently limited musical horizons – you get the impression if it's not by The Beatles or Queen, Everett won't be much interested – it's Mallett who oversees the show's musical content, such as it is.

"We only want the best," Mallett says. "Rod. Cliff. Freddie."

I am aswoon at the thought of such excitements therefore to come, and bleakly amused when I sit in with Mallett on a brief production meeting where he turns down a clip from Martin Scorsese's *The Last Waltz*, featuring The Band and Eric Clapton.

"Bloody rubbish," Mallett announces with a theatrical flourish. "Can't use that," he says, sending on her way, suitably chastised, the production assistant who'd brought him the clip.

We are now gathered around a VCR and Mallett, to my mounting horror, is inserting a show-reel of clips from the first couple of recently-aired *Video Shows*, to demonstrate, I guess, Everett's comic genius. I sit then through about 20 utterly grisly minutes of dismally unfunny skits featuring Everett in a variety of apparently side-splitting comedic roles, the most famous of which will become be-leathered biker Sid Snot and lecherous French lothario, Marcel Wave. What I am forced to sit through here is in all respects ghastly, stroke-inducing stuff that exploits the British public's notorious tolerance for the kind of awful TV that makes you want to chuck a brick through the screen.

Mallett, however, is quickly besides himself, chuckling heartily, while Everett has started making a noise like a hyperventilating gibbon.

"Zat's me!" he announces in a peculiar accent and pointing at the video screen. "Zat's me, zat is."

He's on his feet now, doing a little dance, Mallett clapping along, which is a horrific thing to be witness to. I wonder if Nick's still at the bar, and head that way at a brisk and thirsty trot, eager to be anywhere else but here.

JOHN PEEL

London, August 1978

I arrive at Broadcasting House to interview John Peel for what used to be *Melody Maker,* to find the legendary DJ waiting outside for me with John Walters, his friend and long-time producer.

"Where have you *been*?" Walters wants to know, before I'm half-way out of the cab. "They've been open for 15 minutes," he shouts over his shoulder, heading with some vigour towards a favourite local hostelry.

I know Walters from the better kind of record company reception, to which he is prone to turn up and loudly regale anyone within ear-shot with hilarious tales, usually involving much quaffing with the likes of Keith Moon and Viv Stanshall.

I know Peel from the radio, of course. Growing up in a remote geographical alcove of South Wales, I couldn't get Peel on pirate radio, so didn't hear his *Perfumed Garden* show. But I listened regularly to *Top Gear*, the weekend show on Radio One he originally co-presented before eventually going, as it were, solo. Peel also had a late-night midweek show called *Night Ride*, which featured an amazing mix of exotic music, poetry and weekly updates on the diverse adventures and humorous antics of his pet hamsters, be-whiskered coves who provided him with much raw material for comic banter and whimsical reflection.

Peel and Walters ran *Top Gear* like a private fiefdom within the BBC, untouchable for as long as Peel's popularity is undiminished. This allowed them to get away with, for instance, the appearance on *Top Gear* of classical Indian sitar player Imrat Kahn.

"Now *that*," Walters admits with a huge laugh, banging down pints of fearsomely foaming ale on the table where Peel and I are sitting, "provoked a *great* number of complaints."

"A factory in South London," Peel adds, "went on *strike*."

"He did two 30-minute ragas and we put them both out on the same show," Walters guffaws. "On a *Saturday* afternoon, for God's sake. People went berserk."

Peel has long-since been removed from his influential weekend show, and for the last 18 months has been presenting a show that goes out from 10–12, five nights a week.

"It's a smaller audience than we were used to on *Top Gear*," Peel says, of listening figures for the weekday shows. "I suppose it must fluctuate between 100,000 and 250,000. When you think in terms of the 96 million who are supposed to listen each day with great enthusiasm to Tony Blackburn, it probably doesn't sound like very many. On the other hand, it's Hampden Park filled out a few times – and if you ever got out onto the centre circle to speak to them all it would be a rather intimidating prospect."

So who listens to him these days?

"Apparently, I've got a lot of listeners in places like central Scotland," he says. "In areas where people haven't got a lot of money and there isn't much going on. And a lot of people listen in prisons and borstals. This might sound like romantic, left-wing fantasising, but frankly I'd rather work for them than some of the record companies."

I've been dispatched on this occasion to talk to Peel about his new status and his even more startling reinvention as a champion of punk. Peel, cleverly sensing the general drift of the musical climate and exploiting it totally, left many of his original audience feeling betrayed.

"I get accused of that all the time," Peels says by way of weary explanation when this is brought up. "The thing is, I'm a very opinionated, stubborn bugger and I just make up my own mind, and if people think it's opportunism or there's some cynical reason for doing it, then there's nothing I can do to convince them otherwise. That's what they're going to think, so I just soldier on and do what I think is right.

"I mean, it wasn't a deliberate refusal to grow old gracefully. The first records that moved me strongly were things like Little Richard records and Elvis Presley records and Gene Vincent records. They were very basic and very direct. And then I was moved again by the idealism of the hippies, which I passionately believed in.

"I genuinely believed we were going to change the world and that society was going to be altered by what we did. With punk came a combination of those two things. It was back to basics – to very simple, direct music, and at the same time punks seemed to be hoping, like the hippies, that they could actually make some changes in society that would make for a better way of life. So the two things together I found very exciting, and I was genuinely affected by it.

"I remember going to Virgin records in Marble Arch in 1976 and buying the first Ramones album – I vaguely knew the name. I played it before the programme and felt the same reaction I did to those first Little Richard records. I changed the whole of the programme and played at least half the Ramones album. Immediately, a lot of the traditional listeners wrote in that same night and said, 'For God's sake don't play any more of that. It's *awful*. It's not what we want to hear.' At which point, of course, I realised I should be playing more, not less, of this kind of thing. If there are people in woolly hats living in communes who think I've sold them down the river, I can only apologise."

Walters makes another run for the bar, and Peel waxes mournful about the parlous broadcasting standards of some of his Radio One contemporaries.

"You get the impression sometimes when you listen to them," he says, "that they've just turned up to fill in the time before they go off and make a lot of money opening a boutique somewhere. They see Radio One as a device by which they can procure remunerative outside work, rather than it being, as it should be I think, the main focus of their attention. The place where they should do their hardest work."

"Are you asking Peel why he doesn't earn a few bob opening a shop or a flower show?" Walters asks, returning with more beer.

"I couldn't do it, although it sounds terrible to say it so bluntly," Peel says. "The thing is, I like doing what I do. I want to go on doing it. And I don't stop and think about what it is I do in any kind of sociological terms. I don't think about the future and I don't think about whether it makes me an interesting or fascinating person as a consequence of doing it.

"I like being me. I like going to football matches without people rushing up to me for my autograph. I just like the level on which

I operate. I don't know any stars. I don't feel romantic about this job. If The Clash walked in here and sat at this table, I wouldn't know any of them. That's exactly the way I like it," he says, "and if it continues like that for the years that are left to me, I'll die a very happy man."

THE LEGENDARY ARIOLA JUNCKET

New York | Los Angeles | Portland, August 1978

This starts when lilac-suited *Melody Maker* editor Ray Coleman calls me into his office and tells me he's been offered a trip to America, courtesy of Ariola Records, the German-based record label who've just signed a raft of US bands and now want to show them off. To which end, they've invited Ray and two other editors – Alan Lewis and Alf Martin – on a weeklong US jolly-up.

As Ray drones on about the logistics of the trip – which, apparently, will take in New York, Los Angeles and Portland, Maine – I'm frankly baffled. Is he asking me to drive him to the airport? Carry his luggage? Look after his pets when he's away?

It finally dawns on me that Ray's explaining that he'd like me to go in his place, as a reward of sorts for some recent good work. He doesn't appear to be on drugs so I believe him, the trip now beginning to sound like a bit of a breeze.

Here's the plan, as Ray puts it to me. The Ariola party will be led by glamorous rock PR, Jennie Halsall and a girl from the label's marketing department whose name, ungallantly, I have forgotten. Then, there's me, Alan, Alf, plus photographer Paul Cox. We meet up later that week at Heathrow, discover our flight's been delayed and hit the bar. Alan Lewis has a thirst that seems to have been honed by the Saharan sun and is so drunk by the time we get on the plane he passes out before we get to the end of the runway.

"Bloody punishing schedule," he says, waking up somewhere over the Atlantic, tucking into a packet of nuts and knocking back something with so much vodka in it there's no room for ice.

The first stop on our itinerary is New York, where we are to see two of Ariola's hot new signings, Riot and Prism. First of all, though, we run up a huge bar tab at the Manhattan Sheraton, where Alan Lewis discovers a virtually suicidal taste for extremely strong cocktails washed down with lagoons of lager. I hate to see a man drink himself into oblivion on his own, so by the time we get to The Great Gildersleeves, a club in the Bowery where Riot are playing, Alan and I are fair rocking. The evening then takes a dangerously apocalyptic turn when Jennie Halsall mentions to Riot's manager – who reminds me vaguely of mob-connected Dallas nightclub owner Jack Ruby, who shot Lee Harvey Oswald – that I'm feeling somewhat tired and could do with a "pick me up". Frank knows what she's talking about and, next thing, a balls-hoisting young desperado obviously on his way to audition for a small part as someone lurking viciously at the edge of the frame in a Scorsese movie has taken me aside and starts chopping out lines of coke.

"Help yourself," he says, and I do. "Let me know if you need any more," he adds, which means that not much later I'm in a back room doing large amounts of beak with some very kind people who, if they weren't here might be digging graves in Jersey for the recently whacked. The gig that follows goes by in a blur. So does the rest of the night and most of the next day, of which I have a vague memory of Prism supporting Meat Loaf in Central Park.

The next day we fly into Los Angeles where a couple of Lincoln Continentals are waiting for us, ice buckets full of champagne in the back. As we drive through Beverly Hills, I pour Alan Lewis a glass of bubbly.

"Just to be sociable," he says, draining his glass and offering it for a quick re-fill. We then spend several hours drinking heavily at Ariola's expense at the Hyatt House on Sunset Boulevard, lounging next to the rooftop pool and staring gormlessly at the vast expanse of Los Angeles below us. Then it's off to The Starwood, a club on Santa Monica Boulevard, where we spend a few hours with a group called The Heaters before heading for a night on the town that goes on for a couple of days.

"I'm going to need a holiday after all this," Alan Lewis reflects wearily, hoisting a pina colada to chapped lips in a Malibu bar, and we all drink to that.

We're horribly late for the flight the next morning to Boston, which leaves without us. We're therefore hours late getting to Maine, where Ariola recording artiste Gene Cotton is appearing at the Portland Civic Centre. We meet Gene backstage.

"What did you think of the show?" he asks.

We tell him he was finishing his last number when we arrived.

"Cock up on the catering front," Alan Lewis explains, looking for a drink. Gene looks suitably baffled. Then the promoter appears and invites us to a party at his place, some kind of mansion on the coast, Atlantic breakers pounding the beach outside his back door. As if he's had a premonition of the disaster we're about to visit upon him and his home, the promoter puts us in a sort of alcove, where there's a table stacked with booze.

"We can't take it with us, so we might as well drink it," Alan Lewis says. Pretty soon we're predictably sloshed.

Running along an entire wall of this lavish homestead, there's an intricate metal frieze made up of what looks like medieval weaponry – swords, sabres, scimitars, cutlasses, spears, knives, dirks, daggers, lances, spears. I can't tell if the frieze is one welded piece or separate items artfully interlocked. Neither can Alan, who seems drunkenly fascinated by it and now wanders over to it, staring at its mysteries with an inquisitive eye.

I then watch him reach out to this intricate mesh, fingertips brushing an ornately inscribed blade. Alan gives one of the daggers a little tug and the whole edifice gives a worrying creak. I would've walked away then, into the night, into the surf, into my baby's arms. Alan doesn't. He gives the dagger another tug, and now it's in his hand. There's a groaning in the room then, followed by a worried hush, everybody turning to Alan who's standing there with something in his hand that should be holding up the entire complex structure, this matrix of blades and glinting metal, our host's pride and fucking joy, which is now coming away from the wall, with bits of it starting to fall off. Alan steps back as a sizeable chunk of the frieze unlocks itself and hits the floor with a clatter that makes everyone jump. I notice then that the entire fucking thing is about to collapse, which it does with a fearsome crash, bits of it flying everywhere, like it's been blown off the wall by a bazooka. I don't think the damage could have been worse if someone had driven a tank through the wall. Understandably enough, there's a stunned silence. People are standing there open-mouthed, our host among them.

Alan walks back to the alcove. "One more," he says, pouring a large drink, "then I think we'd better go. Bad form," he adds, "to out-stay our welcome."

AL STEWART

Los Angeles, September 1978

Somewhere over America, there's a problem – something to do with the Boeing's fuel supply that I don't want to know too much about – and we have to make an emergency landing in Montana, where we sit on a runway for about three hours. Not long before take-off, I begin to feel not-quite-with-it, consumed by a feeling of drift and dizziness, a breathlessness I can't shake off. I've been a bit bronchial for a couple of weeks, but now I'm wheezing like an old accordion and coughing like a pit worker.

There's a limo waiting for us at LAX and we pile in, enjoying the largesse of RCA, who are paying for all this, a bunch of us from the UK press flown out for what promises to be another highly entertaining jaunt around the US. In LA, we're meant to be interviewing English singer-songwriter Al Stewart, who's done very well for himself since moving to California, his "Year of the Cat" single topping charts around the world. After we're done with Al, we'll be off to Oregon to meet up with Dolly Parton, who's playing a rodeo – a *rodeo!* – somewhere up there. From Oregon, we'll be heading to Nashville and the annual Country Music Association Awards. After that, it's off to New York for a couple of days with Hall & Oates.

While we're in Los Angeles, we'll be staying at the Beverly Hills Hotel – immortalised for rock fans by The Eagles' "Hotel California". It's a swish old place, it must be said, and room 249, where I am even now unpacking, is roughly the size of a small tennis court. The plan for tonight is a few drinks at the bar and a quick trip down the freeway to Santa Monica, where Al Stewart is playing. I'm still feeling a bit washed out, but a couple of Dos Equis make me feel pretty chipper. Our RCA chaperone, Robin Eggar, has hired an open-topped Toyota jeep to drive us to Santa Monica. Needless to say, we all feel rather swanky on our way to the gig, the breeze in our hair and the sun going down over the Pacific. On the way back, however, it's suddenly very cold. I start shivering and then can't stop. I spend a restless night wracked by heavy-duty sweats and chills. The next morning I can barely stand and I've started coughing blood, to boot.

Robin Eggar takes one look at me and wonders if I'm in a fit state to drive up to Al Stewart's place. I tell him I'll be fine. He doesn't believe me, but off we go, and when we get there the UK press posse are agog at the vertiginous beauty of Laurel Canyon, where Al lives in some splendour. I'm the first one to Al's door, a big oak thing with wrought-iron inlays. It's the kind of door you want to rap robustly. Sadly, all I can muster is a rather weak tap. The door opens, however, and there's Al Stewart looking wealthy and tanned.

"Hi, I'm Al," he says, beaming, holding out a hand. I reach out to take it and am vaguely aware of the look of surprise on Al's face when I pitch forward, falling with a crash through his front door, like a tree keeling over after being cut in half by a chainsaw. I'm aware then of footsteps running up the steps behind me, people leaning over me and then a terrible hush, a graveyard quiet – the keen anticipation of people somewhat regrettably preparing to deal with an unexpected tragedy, a colleague snatched from them by a whim of feckless fate. I want to reassure them that I'm OK, but I can't because I'm losing consciousness, going out, in fact, like a light.

The next thing I hear is birdsong and lapping water, which isn't as reassuring as it sounds. Am I in some benevolent ante-room of heaven, surrounded by fountains, seraphim and much cooing in the afterlife's verdant foliage? This seems rather unlikely, so I take a wild guess and figure I'm still alive – if only just – and probably in Al's garden. Which is of course where I am, stretched out on a recliner by the side of his pool. It's apparently been decided that I need to see a doctor and Al's gone to the trouble of calling his man, who has a surgery on Rodeo Drive, where I am now whisked by a chauffeur named Stan, if memory serves. I've been stretched out on the back seat of Stan's limo, where I lay for most of the drive. Somewhere along the way, I'm aware enough of Stan slowing down to wonder what's going on. I lift my head and through the window see a tall handsome black man returning Stan's wave from the sidewalk across the street. He looks familiar, but I can't quite place him and ask Stan if it might be Jim Brown, the former pro-footballer turned actor, star of things like *Rio Conchos* and *The Dirty Dozen*. It's not Jim, though. It's another NFL legend who's turned to movies after retiring from the game.

"That's OJ," Stan says. "OJ Simpson."

I wish I could at this point say I felt some convenient premonition, a whiff of bloody ghastliness to come, nightmarish images of frenzied stabbings, throat-cuttings, a white Bronco on a Los Angeles freeway. But I don't. The man waving from the sidewalk seems, in fact, like a decent enough cove, if somewhat overdressed.

At the doctor's surgery, I have a ton of blood tests and X-rays before someone who looks like they should have their own TV show tells me I have viral pneumonia, which means I can't travel until further notice and must take immediately to my bed at the Beverly Hills Hotel while my erstwhile travelling companions fly on without me to Oregon and Dolly Parton. The next few days are hell – a procession of room service meals and endless television. I can't sleep, so the TV day starts early, at 6:30am and with a choice between *New Zoo Revue* on Channel 11, *Jake Hess Gospel Time* on Channel 30 and *Captain Andy* on Channel 40. Up next: *Captain Kangaroo*, *Tennessee Tuxedo*, *Bull Markets*, *I Love Lucy* and something called *Hodgepodge Lodge*. The afternoon is full of chat shows, where the guests all look like the undead in a George Romero gorefest, and the hosts have the stricken aspects of the recently embalmed. After the talk shows come the game shows – the completely surreal *Liar's Club*, the incomprehensible *25,000 Dollar Pyramid* and my own favourite, *The Newlywed Game* ("Cindy! Tell us – on your wedding night, was Brad here a spunky monkey or a limp chimp?") where the contestants vie for spectacular prizes, including a year's supply of Porkfest TV dinners.

After three days of this, I am on the brink of insanity, and start to prowl the hotel corridors, a degenerate in the halls of affluence. I hang around the legendary Polo Lounge, where Hollywood's most fabled stars are reportedly wined and dined by fawning studio executives and deals are cut and plans are hatched. There are any number of well-dressed dudes sporting tans from suns none of us have ever seen and teeth that gleam like igloo walls, but the nearest I get to spotting someone you could describe as a star is hunky, square-jawed, barrel-chested Stuart Whitman, memorable opposite John Wayne as a rakish gambler in *The Comancheros*. I try to strike up some conversation with the Polo Lounge barmen, but they're a suspicious lot. Some code of bartending omertà quickly asserts itself and an ominous silence prevails.

By the end of the week, I've had enough and head down Sunset Strip to the Rainbow Bar & Grill, where I have my first drink in what seems a lifetime. I follow it with a few more and a couple after that and by the time I leave, I'm cheerfully drunk. Out in the parking lot, there's dust in the air, headlights sweeping through the night and someone I immediately recognise standing there looking baffled.

Before you know it, I'm walking towards him, hand outstretched.

"Harry Dean Stanton!" I shout in a bizarre hail-fellow-well-met bellow, startling myself in the process.

"Harry Dean Stanton?" he says, the grizzled screen veteran giving me a squinty little look, like he's trying to get me into focus. "Hell of a coincidence, kid," he says then. "That's *my* name, too."

And with that, a car pulls up beside him, he falls backwards into the passenger seat and roars off into the night, one arm waving out the window as the car disappears around a corner and he's gone, gone, gone.

THE CLASH

London, November 1978

I'm having breakfast with Joe Strummer and Paul Simonon of The Clash in a cafe called The Metropole on Edgware Road, just around the corner from Joe's flat. We're trying to make ourselves heard over the clank of cutlery and the sibilant hiss of the Espresso machine, when in walks Paul's girlfriend, Caroline Coon, recently a *Melody Maker* journalist, who's taken over the management of The Clash following the band's recent spectacular falling out with Bernie Rhodes. She takes Strummer aside, looking tense. Their conversation is hurried. Whatever she's telling him is making Strummer fume. By the time he returns to our table, he's furious.

He's just been told that CBS, the band's record company with whom they seem in constant dispute, have somehow got hold of a film of The Clash performing their new single, "Tommy Gun". CBS are trying to get it shown on *Top of the Pops,* without the band's permission. The Clash have already refused unconditionally to ever appear on the programme and Strummer's now determined to stop the record company negotiating a slot for the "Tommy Gun" promo on next week's show.

"It was one of the *shouts*," Joe seethes, "to refuse to have anything to do with *Top of the Pops*. It was one of the things we all wanted to do away with, *right*? It was one of the *shouts*," he shouts. "No one was gonna do *Top of the Pops* to sell their records. Seems *we're* the only ones still shouting. The others have all done it. Maybe they've got their reasons, but it makes me sick it's still on. I want it to *end*. We won't do it, and CB-fucking-S ain't gonna get away with putting any film of us on it behind our backs."

If Strummer sounds somehow under siege, it's because that's apparently how he feels right now. From where he's standing, everyone's got it in for The Clash. Bernie Rhodes has been predictably vindictive since the split, accusing The Clash of the kind of arrogant rock star behaviour they'd originally condemned. He's also gone to the High Court to have their assets frozen and has generally taken his sacking very badly indeed. Further, the band's much-delayed second album, *Give 'Em Enough Rope*, came out a couple of weeks ago and although it charted at Number Two – held off the top of the charts by the *Grease* soundtrack – there have been some notably sniffy reviews. Specifically, Nick Kent in *NME* and Jon Savage in *Melody Maker* have been unsparingly critical of the album's evident shortcomings.

Summer tries to be philosophical about the dismissive critical voices, but you can tell he's been stung and is maybe hurting.

"I could have stood an even worse slagging," he says bravely, if unconvincingly. "The first time you're slagged, it really gets you *here*, you know..." He thumps his chest, not quite sure where his heart is, typically melodramatic. "But after that, you get sort of immune. You get a leather heart, you know?"

The Clash have also come under fire from *NME* double act Tony Parsons and Julie Burchill in their book on punk, *The Boy Looked at Johnny*. Strummer has taken particular offence to the book, because at one point he regarded Parsons as something approaching a friend.

"What disappointed me most," Strummer says of the book, "is that it was boring. And also the fact they'd invented so many lies. They needn't have. They could have put that kind of cynical slant on the *facts*. But they've thrown in, like, five or six outright lies. They're things that *I* know as well as *Tony* knows are just a load of lies."

What really has rankled Strummer recently is the common criticism that The Clash aren't nearly as radical as they like to think they are, for all their rebel posturing. What's Strummer got to say about that? Plenty, actually.

"We're really radical... yeah," he says, warming up, coming to the boil. "We don't do *anything* we don't want to do. We've got a really high standard that we want to maintain, right? And we don't do anything that might cross that standard... All right, you've got to sell records to survive, because a group is such a large machine. It requires a lot of money to keep it running. The money to keep it going has to come from selling records, because you never make money from touring. So we realise we've got to sell records. But we're not prepared to do just *anything* to sell them. We're only prepared to do what fits in with our idea of what it should be like. We're not prepared to go on *Top of the Pops*. We don't feel like it's a real show..."

Yeah, but, you know, on the revolutionary scale, throwing a hissy fit and refusing to appear on a TV pop show is hardly the equivalent of Che and Fidel wading ashore at Playa de las Coloradas with 80 men to bring insurrection to Cuba and throw Batista into the sea.

"You're talking about radical acts, right?" he says, smacking the table in front of him with some force, cups rattling in saucers, spoons flying. "You mean, like planting *bombs?* That's a radical act, isn't it? To actually *blow something up* is an extreme act. There's nothing more extreme you could do to this caff than blow the place up and leave a big hole in the Edgware Road. Maybe you could take your clothes off and dance around on the tables. That would be pretty good. That would turn a few heads. But to blow the place up would be pretty extreme. But the thing is," he says then, "*we never came to destroy*. We never did."

Both Kent and Savage in their reviews of *Give 'Em Enough Rope* had criticised Strummer's sometimes infantile infatuation with revolutionary terrorist groups like the Red Brigades and the Baader-Meinhof crew, and his occasional tendency to romanticise violent insurgency. Predictably enough, Joe thinks he's been misunderstood.

"I really do," he says, rather plaintively. "When we wrote 'White Riot' and all that about Sten guns in Knightsbridge and knives in W11, we imagined that was gonna hit on *us*. I imagined having a knife pointed at *me*, right? I imagined Sten guns in Knightsbridge *pointed at me*. But people took it to mean *we* had them and we were pointing them at other people. That was a song written about the future. I thought the future was gonna do us in. I really did.

"And the only reason I ever brought up people like the Red Brigades was I couldn't believe what they were doing. They were just, like, *normal people*, right? And they've taken up guns. They've gone out robbing banks, kidnapping people and shooting people and murdering them and blowing places up. They've gone to that extreme. So I had to compare *them* to *me*, right?

"Right now, there's loads of people out in their country mansions getting ready to go grouse shooting. And at the same time, there's millions of old age pensioners who have to wrap themselves in bits of cardboard to keep warm because they've got no heating and they have to live for three days on a piece of rotting bread because they've got no food. And I don't think it's fair. And those people in West Germany and Italy, they decided that the only way they can fight is to go out there and start shooting people they consider to be arseholes.

"At once, I'm impressed with what they're doing and at the same time I'm totally frightened by what they're doing." He pauses, assumes a suitably thoughtful impression.

"It's not an easy subject when you think about it," he says then, as if this has not struck him before, splashing ketchup on his eggs, forking a chip and getting on with breakfast.

XTC

New York, December 1978

XTC have been invited by David Byrne, a fan, to support Talking Heads at a glittering New Year's Eve show at New York's Beacon Theatre. I meet up with the excited quartet, whose first trip to America this will be, at Heathrow, where our chaperone, loquacious Virgin PR, Al Clark, returns tight-lipped and ashen-faced from the Air India check-in desk. The bad news is that our flight has been delayed by up to six hours. He's been given some Air India free meal vouchers, however, which he brandishes rather proudly, like they're the tickets that have just won him first prize in a raffle. He suggests we go for something to eat.

"It's nine o'clock in the morning, Al," XTC drummer Terry Chambers points out. "I don't want a fucking *curry*. Let's find a bar and get some bastard beers in."

Which we do, Chambers leading the way and getting merry in a hurry when we get there. Over rather more than several drinks in the hours to come, Chambers gives me a full account of XTC's career to date and reduces me to helpless laughter with innumerable and outrageous stories about the so-called "Penhill Mutants" – these being the eccentric denizens of the Penhill Estate in Swindon, where three of the band are from, who sound like they would not be amiss among the depraved and lunatic cast of something like *The Hills Have Eyes* or *The Texas Chainsaw Massacre*.

Hours later, we assemble again in front of the Air India desk, only to discover our flight has been further delayed.

"Is this *it*, then, Al?" Chambers wants to know. "Fucking marvellous. I'm glad I came. Is the whole of bastard America going to be like this?"

"I think I'm getting lounge lag," Andy Partridge complains, sounding exhausted even though we haven't actually been anywhere yet.

The next day, we're in New York—driving out of it, actually, to Philadelphia, where XTC have a gig at somewhere called The Hot Club. Al Clark is besotted with the New York skyline – the Statue of Liberty, the Twin Towers, the Empire State Building, all that. He suggests any one of these as an ideal location for a band photo-shoot.

"I should feel terribly cheap if we fell for that one, Al," Andy Partridge says. "I mean, it's a bit crass. Like, did The Dead Boys have their picture taken with Blackpool Tower in the background when they came to England. Don't be fucking soft."

We find The Hot Club in what appears to be a derelict part of town. The support band's already here, a nasty bunch of yobs called Diamond Reo. XTC have a look at the hired equipment they'll be using tonight. Chambers is distraught when he sees what passes for a drum kit.

"It's a *boy's* kit," he moans. "It's like the kit I had at school. It should have teddy bears and sheep painted on it."

The group go through a half-hearted sound check which is quickly abandoned and, feeling pretty downcast, they retire, sulking, to their dressing room. I wander back out into the club to watch Diamond Reo's opening set, which is pretty horrendous and notable only for their bass player banging his head against a wall and tearing off his clothes before lashing out at the small crowd with a microphone stand. "I'm gonna piss on you cuz you're a *dawg!*" he screams at no one in particular, the crowd mainly ignoring him.

Backstage, XTC, are glumly considering their American debut, here at The Hot Club.

"Not exactly Shea Stadium, is it?" keyboard player Barry Andrews says, a little forlornly, casting an eye around their dressing room, a miserable place, the walls covered in graffiti, a single lightbulb hanging from the ceiling, a sink half-torn from a wall, puddles on the floor, a few chairs, a rickety table and a plywood door that looks like someone's kicked a hole in it, which now bursts open to reveal an inappropriately cheerful fellow.

"Howzit *gowwwwin*, guys?" he mugs, a messy individual with a greasy T-shirt pulled down over a spreading paunch. One of the club's owners, apparently. "Hey," he goes on, "we gotta great crowd in tonight and they're gonna love the shit outta you guys."

"Love the shit out of us?" Andy asks, incredulous.

"Beat the shit out of us, more likely," Barry Andrews says as the band troop out of the dressing room to the stage.

An hour later, they're back in the dressing room.

"We're going to have to hire a plane to fly over Philadelphia with a streamer flying from the back of it apologising for that gig," Partridge says. "It was terrible."

"Worse than the first time we played London," Barry Andrews agrees. "And we should have been shot after that one."

"The next time you play here," Al Clark, trying to be chipper, insists, "you'll clean up."

"Yeah," Andrews replies morosely, "but only if we bring our own brooms."

We get back to New York at about six in the morning, with everyone in a bad mood. Over lunch the next day, at Virgin's New York HQ on Perry Street where we're staying, Terry is still complaining about last night's gig, a pointless excursion in his much-repeated and rather more colourfully expressed opinion. He's not especially thrilled, either, by the plans for tonight, which include dinner with David Byrne and Jerry Harrison from Talking Heads – Byrne due at Perry Street in a few hours to meet us and take us to the restaurant where Jerry will be waiting. The rest of XTC are flattered by Byrne's affection for them, which seems genuine enough. Terry, on the other hand, thinks there's something a little condescending about Byrne's patronage. "It's like he thinks we're just these amusing *yokels*," he complains. "Country fucking bumpkins, or something." I get the impression there's something about Byrne's studied uptightness that makes Terry want to get far enough under his skin to make it pop.

Al's worried enough about Terry's mood to give him a bit of a talking to, with a final instruction, sternly made, that when Byrne arrives Terry should be on his best behaviour – Al stressing the virtues of a civil tongue, politeness, good manners, a lot less swearing, and not saying anything that might in any respect upset, disconcert or otherwise distress Byrne's apparently fragile sensibilities. I don't think Chambers takes much – if any – of this in. He just sits in front of the TV in an upstairs sitting room at Perry Street, simmering in front of a game show, its hostess a curvaceous blonde with big hair and plenty of cleavage on display who seems to have caught Terry's dubious attention.

Chambers is still there, staring at the TV, when Byrne arrives, looking as pristine as a dashboard Jesus, slightly prim, everything about him unimaginably neat, well-pressed, crisp and rather buttoned-up. He perches on the edge of a couch next to the armchair in which Terry's lolling, knees together, hands in his lap, straight-backed, like someone in a doctor's waiting room, bracing himself for bad news. We sit there for a while in an increasingly uncomfortable silence, Al keeping a wary eye on Chambers, who unexpectedly turns to Byrne with a question.

"'Ere, Dave," he says, laying on the Wiltshire accent a bit thick, a piratical twang accompanied by some understated eyeball-rolling, pointing with his beer can at the game show hostess on the TV. "I wouldn't mind coming my muck in 'er mouth, what about you?"

I just about stop myself from spitting a mouthful of beer 12 feet across the room. Al Clark looks stricken, like someone who's just lost a game of chess to someone in a black hood. Byrne replies with a cartoony chirrup and says he'll meet us downstairs. Chambers watches him go, smirking.

Now, here's Byrne, the next night, on stage at the Beacon Theatre, introducing his special guests.

"This band is XTC," he tells the packed-out Beacon. "They're very good and have two albums out. I love them."

The show goes well and afterwards XTC are in splendid spirits. Al Clark tells them he thought Byrne's introduction was a touching sign of his fondness for them.

"He was all right, but you couldn't *hear* him," Barry Andrews says.

"I thought he spoke clearly and fluently," Al says.

"He's not exactly *Noddy Holder*, though, is he?" Andrews says.

We're invited to Talking Heads' après-gig New Year's Eve party at the Gramercy Park Hotel, but it's a dull affair.

"The night is still young," Al Clark quips, epigrammatically, "but I don't think it's going to get any older here."

So we split, me, Terry and Al, fetching up hours later at a swanky club on Fifth Avenue. Byrne is there with Jerry Casale, Devo's weasel-faced bass player and minister of propaganda. Byrne beckons us over.

"You'll have to excuse us," Chambers announces as we join them. "We're all as pissed as arseholes."

At some point over the next hour, it transpires we've accepted Casale's invitation for XTC to join him the next day for lunch. Which brings us to a restaurant called Il Cortile in Little Italy, just down the road from Umberto's Clam House, where New York mob boss Joey Gallo was gunned down between courses in a shoot-out later immortalised in a song by Bob Dylan. What we imagine will be a convivial snack turns into an uproarious little spat when Andy Partridge takes a serious dislike to Casale. To everyone's surprise, the usually mild-mannered Partridge lays into the hapless Casale with the scathing venom of Lou Reed, flabbergasting the Devo man with a stream of outrageous anecdotes about our old friends, the Penhill Mutants, which climaxes with a long and extraordinarily detailed monologue about masturbation, a subject about which Partridge proves something of an expert, at which point Casale, reddening, makes his excuses and a rather graceless exit.

"Are we not yobs, or what?" Barry Andrews laughs, as Casale, clearly fuming, heads for the door.

"It was just a joust of egos," Partridge says, when we follow a couple of bottles of wine later. "It was just my way of saying, 'Look, pal, where we come from *everybody's* Devo. You're not so fucking special, stop making a circus out of it."

"Come off it," Chambers tell him. "You just didn't like the little fucker."

"Well," says Partridge, stepping out into New Year sunshine, "there was that, too."

THE BOOMTOWN RATS

Los Angeles | Atlanta | Dallas, January 1979

In a suite at the super-swanky L'Ermitage hotel in Beverly Hills, Bob Geldof and Johnnie Fingers, point-men for The Boomtown Rats on a month-long promotional trip to soften up America for the imminent release of their *A Tonic for the Troops* album – and the tour that will follow – are sprawled in front of a giant TV, watching something called *The Love Experts*. Going into a fourth week of interviews, parties, backslapping, handshaking and the general buttering-up of record executives, salesmen, pluggers, DJs, radio programmers, promoters, TV producers and assorted hacks and flunkeys of the US music machine, Bob and Johnnie are beginning to feel extremely sorry for themselves.

"Tomorrow," Geldof moans wearily, "will be our *45th* consecutive press reception." This brings a low groan from Fingers. "If this trip," Geldof goes on, "has achieved *nothing* else, it's cured me of *any* desire to attend any more of these parties. If I *never* go to another lig, if I *never* have another free drink in my entire life, it'll be *too fucking soon*.

"I mean, I *enjoy* talking. Especially about myself and the band. And that's what we're here for. At this stage of the game, though, it's all a bit lick-arse. But I'm prepared to do it. *This* time, anyway. Let's face it – you *have* to. If you leave it to the record company, you'd never get *anywhere*. Left to their own devices, they've got no idea over here. America can be so *backward*, you know?"

I get a taste of what Geldof and Fingers have been going through the next day, which starts at 10:30am, when a limo arrives a L'Ermitage to take us to the offices of KWEST radio for a round of interviews.

"The object of this exercise," Geldof says as we pull up outside KWEST, "is to storm in and make as much noise as possible."

A couple of minutes later, Geldof is doing exactly that, getting into it with a fat, pony-tailed DJ he's apparently taken immediate exception to.

"I suppose you're one of the guys who plays all the crap we hear on the radio," Geldof says, ever the diplomat.

"Uh?" says the DJ.

"Styx. Foreigner. You play shit like that?"

"Not all the time, man."

"You shouldn't be playing them at *all*," Geldof scolds him. "You should be playing *us*."

"Who... uh... who *are* you?"

"We're the most exciting rock 'n' roll band in Britain," Geldof tells him. "But you'll find that out for yourself soon enough when we come back and play."

"Will your album be out then?"

"The album will be *Number One* by then," Geldof announces, grinning, heading off now for rival station KLOS, where programme director Cody tells Bob how much he likes *A Tonic for the Troops*.

"If you like it so much, start fucking *playing* it," Geldof tells him.

"Bob," says Cody, soothingly. "There's a lotta competition, baby."

"No there fucking *isn't*," Geldof insists. "When we come back, you'll be playing us four times an hour. You won't be able to turn on the radio without hearing us."

Next stop, the CBS Tower, near Century City, where the LA music press and sundry hangers-on has turned out in force to meet them. There's lashings of food and drink and the LA hacks pile in. I end up chatting to someone who introduces me to Kim Fowley, who's even more garrulous than Geldof, who spends nearly three hours circulating, schmoozing, having his back slapped and arm punched, laughing, joshing, being a trouper. As the last of the hacks leaves, Geldof collapses into an armchair.

"I am *so* pissed off being polite to absolute morons," he says. "When we get home, I'm going to have to get this smile surgically removed."

The next day, we're in Atlanta. There's a lavish dinner for nearly 100 radio people, flown in by CBS from all over the south, after which we go to see Muddy Waters – an unforgettable sight – at a club called the Agora, which is a bit like being in the same room as God. From there, we move on to what turns out to be a drag club called Sweet Gumheads, where the entertainment's provided by a flamboyant line-up of drag queens in outlandish costumes miming and gyrating to various disco hits.

After the fifth or sixth act, a bewildered Johnnie Fingers leans across the table and whispers in my ear: "They… they're *all men*."

I tell him I know they're all men.

"Jaysus," he says, shaking his head. "This is all new to me."

The next morning in Atlanta, we meet Rich Piombino, a stocky New Yorker and the PD at WKLS.

"I just wanna tell youse guys I think your album is just *fucken great*. I love it. Love it. *Love it*. WKLS *loves* it. We *all* love it. We all think its *fucken tree-mendous*. I ain't bullshitting here, neither. It's guys like you are gonna be taking over, man. Because there ain't no rockanroll happening here no more. You know where rockanroll is at in this country? Gino Vanneli. That's where rockanfuckenroll is in this country. Two years ago, I go see Gino-fucken-Vanneli and that weren't rockanroll. That was *shit*. He kept the audience waiting two fucken hours. You know why? *His fucken hair was wet.* I wanted to go backstage and kick the shit outta his face. You guys gotta come back, man, soon. I love youse guys. WKLS loves youse."

"It's amazing," Fingers says on our way out. "We keep meeting guys like that. They can even talk the face off Geldof. I can't remember the last time anyone did that."

Soon, it's TV time! Geldof and Fingers are led into a small garishly coloured studio, to be interviewed by Ms Terri Tingle, an ex-topless dancer and now host of a show called *Entertainment Page*. The final chorus of "Me and Howard Hughes", a track from *A Tonic for the Troops*, fades quickly and Terri's suddenly talking to Atlanta.

"Hi!" she beams, her smile as bright as a thousand suns, too many teeth for one mouth. "You've just been listening to The Boomertown Rats – and I have with me in the studio two members of the band, Johnnie Fingers and Bob Goodolf!"

"*Geldof*," says Geldof.

"I'm sorry," Terri says, simperingly apologetic when she obviously couldn't give a fuck what Geldof's name is. "I've never been to Ireland."

"That's all right, love," Geldof says. "I've never been to Atlanta before."

Terri clearly wonders what this has to do with anything, but presses on anyway.

"I *luurve* your album," Terri gushes. "How do you write your songs?"

"With a pencil and paper, usually," Bob smiles.

"And where... where are the rest of the band? At home? Why aren't they with you?"

"Because they're boring," Geldof tells her. "I'm here because I talk a lot and he's here because he wears pyjamas," he adds, nodding at Fingers.

The following day. A reception at CBS Atlanta. More drinks. More food. More smiling. More people who *luurve* the album. More back-slapping. More small talk. The "Rat Rap" video, again. At least 17 times. Bob and Johnnie go off to be interviewed by Tony Parris of *The Atlanta Gazette*. They come back a few minutes later, Geldof fuming.

"You're just trying to look like a star," Parris, according to Geldof, had told him.

"I *am* a star," Geldof, according to Geldof, had replied.

"Maybe in England, but not here."

"Some people are stars *wherever* they are," is what Geldof comes back with then, adding "Just like some people are stars and others aren't. *I'm* a star. *You're* not. It's as simple as that."

We're in Dallas now, where on our first morning Geldof causes a bit of a fuss during a radio interview when the DJ asks him where the Rats will be playing when they finally come to town. Geldof tells her they'll be playing at the Texas Book Depository on Dealey Plaza – from where, of course, Lee Harvey Oswald is meant to have shot John Kennedy. This effectively ends the interview. "There are just some things we don't joke about, sir," Geldof's told as he's shown the door.

We're in Dallas so that Geldof and Fingers can put in an appearance at the annual CBS National Convention. This is being held at the Fairmount Hotel, a kind of Disneyland castle awash with satin tour jackets, walrus moustaches and the raucous laughter of people trying too hard to have a good time. As we go into dinner on our first night, we're given fancy little name tags.

"Jaysus!" Geldof groans. "Will you look at *this!*" He holds out his name tag, which has been made out to someone called BRAD GANDALF. This makes us all laugh, although Geldof's not so amused and sulks through a couple of courses.

CBS president Bruce Lunvall makes a speech reminding everyone – all those reps from every commercial outpost of America – that they're here because they're swell guys, doing swell jobs, shifting unit after unit for the company. "And I want to tell you," he tells them, "CBS is *more* than a company – it's a *family!*"

Oh, what a cheer this brings.

Then CBS MD Jack Craigo is introducing Geldof, lead singer with the label's hot new act, The Boomtown Rats. Geldof walks nervously to the speaker's podium.

"You've been told over the last few days that CBS is a real family," he begins, a couple of weeks of growing resentment finally coming to the surface, "full of warm and wonderful human beings. Frankly," he goes on, "I didn't know there were that many warm and wonderful human beings in the entire world, let alone one record company. I think you all know that really you're all just a bunch of fucking bastards."

There's more of this, but no one's listening because they're all *cheering*. For the moment, anyway.

Geldof returns to our table, exchanging handshakes with the CBS top-brass and their underlings.

"Fucking morons," he mutters, giving a big friendly wave to a couple of passing vice presidents. "What a bunch of absolute fucking morons."

THE CLASH

Cleveland | Washington DC, January 1979

I fly into Cleveland to meet The Clash in the middle of a blizzard that people from around here later tell me is the worst they can remember. What I don't know, as the TWA flight out of New York taxis across the runway through driving snow, is that The Clash are currently thousands of miles away. Their first American tour opened on January 31st in Vancouver, with dates quickly following in San Francisco and Los Angeles. They were then meant to drive straight to Cleveland for a show tomorrow night at the Agora Ballroom, but on a whim decided to light out on a three-day excursion to the southwest, taking in the sights of Arizona, New Mexico and Texas before swinging north. At some point, their tour bus has broken down and been taken to Nashville for repair. Which means that even as I'm being flung all over the sky by buffeting winds on the last flight into Cleveland before the weather shuts the airport down, they're in Oklahoma waiting for a flight of their own that now won't get them here until who knows when.

Meanwhile, I'm being driven through the freezing dark in the one local cab I've been able to find, a battered Pontiac held together, from what I can tell, by not much more than rust, a cabbie at the wheel named Lisa who – when she realises where I'm from – asks me if I know Benny Hill. She's a big fan, watches him on cable, cracking up at his smutty mugging. "I love it," Lisa chuckles, "when he slaps the little bald fella on the head." She laughs out loud, just thinking about it. "You sure you ain't met him?"

There are banks of snow piled high on both sides of the highway, emergency lights flashing wherever you look, snow coming down in relentless flurries, whipped against Lisa's windscreen by a ghastly wind. At times, she's forced to drive virtually blind. The huge car, which in many ways is more like a fucking boat, slides beneath her, at one point skidding at some speed across several lanes. We drive on through derelict downtown areas, creeping through the treacherous slush. The streets we're skating through are lit by the dull, exhausted glow of neon lights, flickering from pool halls, bars, porno cinemas – "Eroticinemas", as they have it locally – and assorted all-night dives. Groups of shivering men gather in windswept doorways along the route, stamping their feet, passing bottles, their breath frozen on the night air.

A drunk wrapped from head to foot in newspapers staggers out into the road in front of us, forcing Lisa to break hard enough for the rear of the Pontiac to get away on her again. She lets the car glide, does some fancy clutch work and we're back on beam and driving around the drunk. Looking back, I watch him walk unsteadily back to the sidewalk and fall headfirst into a snowdrift. Lisa says on a night like this there ain't no one on the streets who ain't up to something bad. Unemployment and violent crime are partners here in a typically unholy marriage. The city, formerly home to industrial dynasties like Standard Oil, the Hanna Mining Corporation, Republic Steel and the Consolidation Coal Company, is now heading for economic disaster, bankruptcy looming, Cleveland in debt to the tune of $16 million to six Ohio banks that want either their money back or financial control of the city. Its young mayor, Dennis Kucinich, has said he won't give up. As far as Lisa's concerned, the place is primed to blow.

"It's not so bad in the winter," Lisa says. "People are too cold to kill each other. In the summer, it's like someone declared war. There's so many unemployed, they get drunk, they get restless, they kill people. There's a lot of drugs murders, a lot of drunk killing. Most of the men who get killed, they know each other. They hang out together in bars and they got no one else to fight. They got no work so they get intoxicated and argue and start fighting and bang! Someone's dead. They say the unemployment ain't so bad no more. But I don't see my man in work. Here's your hotel," she says, pulling up outside Swingo's Celebrity Hotel, where at the time I'm still expecting to meet The Clash. "I'll drop you around the back. It's kinda safer," she adds, before driving off slowly, with a honk of her horn and a wave of a hand through a quickly closed window.

I'm now at the reception desk of the splendidly named Swingo's, looking forward to getting my room key and thawing out with a drink in what I'm sure will be luxurious accommodation. Things then go a bit Bethlehem on me, no room at the fucking inn, that sort of thing. The receptionist, whose name is Brett, checks one list, then another, makes a sort of sucking noise, like water disappearing down a plughole, taps his teeth with his hotel ballpoint, purses his lips and shakes his head. "Our system's never heard of you," he says, and I wonder if Brett's gloating a bit at this. He certainly doesn't look as distressed as I feel, in fact he seems annoyingly perky. He skims through some more paperwork. "No," he says with a certain triumphant relish that makes me want to set him on fire. "There's definitely no booking for you."

I ask him to put me through to Caroline Coon, who's managing The Clash at the time. Brett tells me the band haven't arrived yet, which puzzles me as they should have been here hours ago. I tell Brett I'll take a room anyway, and bill it later to the band. Brett gives me a creepy little smile.

"I'm sorry, sir," he says with as much sincerity as he can muster, which really isn't very much at all. "We're completely full."

He suggests I try the Holiday Inn on East 22nd Street, as if I know where that is.

"It's not too far," Brett now tells me. "You can go out the back way. That's quicker. But if I were you, I'd go out the front. It's a longer walk, but there's more light. You'll be able to see anyone coming at you."

I leave a message for The Clash, step back out into the blizzard – which is blowing harder than ever – and begin a long head-down trudge through the snow to the Holiday Inn. I'm a couple of blocks from the hotel when someone wearing about four overcoats and a woollen cap pulled low over his eyes steps out of a doorway, a huge looming figure who now blocks the sidewalk.

"Carry your bag, man?"

I tell him I'm fine, thank him for his courtesy and walk on, the freelance bell hop in somewhat stumbling pursuit.

"C'mon, man, where you goin', uh?" he wants to know, getting closer and sounding to me a little testy. He's right behind me when a

199

police car appears through the swirling murk, cruising slowly down the street. I turn to face the fellow following me, but he's gone, vanished into the night, fortunately without my bags, and now I'm at the Holiday Inn. I almost weep with relief when the receptionist tells me they have a room and hands over the key to it, which I hold like a sacred relic, the rib of a saint or something. I wait in the hotel room for an hour but there's no word from The Clash. I can't settle so end up in a bar called Bumper's that's attached to the Holiday Inn, where not much is happening in the sad fluorescent light that gives the place a mortuary sheen. There's an off-duty cop at the bar who tells me his name is Don and then doesn't say another word. There's also a pianist on a small dais who, when he smiles, looks to have more teeth than you'd find in the mouth of something with a tail in a paddock at the races. He's playing Billy Joel's "My Life" and attempting to catch the eye of one of the two women at a table across the room from him. Both women are made up like they're trying to scare people with a look that Heath Ledger, years later, will pick up for his turn as The Joker in *The Dark Knight*. There's a cage hanging from the ceiling above them, with two parakeets in it squawking hysterically.

"*Shut those fucken birds up,*" Don suddenly yells, making me jump.

A passing waitress smacks the bars of the cage with a plastic tray, provoking more squawking from the parakeets. Don's got his hands over his ears. Feathers float down into the drinks of the two women. The pianist starts playing "Help Me Make It Through the Night", which gets a smile you wouldn't describe as coy from one of the women. Back in my room at the Holiday Inn, there's a call from Caroline Coon. The Clash are finally in Cleveland after being stuck for five hours at an airport in Oklahoma because of fog. They're in the bar at Swingo's if I want to join them, which I would if I could be bothered, which I can't. I tell her I'll meet up with the band in the morning before they head to the Agora for their sound check.

The next day, I'm in the cocktail bar at Swingo's when Joe Strummer walks in, resplendent in a shocking pink jacket and shades, hair swept back in an impressive quiff. He's just back from a visit to a Cleveland dentist, his face swollen from an abscess on a tooth that he refuses to have pulled. He's also still suffering from the prolonged after-effects of the hepatitis that put him in hospital last year and, furthermore, has a savage gash on his lower right arm, after an unexplained incident in Vancouver.

"I keep ripping it open," he says. "I have to kind of bind it up with gaffer tape before we play. I think it's turning septic, though," he adds, rolling up a sleeve to show me the weeping wound, which makes me wince.

On our way in a taxi to the Agora for the band's sound check, with Caroline Coon now also in tow, Strummer gets worked up about freeloading record company types, the vice-presidents, area vice-presidents, regional managers, regional vice-managers and the like who had been flown from all over America to see The Clash at the Santa Monica Civic and otherwise party in LA at the band's eventual expense.

"I was disgusted they were there," Strummer says. "They've done nothing for us and there they were, poncing about backstage with their slimy handshakes and big smiles. I just ignored them. I don't have any time for it, all that record company bullshit. And, like, I heard they'd been taking journalists who'd come to see us out for nine-course meals before the gig. *Nine-course meals?* I've never had a nine-course meal in my life. I can't even imagine what a nine-course meal even *looks* like. I mean, what kind of person eats a nine-course fucking meal before a rock 'n' roll show? It's a disgrace that we should be associated with something like that."

Joe stomps off to make some noise at the sound check. Caroline and I wander backstage, where we run into Bo Diddley – Bo Diddley! – who's supporting The Clash on this tour, despite the evident hostility of CBS, who've been at odds with The Clash over just about every aspect of it, especially the budget and what they have made clear they consider a foolhardy choice of opening act.

"Even the promoters who were enthusiastic about The Clash didn't think it would be a good idea to tour with Bo," Caroline says. "They said he'd get bottles thrown at him. I told them that if Bo Diddley got bottles thrown at him, The Clash wouldn't play. It was absurd."

Anyway, here's Bo asking about Joe's inflamed molar. Turns out Bo's had problems in this department himself, as he now tells us with somewhat theatrical relish.

"I was on tour one time," he begins, and I look around for a chair, something telling me we might be here for a while. "Got this sumbitch tooth playin' hell, man. I went to the dentist. Dentist told me I'd be fine. I was halfway across Texas when that dude went. No warnin', nothin'. Sonuvagun. I made my driver pull over right there. Got to the nearest dentist and got him outta bed. Made him chisel that bad dude right outta my head. So you tell that boy, Joe, to watch hisself.

"An' tell him not to worry," Bo goes on. "If he can make the gig, he's doin' all right. You make the gig, you make the money. Take it from an old hand. Take that dollar. And fuck the rest. As long as you got that dollar in you hand, you doin' all right. One day you'll *need* that dollar. Because when you finished, that's it. Ain't no one gonna come from nowhere with money for you when you's finished. When a bucket loses its bottom," he adds sagely, a wise old road warrior, "*everything* goes, man."

The Clash that night are by turns sloppy and inspired and if they never really catch fire Cleveland nevertheless loves them, with most of the Agora crowd following the band back to Swingo's for a party that rocks on late into the night. Hence the many sore heads among us the following morning when we gather ourselves in the lobby at Swingo's for the long drive to Washington DC in the bus The Clash have rented for the tour from country hellraiser Waylon Jennings. According to tour manager Johnny Green's original schedule, we were meant to have left Cleveland at noon. Two hours after we should have hit the road, we're still, however, hanging around the hotel lobby. There's been a problem with the hotel bill, which CBS were meant to cover and evidently haven't. The Clash can't pay it because they haven't got any money. So Caroline Coon's been on the phone all morning, trying to get through to someone at the CBS office in New York to wire enough money to pay the bill. Whoever's got the clout to authorise the payment is in a meeting and can't be disturbed, she's told when someone eventually takes her call, which makes her fume. At one point it looks like we'll have to do a runner, but eventually the money comes through and at around 3:00pm, we get on the tour bus. By now, the skies are darkening, another storm front moving in, snow starting to fall, the wind already howling like something screeching across the tundra.

Bo Diddley pauses at the steps to the bus, looks at the weather and shakes his head.

"This ain't gonna get nothin' but worse," he says, a doomy prediction but true enough. We drive into the gathering dark, through a chill and barren landscape, vast plains of snow and ice on either side of the highway, frozen rivers and lakes out there, too, isolated farmhouses, truck stops, giant Exxon signs flashing through the accumulating gloom, the snow piling down, the windscreens of the bus freezing over. We have to stop regularly to chip off the ice.

The bus is split into three sections: there's a main compartment up front with coach seats, a TV and video, a middle section with bunk beds and a kind of lounge at the back, where Mick Jones is rolling a couple of spliffs. Bo Diddley's already grabbed a bunk and pretty soon everyone else is crashing out, too. Before he heads off for whatever passes here for a bed, Mick hands me one of the joints and says he'll see me later and makes his way unsteadily to wherever it is he's planning to get his head down. I can't sleep so make my way to the front of the bus, now empty, and sit with the driver, one of Waylon's good old boys, hired with the bus, who now regales me with wild tales of Waylon.

"These boys don't seem half-bad," he says of The Clash. "But if you want to put some colour in your cheeks, by God, go on the road with Waylon," he laughs, chuckles turning into a cackle, the driver madly tickled by some outrageous memory of Waylon and his legendary wrecking crew. Tonight's the TV premiere of John Carpenter's *Elvis* biopic, starring Kurt Russell, which I now start watching, lighting Mick's reefer as the credits roll and quickly drifting elsewhere. After I don't know how long, I'm vaguely aware of some heaving bulk settling into the seats across the aisle from me.

"Man," I now hear, and it's a low rumble on the edge of the consciousness I've been slipping away from. "This is a bad, bad night."

I can now hear the top of a bottle being unscrewed, followed by a lot of glugging and a surely satisfied sigh at the end of it all. Someone is now tapping me on the shoulder.

"If you ain't dead," a voice says then, "will you take a drink?"

At which point, I sit bolt upright. It's Bo Diddley sitting across the aisle there, the great rock 'n' roll legend swigging on a bottle of something that doesn't appear to have any kind of label. He offers it to me and I tell him I'd be variously honoured, grateful and happy to have a drink with him.

"No need for a *speech*, man," he says. "Just take the bottle." Which I do, taking the hefty swig recommended by Bo. I'm expecting a throat-burning moment, some fearsome roar in my head. But whatever Bo's plied me with here goes down incredibly smoothly, and I tell him so.

He smiles, sweetly. "Give it a moment," he says.

Next thing I know, the inside of the bus is filled with a brilliant light and for a moment I think we're under fire, tracer rounds lighting up the black night, trees bursting into flames, helicopters exploding over burning cities. All of which is followed by a fiery wind that appears to burn the skin off my face as it roars down the length of the coach, taking my hair with it.

"Thought you'd find it a bit of an eye-opener," Bo says, laughing again. I ask him what the fuck was in the drink. "Personal recipe," he says. "Not even the government could get it out of me."

He takes the bottle back, has another long pull on it and starts watching Kurt Russell as Elvis, which brings on a bit of a frown.

"Where did he get that *hair?*" he wants to know. "Never known Elvis to have hair like that," he says, clearly troubled, handing me the bottle of nuclear-strength moonshine.

"I was driving this way once," Bo says, pushing back in his seat, getting comfortable. "The road just went out from under me, *whooosh*." His large hand glides through the air. "Whoosh," he says again.

I ask him how much trouble he's been in, all these years on the road. This cracks him up.

"You a *comic* sumbitch," he laughs. "Listen. I'm 50 years old. I've lived all my life in the USA, travelled in every goddam state. And I'm *black*. And you want to know if I've ever been in any *trouble?* Shit. I been in the kinda trouble I don't even care to recall. I've had dudes come up to me and put a gun to my head. They'd say, 'Nigger, we gonna blow the shit outta your brains.' I'd always be po-lite and say, 'Yessuh, sho you are.' Then I'd get the hell outta there."

And where did this mostly happen?

"Texas," he says. Then after a pause, "and Alabama and Kansas and Virginia and Mississippi and Georgia and Tennessee and Missouri. All goddam over. This is America, baby. They got *problems* here with people like me."

It's around 2.30 in the morning when we finally roll into Washington, where we're supposed to be staying at the Barbizon Terrace hotel and where the receptionist tells Caroline Coon no rooms have been booked for The Clash.

"Fucking CBS," she laments. "They're really trying to kill us."

Alternative accommodation is eventually found at a nearby hotel called the Americana. Some of us still aren't ready for sleep. Johnny Green, Paul Simonon, Mick, Joe, tour DJ Barry Myers and I end up in an all-night diner. Mick's got a map of Washington and despite the unlikely hour wants to go sightseeing. It's 4.00 am now and Mick fancies visiting Arlington, the military cemetery, where burns an eternal flame in memory of the assassinated JFK.

"Great," Strummer says. "Let's go and piss on it and put it out."

We decide we'll go to the White House, instead. Mick, Joe, me and Johnny Green find a cab, Johnny hands the driver a bunch of notes and he agrees to take us to Pennsylvania Avenue, eerily quiet at this hour, the street deserted, nothing moving anywhere that we can see. The cab pulls up, across the street from the White House. Johnny Green's not impressed.

"That it?" he asks. "Looks like a toilet or someone's garden shed. Don't tell me they run the entire bleedin' world from that."

"Just think," Strummer says. "If we had a mortar or a bazooka or some machine guns, we could blow it away. Just lob a few grenades over the garden wall and wipe them all out. It's worth thinking about."

Mick's starting to look a bit worried.

"Can we go, please?" he asks the driver, his voice suddenly small and spooked. "I'm getting nervous sitting here. I can feel people looking at us, loading their guns. I don't want to be here when the bullets start flying."

He pulls his hat over his eyes, sinks deep into the back seat of the cab, slumped low, not much of a target. The cab starts rolling down Pennsylvania Avenue, Joe squirming in his seat, on his knees, looking out the back window at the vanishing White House, like he's wondering what it would look like after a direct hit from something with a nuclear war-head. Then the cab turns a corner and the White House disappears in the Washington night which, as we drive into it, swallows us up, too.

MIKE OLDFIELD

Berlin, April 1979

Mike Oldfield, in an earlier incarnation the shy retiring boy genius behind *Tubular Bells*, pours me a very large glass of Rhine wine, staring deeply into my eyes as he does so. We're sitting in the bar of Berlin's Intercontinental Hotel, the night noisy around us, but Mike quite oblivious to its rowdy hum.

My glass full, Mike slides it across the table towards me, leans forward until he's close enough to kiss me, which for a worrying moment I think he might. He smiles instead, mischievously.

"You've got lovely hair," he says.

I thank him for this unexpected compliment and try to get the interview back on track. A couple of hours earlier, Oldfield had played Berlin's Eissporthalle, a cavernous arena. He's currently touring Europe, promoting his *Incantations* album, which may be the most uneventful piece of music I've ever heard, but which to perform nevertheless takes a 10-man rock band, a 24-piece orchestra, the Queen's College Girls Choir and Maddy Prior, who takes the vocal lead on a preposterous arrangement (by Oldfield) of Longfellow's epic poem, "Hiawatha".

A couple of nights earlier, in Dusseldorf, a huge crowd had been reduced to a collective doze by its interminable length. Tonight, just as heads start nodding, the mixing desk blows up, waking everyone with a fright.

"That was my fault," Mike tells me now.

Why?

"Because," he confides, looking like he's going to reveal some inner secret he's kept to himself for years, "I had a very unhappy childhood. I made my parents reject me. I wanted them to fuck me up. So they did."

He can see I'm bemused.

"This is all perfectly true," he insists. "I'm responsible for everything that happens. The mixing desk blowing up, the audience being bored by the concert..."

Bored, why?

"Because I wrote *Incantations*."

And you think it's boring?

"I think," he says, "it's *rubbish*."

Then why inflict it on these poor people?

"Because I *want* to bore them. I want them to reject me. Then I want them to understand *why* they're rejecting me. And if they can understand that, we can all have a good time."

He can tell I'm having trouble making sense of this.

"It makes perfect sense. It really does," he says. "But I don't expect you to understand. I think you're probably an idiot."

Thanks a lot.

"But that's all right," Mike adds quickly, splashing another half bottle of wine into my glass. "I'm an idiot, too. That's the whole point. *Incantations* can only succeed if I can prove to the audience I'm an idiot."

I look at him, blankly, it must be said.

"You don't really understand what I'm talking about, do you?" he asks now, and starts stroking the back of my hand. "But that's *great*. It means *you're* probably fucked-up, too."

And that's a good thing?

"Certainly! I felt great when I realised how fucked-up *I* was. Because it meant I didn't feel fucked-up anymore. I could feel happy without feeling guilty. The only way I could feel happy before was by making people feel sorry for me. Then I could hate them, and that made me even more fucked-up."

This is certainly clarifying a few issues, Mike.

"I think so," he says, giving my hand a squeeze. "You know," he goes on, "before, I used to have these moments of blind panic – they were *dreadful*. I used to have to stop whatever it was I was doing and just scream. I used to be *so frightened*. I'd be incapable of doing *anything* for days. For *months*. I'd just stop. I just used to think 'Why?' I just couldn't feel *happy*. If people said they liked me, I hated them.

207

"I remember when I played the Queen Elizabeth Hall just after *Tubular Bells* came out. I stood on the stage at the end of the concert and looked at the audience. And they looked at me. And do you know what they *did?*"

I didn't.

"They actually *applauded.*"

Fuck me.

"I was amazed," Oldfield says. "I *hated* that concert. I thought we were terrible. And people came backstage and said they'd loved it. I couldn't believe it. The only way I could even begin to enjoy it was by reminding myself how *bad* I thought it had been. I used to feel bad about everything. The more they loved it, the worse I thought it was. And that was the only thing that made me feel happy."

So in some way, you used to relish your own misery?

"Definitely!" Mike exclaims, excited, as if he's made some sort of breakthrough here. "I used to love playing the martyr."

But that's behind you now?

"Yes. I simply realised that having a good time didn't mean I had to feel miserable. It was about the time of *Ommadawn*. I realised what had been fucking me up was being born. So I decided I was just going to have to be re-born. It was the only answer. I had to recreate the circumstances of my own birth. It's something I'd really recommend."

I'll think about it, I tell him, trying to slip my hand from his.

"You really should," he says, flicking the hair out of my eyes.

"The end of side one of *Ommadawn*," he says then, "do you know what that is?"

Again, I didn't.

"It's the sound, Allan," he says, tucking my hair behind my ear, "of me exploding from my mother's vagina."

I'm briefly worried that Mike is going to go into even more gynaecological detail, and brace myself for what might come next, instead of which Mike suddenly announces he's ready for bed and is quickly off, followed it must be said by my somewhat huge sighs of relief.

For years, of course, the notoriously press-shy Oldfield baffled and frustrated his record company by refusing to do interviews, encounters with journalists something he found nerve-racking. When *Incantations* comes out, however, he shocks Virgin by demanding interviews with anyone who wants to talk to him, Mike expressing to everyone's amazement a particular yen to appear in the pages of both *Penthouse* and *Woman's Own*.

What we have to thank for this new extrovert and unpredictably eccentric incarnation is Oldfield's recent engagement with Exegesis, a course of psychological therapy he underwent to liberate him from his painful timidity and "bring him out of himself." He even agrees to allow a party of music hacks to accompany him on tour in Germany, and that's us, gathering outside the Dusseldorf Hilton, the morning after a show at the Philipshalle that drags on for so long I am sure I'll be claimed by old age before it's over.

Oldfield has already flown ahead to Berlin, leaving the rest of his vast touring party to travel across Germany in a convoy of coaches, a 13 hour journey ahead of us, by road to Berlin. We are a motley assortment. There's me and laconic lensman Tom Sheehan from *Melody Maker*, Pauline McLeod from *The Daily Mirror*, Danae Brook, who has the slightly frazzled look of a Sixties wild child, from *The London Evening News*, photographer Jill Furmanovsky and someone with a beard and wearing a parka named Bob Edmands, who claims he's from the *NME*. Oh, and that's Virgin press supremo Al Clark, just stepping onto one of the coaches to tell us that we'll be leaving shortly and that for the benefit of anyone who might fancy a drink en route – why he's looking gimlet-eyed at me and Sheehan at this point, I can only hazard the wildest possible guess – we'll be stopping briefly at a service station for suitable provisions before hitting the autobahn. Of course, we take full opportunity to stock up on what turns out to be some formidably strong local beer and then we're back on the road. Three hours later, we're still in the Dusseldorf suburbs, trapped in a massive traffic jam, moving very slowly in the direction of nowhere in particular, most of the beer already gone and some of us on our way to being very drunk indeed.

Al's originally split us journalists into two groups. Me, Sheehan and Pauline McLeod start the journey on the coach with the gals from the Queen's College Choir and their musical director, David Bedford, who I know from his string arrangements for Roy Harper and, earlier, as a member of Kevin Ayers' band, The Whole World. The coach is fitted out with a video player, but Bedford announces there'll be no films shown today. The girls are under a bit of a cloud after getting somewhat out of hand the previous day during a screening of

The Ups and Downs of a Handyman, a soft-core feature about the sexual adventures of bored housewives that had them all screeching with laughter and making such lewd comments that a blushing Bedford had turned the film off. After we stop for a very late lunch somewhere on our way to distant Berlin, Al decides we should all now travel on the same coach, making the mistake of treating us to another couple of cases of highly-debilitating Schulteissbier. There's a definite whiff of journalistic competition in the air now. Danae Brook interviews everyone in sight, including Tom Sheehan, who's by now talking in an incomprehensible cockney esperanto. She disappears up the coach, armed with notebooks and a cassette recorder, as if she's on some crucial mission in the field of human endeavour, a model of industry to us all, especially Ben Edmands, who's fallen asleep – an early victim of the dreaded Schulteissbier. Pauline McLeod, meanwhile, spends about an hour discussing the intricacies of the tour's sound system and its operation with Kurt Munkasci, a pony-tailed American engineer. She stares with increasing bafflement as Kurt spews out a torrent of mind-boggling data, statistics and stuff about advanced circuitry techniques, and just sort of slowly deflates when Kurt eventually ups and leaves to take care of business elsewhere.

"I didn't understand a word," Pauline says, fanning herself with a notebook full of indigestible facts.

Darkness falls and brings with it a moment of high drama! One of the girls in the choir has been taken sick. She had complained earlier of an upset stomach. Jill Furmanovsky, intending only to help, had given her an aspirin, but has succeeded only in aggravating the poor lamb's condition. She's now in considerable distress and Jill becomes terribly upset when I accuse her of thoughtlessly poisoning the afflicted chorister, who is even now being carried to the back of the coach, where she and her tortured intestines are laid out on the back seat. Much weeping and groaning ensues, embellished by some high-end lamentations from the stricken warbler's distraught friends. After about an hour of their keening wails and the continued loud misery of the ailing missy, I've had enough. If she's not going to make it to Berlin, why don't we just wrap her in a blanket and dump her on the side of the road? There's a river coming up. We could pitch her through a window, her travails ending with a splash. Curiously, only Sheehan thinks this is anything like a reasonable course of action, although Pauline looks like she thinks the idea might have some merit. Everyone else just glowers at me, including Ben Edmands, who's just woken up, doesn't have a clue what's going on, but clearly thinks I'm to blame for something. Al Clark now confiscates what's left of the beer and admonishes me for my insensitivity, like I even fucking care at this point. We continue on into the German night.

Many – *many* – hours later, we find ourselves at an East German border crossing. By now, we're so far behind schedule we'll be lucky to get to Berlin by dawn. Everyone's tired and cranky, eager to get this trip over with. We hope, therefore, to breeze through this checkpoint and be on our way. The coaches are waved into a special security area. A low mist swirls around the jackboots of the East German border guards. Searchlights cut through the dark. There's a lot of barbed wire. Sharp commands are barked out and echo through the night. There are big dogs, snarling, straining on their leads, eager for action. Machine-gun posts are lit up by tracking searchlight beams.

A couple of border guards, automatic weapons slung over their shoulders, get on the coach and tell us to hold up our passports for inspection, *pliss*. I try to get the people around me to quickly scribble little black moustaches on their passport pictures, but the humourless bastards don't want to know. Anyway, here come the grim-faced goons with their guns, checking everyone's passports. And here's Tom Sheehan, frantically rummaging through pockets and bags. He's looking for his passport, which he evidently *can't find*. Where is it? In his suitcase. Where's his suitcase? In the luggage compartment, *in the very belly of the coach*. Can he get to it easily? Of course not. He was the first one on the coach this morning. The entire luggage compartment will have to be unloaded. We're going to be here for hours. No one speaks to us for the rest of the journey.

The next night, the UK press posse is gathered in a dressing room, backstage at the Berlin Eissensportshalle. Oldfield arrives with David Bedford, having spent an hour or so in a local bar. He's clearly in what Al Clark describes as "one of his more disquietingly impish moods". We are, in fact, to be subject throughout the evening ahead of us to a veritable Niagara of pranks and assorted japes, Oldfield liberated from his former uptight sobriety by his recent brush with Exegesis. He begins by accosting Ben Edmands.

"What *frightens* you?" he demands of the flustered Edmands, who Oldfield now attempts to embrace. *"Affection!"* Oldfield declares, hugging Edmands and kissing him – a big smacker, right on the lips – much to the *NME* man's obvious distress. Bob tries to bat Oldfield away. Oldfield ruffles Bob's hair and walks off, chuckling, no one keen to make eye contact with him if it means they'll end up with his tongue down their throat. Anyway, here's Al with news from David Bedford, with whom he's been in rapt discussion. Al now tells us that according to what Bedford's just been telling him, Oldfield wants the UK press contingent to join him tonight on stage. We're apparently to join the percussion section during the "Sailor's Hornpipe" routine at the end of *Tubular Bells*, which follows the complete performance of *Incantations*. Marvellous! I venture into the backstage corridor to discuss my potential contribution with the gifted young composer and his musical director, but there's no sign of them. Looks like I'll have to wing it.

What seems like a lifetime later, the gruelling *Incantations* mercifully out of the way, Oldfield leads the band and orchestra into *Tubular Bells*. David Bedford collects us from the dressing room where we are eagerly waiting our call. We now assemble in the wings, led by Al Clark, who's determined to get in on the act. We ask Bedford if we can be introduced as The Hackettes. He ignores this and starts distributing various percussion instruments. I'm given something I take to be a Romanian mousetrap, handed out by Bedford in error. I don't know whether to beat it, shake it or hit Al Clark over the head with it. Sadly, it doesn't seem like the kind of thing upon which I might play an extended solo with my teeth before setting it alight in fiery sacrifice to the gods of rock 'n' roll.

But, hey, what's this? Oldfield, the band and orchestra are going into "The Sailor's Hornpipe". *Achtung!* Time for action! Al Clark pushes his way to the front of the gathered hacks, barges past Bedford and rushes to the front of the stage. "*Berlin!* Are you ready to rock 'n' roll," he's shouting now, simultaneously banging two bits of wood above his head and shaking his hips like Elvis in *Jailhouse Rock*. Danae Brook goes quite berserk, gyrating wildly in the manner of Tina Turner and wailing in Pentecostal tongues. Despite an initial reluctance to participate in this fiasco, Bob Edmands launches into a rather free form improvisation. It brings him a look of stern rebuke from the increasingly exasperated Bedford, who takes this opportunity to inform me that I'm holding my mousetrap or whatever it is *upside down*, thus rendering my contribution to the unfolding spectacle quite redundant. Al, meanwhile, for reasons I can't immediately fathom, has started shrieking in Spanish, which makes him sound like he's being tortured by the Inquisition. Then it's over. David Bedford grabs the instruments from us and tries to bundle us off stage, but Al and I are going nowhere fast, made giddy and star struck by our moment in the spotlight, savouring the applause of the highly-appreciative crowd.

"Good night, Berlin!" I shout. *"You were great! See you soon!"*

"For goodness sake," Bedford says, seething now, *"get off."*

LOU REED AND DAVID BOWIE

London, April 1979

Lou Reed's just played a famously confrontational show at London's Hammersmith Odeon that gets off to a bad start when he insists the theatre's house lights are kept on during his set, which makes large sections of the audience feel uncomfortable, exposed and nervous. Lou then plays most of his new album, *The Bells*, which hardly anyone here has heard – Lou standing with his back to the room, conducting the band, the crowd growing impatient for something a bit more familiar. There are calls for "Heroin", "Sweet Jane", "Walk on the Wild Side" and other signature Lou tunes, which Lou announces he won't be playing, so anyone who's come to hear them might as well leave now, which a good part of the crowd does. Lou watches them leave, a disgruntled exodus, and "Heroin" is the first song he plays after the last of them is out the door. The set ends after an interminable version of "You Keep Me Hanging On", which is sung by Lou's bass player Ellard "Moose" Bowles and played at excruciating volume.

People on the way out look dazed, deafened by the recent cacophony, drifting towards the exits like they've just survived a plane crash. Among them, I notice Lou's record company PR, Howard Harding, who's been sent by Lou to find me, with an invitation to meet Lou backstage for a drink. When we get to the backstage bar, however, there's no sign of Lou. Howard goes off to look for him and returns moments later. Lou's already on his way with David Bowie for dinner at the Chelsea Rendezvous, a restaurant in South Kensington, where he'd like us to join him. Dinner with Lou and The Thin White Duke? I'm off like a shot.

This is what we find at the restaurant when we arrive: Lou and David in a chummy huddle at the head of their table. Lou's got his arm around David's shoulder. David is smiling. Lou's laughing, slapping the table, dangerously boisterous. Lou sees me, calls me over.

David looks up at me.

"Allan, nice to see you," he says, extending a hand. "How are you?"

His charm is unnerving.

"ALLAN!" Lou roars, grabbing my hand, nearly breaking a couple of fingers. He yanks me across the table. I almost end up in Bowie's lap, an elbow in what's left of Lou's dinner.

"Do you know Allan?" Lou asks Bowie.

"We meet occasionally," Bowie tells Lou.

"Did you see the show tonight?" Lou wants to know. I tell him I'm still recovering, which makes him laugh.

"Good," he says. "What did you think?"

I tell him I felt like I was being given a good pistol-whipping.

"You probably deserved it," Lou says, snappily.

I decide to leave them to the rest of their supper.

"Yeah," Lou says. "Go."

I go. Lou turns back to Bowie. They get their heads down together, an old pals' act well under way. Lou gets up and waddles down the restaurant to talk to some people at a nearby table. He grabs a chair for Bowie, who's followed him. There's a great deal of mutual backslapping, good times remembered. Lou orders Irish coffee, Lou and David raise their glasses in a toast. "To friends." It's all rather touching.

They now return to their original places, resume their conversation, getting deep into something, foreheads almost touching over the table. Five minutes later, the place is in uproar. Bowie's said something to Lou that clearly hasn't amused him. Lou replies by smacking Bowie in the face, a real clout. Fists are quickly flying. Most of them are Lou's and they're being aimed at Bowie, all of them landing with percussive force. Bowie flaps at Lou, uselessly. He ducks, trying to protect himself. Lou's on his feet, screaming furiously at Bowie, still lashing out. "Don't you EVER say that to me!" he bellows hysterically. "Don't you EVER fucking say that to me!" About nine people pile on Lou and wrestle him away from Bowie. There's an arm around Lou's throat. He continues to spit insults at Bowie, who sits

215

at the table staring impassively, clearly hoping Lou will go away, just fuck off, calm down, whatever.

Lou shrugs off his minders. There's a terrible silence – a heavy-hanging thing, ominous. People are watching, open-mouthed, frozen in mute surprise. Lou sits down next to Bowie, whispers something. They embrace. There's a collective sigh of relief. Lou and Bowie kiss and make up. Meals are resumed, more drinks delivered. It looks like the tiff or whatever it was has blown over. But the next thing I know, Lou is dragging Bowie across the table by his shirt and smacking him in the face. The place explodes in chaos again. Whatever David said to precipitate the first frank exchange of conflicting opinions, he has rather foolishly repeated.

"I told you NEVER to say that," Lou screeches, batting David about the top of his head. David cowers. Lou gets in a few more solid punches before he's hauled off the whimpering Bowie. Lou struggles with his minders, tries again to launch himself at Bowie. The silence that follows is this time ghastly. Lou's people decide to get him out of the place before he blows again. He's escorted out of the room by an especially burly minder, who frogmarches him to the exit, a restraining arm around his shoulders. Lou's face is set in a demented dead-eyed scowl. He doesn't look back. Bowie's at the head of the table, alone in the evening's debris. He's sitting with his head in his hands and appears to be sobbing. I wander over. Bowie asks me to join him.

"There isn't a chair," I tell him.

"Then sit on the fucking *table*," he says, a little testily. I sit on the table, tell him I'm sorry his reunion with Lou seems to have gone somewhat disastrously awry.

I mention as casually as possible that while I couldn't quite hear what had been said between them, Lou seemed very upset.

"Yes," Bowie says, wearily. He seems close to tears.

"It was nothing," I'm now being told by one of Bowie's assistants, who looks like she's just been collecting their coats from the cloak-room. "It's all over," she adds.

"It isn't," Bowie says then, eyes glaring.

"Are you a reporter?" another of Bowie's reassembling entourage wants to know. After a fashion I admit. I'm then told to leave.

I protest, tell them Bowie's just asked me to sit down, suitably indignant. Basically, I just want to know what happened.

This does it for Bowie, who's on his feet in a flash.

"FUCK OFF!" he shouts. He means me. "If you want to know what happened, you'll have to ask fucking Lou. He knows what fucking happened."

Lou's gone, I remind Bowie.

Bowie, apoplectic now, grabs me by my lapels and starts shaking me. If he hits me, I wonder if I'll hit him back. Probably.

"Just FUCK OFF!" he yells, shoving me hard. "You're supposed to be a journalist, go and fucking *find* him. Ask *him* what happened. *I* don't know."

He pushes me again, turns away, trips over an upturned chair. I'm grabbed from behind, dragged back to my table. Bowie sits down. Then he stands up. He starts throwing things around, tips the table over. "Ahhhhh, FUCK!" he shouts.

He pushes his way through the restaurant, kicking chairs out of his way, clearly in a fearful flap. He starts to climb the stairs to the street. There's a potted plant on each step. Bowie smashes most of them on his way out. The remaining guests are speechless. The waiters look on, astonished. Just as Bowie gets to the top of the stairs, I am prompted to call up to him.

Good night, then, Dave!

There's a kind anguished howl from above, followed by a plant pot that sails over my head and shatters against the wall behind me. Bowie then disappears, still wailing, into the night.

ROBERT FRIPP

Bournemouth, April 1979

I get the train down to Bournemouth to interview Robert Fripp about *Exposure*, the former King Crimson guitarist's first solo album. He drives over from the nearby village of Wimborne – where he has a cottage – to meet me at the station, starts talking before I have both feet on the platform and doesn't stop for what seems like about four days of torrential chat that, even as he negotiates the lunchtime traffic into the town centre in his neat green Volvo, leaves me reeling and queasy and in danger of throwing up, which I later do.

I am at the time of writing already sick – have in fact spent the last week coughing like a consumptive young Romantic poet, the doomed Chatterton, perhaps, pale unto death in a very big blouse and knicker-bockers, fading away in a damp attic, adrift in bilious dreams. Fripp's yapping is now making me feel wholly delirious.

We go for a snack in a ghastly vegetarian place Fripp knows, where over some kind of nut cutlet, we review his post-Crimson career – which notably takes in recordings with Peter Gabriel and with David Bowie and Eno on *"Heroes"*, as well as a lengthy spell at the International Academy for Continuous Education in Sherbourne, where he studied the teachings of mystic philosophers GI Gurdjieff and PD Ouspensky, the Sherbourne academy based on Gurdjieff's own Institute for the Harmonious Development of Man. Cutlets consumed and washed down with some sludgy vegetarian drink that looks like something a cat might have vomited up, we find ourselves in a local hostelry, packed with lunchtime drinkers. Fripp finds us a table, which we share with two businessmen who give us suspicious looks when I set up my tape recorder. This is when Fripp says

218

he'd like – if I have no objection – to preface our interview with a statement he's prepared, in which he will outline what he describes as a three-year career plan called The Drive to 1981. I tell him to go ahead.

"Thank you so much," he says, and begins to speak directly into my microphone as if he's addressing a public meeting or a planning enquiry. Fully 40 minutes later, almost without taking a breath, he's filled almost an entire side of C90 tape and is still going strong, eventually shedding light on what *Exposure's* all about.

"*Exposure*," he says, "deals with tweaking the vocabulary of, for want of a better word, 'rock' music. It investigates the vocabulary and, hopefully, expands the possibilities of expression and introduces a more sophisticated emotional dynamic than one would normally find within 'rock'."

Thus concludes Fripp's opening statement, which he had begun nearly an hour ago. He looks at me. I'm speechless, quite overwhelmed.

"ONE LANCASHIRE HOTPOT AND A CHEESE FLAN – THANKYEWWWW!" bellows the barmaid over the heads of the crowd.

Fripp winces at the sound of her voice, which is not unlike a chainsaw howling through teak, but is quickly back in the conversational swing of things and soon telling me about his monastic tenure at the institute in Sherbourne, which sounds to me like a hell on earth.

"There were 100 people living in the house," he recalls breezily. "They'd come from all different walks of life, from different countries. In my year, we lost about 20 pupils, three of them to the asylum. It was very hard going, one of the most uncomfortable physical experiences of my life. It was always horribly cold. And it wasn't just the *physical* cold. There was a kind of cold," he says, voice lowering conspiratorially, the businessmen who have been listening to him with baffled fascination now leaning forward to catch what he says next, "that at times could *chill the soul...*"

"ONE SAUSAGE EGG AND BEANS AND A CHEESE FLAN – THANKYEWWWW!" the barmaid screeches.

"I shared a dormitory with five other men," Fripp ploughs on. "One from Alaska, two Americans, an Irishman, a Polish American and an Italian..."

("*Heard* it," I'm tempted to interrupt.)

"The Italian," Fripp goes on, "would wake up most mornings at 3am and fart sufficiently loudly to wake me up. The Alaskan had his bed next to mine. He was always rather depressed and unhappy. His head was hunched into his shoulders, like this. . ."

Fripp does an impression of a somewhat deformed Alaskan. The businessmen move nervously away from us.

"One of my favourite memories of Sherbourne," Fripp's telling me now, "is of being in a trench, digging for a water main. There I was at the bottom of an eight-foot trench, which has taken two days to dig, with 28 other people, all of whom without distinction I detest. Suddenly it begins to rain. And then a cheerful voice at the top of this trench as one looks up says, 'Hello! We're digging in the wrong place! The water main's over here! You'll have to start again.'

"It was *marvellous*," he says with a note of truly sombre reflection, "to have one's lofty ideas of oneself so deflated. I mean, I think everyone who went into Sherbourne thought that God had selected them uniquely and specifically to save the universe, so it was a very, very useful deflation."

"LAST ORDERS, LADEEZNGENMEN, PERLEEESE," the barmaid howls.

"Time to move on," Fripp announces, so we do – to somewhere called The Salad Centre, where we have some herbal tea that tastes like it's been strained through someone's dirty socks and Fripp talks and talks and talks and I begin to feel even more strangely disembodied and start wondering if I am going to be stuck forever in this strange purgatory where I will have to listen to Fripp's apparently endless discourse as eternity unfolds, Fripp's voice haunting me lo until the end of all time. I stare blankly at him, whatever he's saying (something about "riding the dynamics of disaster") reduced to mystical static that means nothing to me. On and on he goes, until the light starts to drain from the day, even as all life begins to drain from me.

We're back at the station now, Fripp still talking. I want, frankly, to scream—beg him for a moment just to *stop*. But on he goes. I feel like stabbing myself. Bile is rising in my throat. Where – oh, where – is my train?

"I'm currently working on a completely new theory," he says, and I'm afraid he's going to tell me what it is, which he does. "I'm working on the theory that Christ spent the missing 12 years of his life in Wimborne," he begins, at which point I can stand it no more and promptly chuck up where I stand.

"Oh, dear," says Fripp. "Might it have been the nut cutlets?"

THE PRETENDERS

Chester | Blackburn, July 1979

A week before they start their first UK tour, The Pretenders are shooting the video for their new single, "Kid", at a fairground in Gerrards Cross, just west of London. I head out that way, with photographer Tom Sheehan in tow. We find them in a field on a blisteringly hot afternoon, hanging around while the film crew wander about setting up their gear. Guitarist Jimmy Honeyman-Scott and bass player Pete Farndon come over and introduce themselves. Jimmy is all yap and brashness, relentlessly good-humoured, on the lookout for the funny side of everything. Farndon is all leather, quiff and cool. Drummer Martin Chambers now joins us, a bluff, hearty type. Chrissie Hynde, meanwhile, is at first a little more circumspect, a tad wary of journalistic attentions. She's not quite the scowling harridan of legend, the stroppy and obnoxious "loudmouthed American boiler" described by The Damned's Rat Scabies, who knew her back in the fledgling days of punk, when she was famously trying to put a band together. But she has a fairly intimidating presence, eyes glowering beneath what will become a trademark fringe, no doubt about that.

Sheehan leads her off to take some pictures with a group of fairground workers. Whatever he says to her, over there by the waltzer, makes her laugh, loudly. By the time they return, the photogtapher's magic has worked again. Now we're all laughing, Chrissie is punching me on the shoulder and doing an improbable impersonation of Tony Iommi, her Brummie accent comically unconvincing, all this a reference to the beating I took from the Black Sabbath guitarist in a Glasgow car park, said encounter evidently the source of much thigh-slapping mirth among the band. We head for a nearby pub and the

222

drinks keep coming at a fair old rate until we're summoned with some urgency from the accommodating hostelry to the video shoot. Keef, the director, wants Chrissie singing aboard what looks like a pretty half-arsed excuse for a roller-coaster, with Jimmy miming his guitar solo in the car behind her. The video budget doesn't extend to a crowd scene, but Keef wants some bodies on the ride. Sheehan and I are duly recruited as extras. I immediately seek out Keef and ask if he perhaps has a moment to discuss, for instance, character, tone and what my motivation might be in the scene ahead. What, you know, does he *want* from me?

"Just wave every time you pass the fucking camera and try to look like you're having a good time," he tells me, by way of curt reply.

The first take seems good enough for me, and I'm already feeling windswept and bilious, the ride turning out to be rather more raucous than any of us had imagined. But Keef is a brutal perfectionist, the Michael Cimino of the nascent pop video. We shoot and shoot again until he's satisfied and we stagger off the ride, as unsteady on our feet as jack tars hitting the dock after a year at sea.

"Right!" says Jimmy, hair standing up like he's been electrocuted, legs a-wobble and eyes rolling. "Everyone back in the pub for 20 pints, a couple of lines of speed and then back on that bastard for another 40 minutes! Who's up for that?" he shouts at our retreating backs, Sheehan and I beating a dizzy retreat and promising to meet up with the band the following week in Chester.

Which we do, at a club called Smartyz, where The Pretenders are playing the opening night of their tour. I'm sitting with Chrissie in the band's dressing room going over the lyrics of Neil Young's "Hey Hey, My My (Into the Black)" from *Rust Never Sleeps*, which I played her earlier and which she now wants to cover in tonight's set. At this point, Elvis Costello pops his head around the dressing room door, a totally unexpected visitor. Elvis proceeds to give The Pretenders a bit of a pep talk, says he'll see them in the charts and disappears.

"He's a nice cat," Chrissie says of the retreating Costello. "An aggressive little bastard, though."

The Pretenders then play the kind of show that generally puts bands in a mood to celebrate, and head for their hotel to do just that. Unfortunately, the hotel bar is closed and dynamite won't open it now. A night porter who looks like he's been on duty since the early middle ages points us in the direction of The Dunkirk, which he describes somewhat optimistically as "an all-night restaurant" but in grim reality turns out to be a 24-hour truck stop. "Lorry Drivers Will Be Served First At All Times" announces a sign tacked on the kitchen wall, and we aren't inclined to dispute the fact. Pete Farndon heads straight for the nearest pinball machine. Martin Chambers takes on a couple of local nighthawks at pool. Jimmy sits at a table sulking because he can't get a drink. Chrissie leans against the jukebox, which is playing Willie Nelson's "Blue Eyes Crying in the Rain". Pretty soon, she's ready to split. It's 3.30am, something like that. We head for the band's van, where Pretender's manager Dave Hill and Jimmy are waiting for us. There's no sign of Pete or Martin.

"Martin will be here until he beats those cowboys," Dave Hill says, wearily.

"Let's just fucking *leave* them," Chrissie harrumphs. "I come all the way from Akron, O-fucking-hio, and end up with a buncha hicks who just wanna play pinball and shoot pool all the time. It's fucking disgusting."

"Here they come," Jimmy says now, as Pete and Martin stroll out of The Dunkirk, Martin with a raffish swagger that suggests he's won his game of pool.

"Good," says Chrissie. "Let's sleep."

Early the next evening, The Pretenders roll into Blackburn, where they are playing tonight at St George's Hall. When we get there, the town is oddly deserted, the streets empty, like the place has been evacuated. Where is everyone? Have we missed something on the news? We spot a weather-beaten poster for tonight's gig, the only one we see, which seems a bit unpromising. We drive around Blackburn's one-way system for a while and finally fetch up at St George's Hall. There are maybe six or seven kids outside, just hanging around with a general air of being up to no good. They give us a surly look as we pull up.

"Is that the audience, do you think?" Martin Chambers wonders. It very nearly is. By the time The Pretenders are ready to go on stage, there are a mere 152 people in the crowd. The show's already been moved from the main auditorium upstairs to the smaller Windsor Hall.

"If we'd put them on oopstairs, where they were originally going to play," we're told by a local jobsworth, a gimlet-eyed man, dour as an undertaker, "the audience would've looked like a threepenny bit on that dancefloor." He goes on to tell us that when weasly punk band The Members played here only 50 people turned up. This cheers the band a bit, but only briefly. The old duffer then tells us that even more recently The Damned pulled a crowd of over 1000, a record apparently for the venerable venue. The mood in The Pretenders' dressing room takes a turn towards the glum.

"Let's cancel the gig and go for a drink," Chrissie Hynde says, and it doesn't sound like she's joking. "Have we really got to go out there and play? There's hardly anyone out there, man."

"We could invite them all in here, I suppose," Pete Farndon suggests. "We could have quite an intimate evening." Chrissie, unamused, gives him a withering look.

"Fuck it. Let's just go out there and *do* it," she says then, heading for the stage and the best show I ever see The Pretenders play.

The next day is a day off for the band and we're going to be driving to Hereford, hometown to Jimmy, Pete and Martin, for no better reason apparently than Jimmy wanting to take us for a drink at his local working man's club – the kind of place, as it turns out, where people have more tattoos than teeth, but where Jimmy nevertheless feels quite at home. Tom Sheehan is heading back to London, so we see him off with a couple of quick ones and a lot of laughter at the hotel bar and then haul our bags out to the parking lot, pile into the band's van and are soon hurtling down the motorway. Jimmy's in the front seat next to Dave, the driver. Martin is sitting behind Jimmy, Dave Hill dozing next to him. I'm in the seat behind Dave, talking to Pete Farndon who's sitting next to me. Chrissie's curled up at the back of the van, in a space behind Pete, reading Raymond Chandler's *The Little Sister*.

The next thing anyone knows, there's an enormous noise, like something blowing up—an actual, you know, *explosion*. The windscreen has shattered and there's glass flying everywhere, a blizzard of shards blinding Dave the driver. Wind blows through the van with a keening *whoosh*, the van itself is momentarily out of control, doing its own thing, heading who-knows-where at high speed. Plucky Dave, however, instinctively jerks the steering wheel to the left, keeping us on our side of the motorway's central reservation and out of the path of oncoming traffic – a head-on collision with something coming the other way being the last thing we need right now. A couple of cars and at least one lorry swerve around us, horns blaring, tyres squealing, that kind of pandemonium.

We make it somehow across the motorway – all three lanes – without being sideswiped, rammed or shunted, pull up on the hard shoulder, brakes screeching while the van jerks to a bone-rattling stop. We stagger out, shocked and breathless. No one's seriously hurt, though Dave the driver's face is bleeding, Jimmy's arms are covered in nasty-looking cuts and a piece of flying glass has sliced Chrissie's face. We're all a bit shaken.

I look at Jimmy. Jimmy looks back at me, smiles.

"Bet *that's* given you something to write about," he says, shaking glass out of his hair.

"Things *were* getting a bit dull," says Martin Chambers, as if he's used to this kind of thing which, as a former driving instructor, may well be the case.

"Anyone got a mini-cab number?" Pete wants to know, digging a lump of glass out of his leg.

A lot of phew-that-was-close laughter follows, a strange elation, weird intimations of immortality. The feeling being that if we've survived this, we'll get through anything, live forever.

It doesn't turn out like that, of course. A friendship with Pete and Jimmy that starts on this trip lasts as long as they do, but that isn't very long at all. Within four years they're both dead, claimed by the drugs we were all mad for in those days. In that time, The Pretenders become a big noise everywhere, one of the hardest-working bands in the world, long gruelling tour following long gruelling tour that will leave them at each other's throats, personal animosities fuelled by jealousy, exhaustion and drugs taking an eventually fatal toll.

In June 1999, almost exactly 20 years since that first UK tour, there's a new Pretenders album called *Viva El Amor* coming out, and Chrissie Hynde as part of a long interview looks back on the band's unravelling. We're sitting in the chintzy parlour of a private member's club, somewhere off Oxford Street, and her mood is rueful to say the least.

"Dave Hill was really smart," she says of her former manager. "He got us over to America and we toured our asses off over there. It burned the band out in the end. You documented one of those tours, so you know what it was like."

She's thinking of the time Sheehan and I spend with the band in San Francisco in September 1981. *Pretenders II* was already screaming up the US charts and the band were in town for two shows at the Warfield Theatre, the first dates of another long American tour. Backstage, everyone seemed on edge. There were tantrums in the air: Chrissie was locked in her dressing room, refusing to see anyone; Jimmy was drunk; Martin was nowhere to be seen and Pete Farndon was wandering around dressed like a samurai (his stage gear for the tour) and looking pretty sullen about everything. The corridors, meanwhile, were full of people who seemed to have nothing much to do with the band, hanging out, trying to look cool and important, but mostly just getting in the way, milling about, bumping into things, full of vacuous chat.

"It's like the fucking casbah," Sheehan complained, the photographer being buffeted, nudged and elbowed by the crowd, whose number seemed to be increasing by the minute, a parade of dubious pin-eyed mutants. People kept asking us if we had any drugs and when we told them we hadn't they'd ask us if we wanted to buy some. Everybody was high and wanted the band and everyone with them to get high, too. There was cocaine everywhere.

"Well that was the thing," Chrissie says. "These assholes could always use cocaine as a calling card to get backstage. I hated them for that. It pissed me off big time. But Jimmy and Pete, they couldn't get enough of that shit. I didn't mind the drugs. I just minded the assholes. I hated people using drugs as a way of getting close to the band. I never liked that. So I always went off on my own. But, yeah, there were lots of drugs. Jimmy was a speed freak. Cocaine was too expensive for us when we started. And there was always that smack element hanging around. When Johnny Thunders and the Heartbreakers came over to London, smack really became the cool thing. Pete was absolutely mesmerised by Johnny Thunders. When Johnny Thunders left a blood-soaked tea towel in Pete's kitchen, that to Pete was like an example of rock 'n' roll genius. The writing was on the wall from then on, I'm afraid.

"But, you know, when I look back on it – hey! These were just guys from Hereford. They didn't know what hit them. Like you say, it was too much too soon for them. But for me – I'd been crawling in the gutter for years. It wasn't too soon for me at all. But, shit. They'd never even been to America. And when they do get there, there's limos and stuff and, of course, they thought it was the greatest."

Pete and Jimmy certainly seemed to throw themselves into what I guess we'll have to call the rock 'n' roll lifestyle.

"They didn't *throw* themselves into it," Chrissie says with a bitter chuckle, a grim laugh. "They fucking *hurled* themselves into it."

She pauses, seems to be gathering some last thoughts about The Pretenders and what happened to the band she had fought so hard for so long to put together.

"We were a *great* rock 'n' roll band, you know," she says, regret and defiance in her voice. "And we loved rock 'n' roll. But in the end, it was rock 'n' roll that killed us."

THE SEARCHERS

Rhydyfelen, South Wales, November 1979

The rain's coming at us almost horizontally, driven by a wild Rhondda wind. Walking into it is like being stabbed in the face by someone with a fork and a colourful grudge. I grew up near here, on the coast where, when the weather was bad, it was often even worse than this. I'm therefore stoically uncomplaining, unlike the company I presently find myself in, among them grizzling photographer Tom Sheehan who you'd think had never seen rain before.

We're heading for the Rhydyfelen Non-Political Club, which turns out to be a great concrete box at the end of Poplar Road, its bulk barely visible through the downpour, a blinding thing. Anyway, upon arrival we push open some doors and are suddenly standing in a garishly-lit bar, shipwrecked sailors washed up on some alien shore from storm-tossed seas, dripping like people melting in a John Carpenter film.

The bar in front of us is host to a couple of pool tables, groups of men standing idly around them, eyeing us suspiciously, others at the bar itself, smoking and drinking and looking at us with a certain surliness.

There's music coming from upstairs. We can hear the twang of electric guitars, the muffled thud of drums, something that might be described as singing but in actual fact possibly more closely resembles the sound of expiring wildlife, things with whiskers, paws and fur being noisily annihilated.

Wherever the noise is coming from is where we want to be, so we squelch across the bar and up some stairs, at the top of which there's a poster taped to the wall advertising tonight's appearance by

Merseybeat legends, The Searchers. And here, waiting for us, is the band's Mike Pender, who now tells us to follow him to what tonight passes for their dressing room.

He pushes through some doors into a smoky cacophony, a packed room, the size of an aircraft hanger, with rows and rows of tables running its length, from the bar where we briefly pause, to – at the far end – a small stage with a painted backdrop of a Spanish village. This is where the local band we could hear downstairs are just finishing their set. Pender goes before us, intrepidly negotiating a tortuous passage through suddenly shrieking fans who have maybe just recognised him from a time when in the early 60s he would have been on the telly and in the papers all the time, his face also then staring out at them from album sleeves in the windows of their local record shops.

The band's dressing room turns out to be a small cluttered place, beer crates and chairs stacked against the walls. This is where we find John McNally, with Pender the only other original member of The Searchers still with the band, although bassist Frank Allen has been with them since 1964 and drummer Billy Adamson's been on board for almost as long.

"Not exactly the London Palladium," McNally laughs, hopping on one leg as he tries to get into his stage trousers. "But we've played worse places. When you're trying to survive, you'll play anywhere."

Remember this. Between 1963 and 1966, The Searchers were second only to The Beatles in popularity. Their debut single, "Sweets for My Sweet", was the first of three number ones, alongside "Needles and Pins" and "Don't Throw Your Love Away". Another of their signature tunes, "Sugar and Spice" went to number two.

They were big in America, also, where they once had three singles simultaneously on the Billboard chart and where their distinctive harmonies and Pender's chiming 12-string electric guitar was credited as a direct influence on the emerging West Coast sound of The Byrds, Love and Buffalo Springfield.

Towards the end of 1966, however, the hits ran out. Their popularity had been on the wane for a year but they ignored the warning signs. Their record contract expired and wasn't renewed. They weren't on telly any more. They moved further down the bill on package tours. Working men's clubs, holiday camps and cabaret loomed, to which circuit they seemed doomed until a Ramones cover of "Needles and

Pins" made Sire label boss Seymour Stein wonder what had become of them. Stein's people found them somewhere on the Northern cabaret circuit and offered them a deal to make a new album. They didn't have to be asked twice. A successful second crack at the big time would get them out of places like this, for a start.

"Not that we're ungrateful," says Frank Allen. "People can take the piss out of the clubs all they want, they're an obvious target. But if it wasn't for that circuit, we wouldn't have survived. Neither would a lot of other people."

It couldn't have been easy adjusting, though, after their glory years, brief as they were.

"It was surprisingly easy, actually," says McNally, "when we realised how much we could earn."

"And you've got to remember," adds Frank, "we've never actually done a cabaret act as such. We've never run around dropping our trousers, doing impressions, telling jokes. We've never done that."

"Yes, we *have*," McNally laughs out loud.

"Well, maybe a couple of times," Allen admits sheepishly. "But let's keep it to ourselves."

"People who come to see us at these places basically just want to hear the hits," says McNally. "They want to be reminded of what they were doing or who they were with when 'Needles and Pins' came out."

"You can see them looking around dead shocked when we do anything new," says Pender. "They think we haven't learned anything new since about 1964."

"It does get to you some nights," McNally says. "When you're a bit down and you see all these people who are just interested in the past. Some nights I hate doing 'Sugar and Spice'. Can you imagine playing that every night for 10 years? It's a pain in the neck."

"It's funny sometimes," says Pender. "These kids come to us and say, 'Hey – you're really good, you can really play. You should be making records.' They don't realise. And what do you say to them? 'Oh, well, we *used* to...' "

"We were very green," Pender says of their fall from grace. "We were taken advantage of."

"People come up to us," Allen says, "and say, 'Hey – you must be millionaires now.' But we're not. It was the record company and the manager who made all the money. We saw very little of it."

231

Were they bitter?

"There's no point in feeling bitter," says Pender. "You can't hate people. I resent being screwed out of a lot of money, but we weren't the only ones. Even The Beatles got screwed. Ask them, they'll tell you."

The new album represents a possible new future for them, which they worry Sire won't help them reach.

"We were meant to be opening for The B-52s this month at the Electric Ballroom, but Sire had second thoughts and cancelled. I guess they're trying to protect us," says Pender. "But if we're going to sell this record, we're going to have to dive in and do it. Why waste time? Given a fair chance, I think we could be successful all over again. All we need," he adds yearningly, "is the chance."

They don't get it. The album, which is good, sells poorly. Sire drop them. They are very soon back on the club circuit, rainy nights in Rhydyfelen and places like it once again their only future.

JERRY DAMMERS

Hemel Hempstead, December 1979

Jerry is lurching through the drizzle, coat collar up against the cold, wondering where we are.

"I'd ask these kids," he says, lost now and finally admitting it, "but I'm afraid they'd beat me up."

There are six of them, cocky little skinheads, coming down the road towards us, on their way to the Pavilion to see The Specials.

"You goin' to the concert?" one of them asks Dammers.

"'Spose so," says Dammers, and we turn to walk back with them into Hemel Hempstead.

"Where you from?" they ask him.

"Coventry," Dammers tells them.

"You come all the way down from Coventry just for the concert?" they ask, amused by this.

"Sort of," says Dammers.

"Why?" they all want to know.

"I'm in the group," Dammers says.

"The *Specials?*" they all shout, an excited chorus.

"'Sright," says Dammers.

"Who are you then?" they ask. "'Orace?"

"I'm Jerry," says Dammers from the depths of his overcoat.

"Jerry who?" they all laugh, wondering if they're being wound up.

"Jerry-who-plays-keyboards," says Dammers.

"I don't remember you on *Top of the Pops,*" says the little skinhead who'd first spoken to us.

"I was probably hiding," Dammers says. The kids all laugh at this, and so does Jerry.

233

"See you then," he tells them and turns and walks away, although I'm not sure he knows where he's going.

Not long after this, I'm sitting in The Specials' dressing room, backstage at Hemel Hempstead Pavilion, talking to vocalist Terry Hall and the band's manager Rick Rodgers. Dammers, meanwhile, is asleep under a table, oblivious to the banter and chat, the various to-ings and fro-ings, going on around him. You wouldn't think to look at him there, dribbling onto the sleeve of his crumpled black overcoat, that this is the architect of the 2-Tone revolution, the mastermind behind The Specials' spectacular assault on the charts.

At the time of which I'm writing, I've spent nearly three months chasing the dozing Dammers for a *Melody Maker* cover story. I spend a week, for instance, on October's 2-Tone tour with The Specials, Madness and The Selecter, and speak to everyone who'll talk to me about Dammers, but Jerry himself remains cheerfully elusive.

When The Specials play Dublin and Belfast in late November, supporting Dr Feelgood on a memorably lively couple of dates, I am still in pursuit of the *MM* cover story. I spend even more time with Jerry then, every minute a gas, Jerry by some distance one of the better kind of people I have come across in the so-called music business. Whenever the subject of an interview comes up, however, he suddenly finds himself with something else to do. I am, though, dogged in the chase, and finally run the blighter to ground in a bleak and empty cafeteria at the Hemel Hempstead Pavilion, a grim room, brutally illuminated by fluorescent lighting strips. We sit at a table, shivering. I ask Jerry about his childhood, and he squirms uncomfortably, like he's being interrogated by the Gestapo, bracing himself for the application of pliers, red-hot pokers and sundry other instruments of torture.

"I don't know what to say," he finally admits. "My father was a vicar. I grew up in a vicarage. It was a bit weird, a bit oppressive. I didn't like it. In fact," he says, suddenly vehement, "I *hated* it. It was very strict, and when I was about 13 I started to rebel against it. I refused to accept all the things my family stood for.

"I used to go a bit mad," he goes on. "I suppose when I was about 13, I used to be a mod. A mini-mod. Then I grew my hair and ran away from home when I was 15. I went with a friend to Ireland, some island off the coast that John Lennon had bought, sort of a hippie commune. I stuck it out for two weeks, went home and freaked out completely. I got really badly into drinking and vandalism. I used to get really pissed up and put my feet through shop windows, things like that."

One summer in Torquay, his career as a vandal came to an abrupt climax.

"A whole load of us went down there on holiday," he remembers. "We were drinking scrumpy and got really pissed up. We were walking down the road and this car was coming toward us, so we stood in the middle of the road. But the car didn't stop. So I jumped on the roof and started jumping up and down. There was this family of holiday makers inside, looking horrified. I was jumping up and down, and the roof finally collapsed. I was arrested and fined £250. The judge said that had to be the last time I was brought before the court. It was."

We are soon whipping through the pages of his life story. Here, for instance, is Jerry at art school, playing in bands like Peggy Penguin and The Southside Greeks and The Sissy Stone Band.

"We worked mostly discos and clubs and played all over the place," he remembers. "But we couldn't afford hotels, so we had to travel home every night from gigs. If you're playing in somewhere like Egremont or Sunderland and you have to travel 900 miles to get home, it gets a bit desperate. I used to take lots of sulphate then. Not because I got a buzz off it. I was just scared the driver would fall asleep. I used to sit in the front with him, and chat to him all night."

And, here is Jerry putting together first The Coventry Automatics, then The Specials, raiding other local bands for the people he wanted, including Terry Hall from The Squad and guitarist Roddy Radiation from The Wild Boys, his determination holding the early Specials together through all manner of colourfully-described adversity, Jerry now quite the accomplished anecdotist, using up a lot of tape for someone with nothing to say. He remembers the Automatics supporting The Saints at The Marquee. It was an Easter Monday, and nobody came. They had to borrow 10 quid to get home to Coventry, where Dammers plotted and planned, hustled a support slot on The Clash's On Parole tour, for which Bernie Rhodes paid them £25 a night, a pittance they put towards the cost of recording a single, "Gangsters", which they release on their own label, 2-Tone.

"It was as much a reaction to Bernie as anything," Dammers says. "He didn't think we were good enough to make it, had no confidence in the band. I was determined to prove him wrong. Actually, we didn't have enough money to finish the B-side, so we had The Selecter on that side. They had made this tape about two years earlier, and we just overdubbed a ska guitar and hey, presto – that was The Selecter B-side and the birth of 2-Tone."

About then, Rick Rodgers turns up in the cafeteria, tells Jerry that he's needed for a band meeting.

"But I'm doing an *interview*," he protests. Now that he's talking Jerry can't apparently stop, and he doesn't, the batteries in my tape recorder giving out long before he gives up.

Melody Maker HQ, December 1979

At the time of which I'm writing, *Melody Maker* is housed in a Nissen hut in south London, the kind of place you'd expect to see illuminated at night by searchlights, with guard dogs barking somewhere in the shadows. As you join us, it's a Monday morning somewhat frantic with activity. It's about 10:15am now, and I'm saying good morning to *MM's* legendary jazz correspondent, Max Jones.

"Hope you'll join me, old boy," Max says, pouring typically generous amounts of rather good scotch into our coffee.

I sit back to back with Max, have done for a couple of hugely entertaining years. Max spends a great deal of his time in the office in creative engagement with his expenses sheets, manipulating columns of figures like a quick-witted mob accountant and telling me outrageous stories.

Here's one about the time he went to interview Billie Holiday. The way he tells it, inimitably, Max turns up at her hotel, knocks on her door and is told to enter. Which he does, to find Lady Day naked on her bed, legs spread wide and her pet dog, whose name apparently is Mister, head down between them, tail wagging as it goes at her sex, slurping noisily away with cunnilingual vigour.

Ever the gentleman, Max averts his eyes and adjusts his beret.

"Don't mind Mister," Billie tells Max. "He's jes enjoyin' his breakfast."

Anyway, back to this morning. Most of the regular *MM* staff are in by now – journalists writing up final copy for the news and reviews pages, subs hacking away at copy, one eye on the clock waiting for the pubs to open, assistant editor Mick Watts and editor Richard Williams dithering over the punctuation in a headline.

It's about this time that stylishly bedraggled production editor John Barton, squinting through a cloud of Gitane smoke and looking as sweatily grubby as someone you might meet recruiting mercenaries in a Mombassa gin-house, points out to Richard that we are still waiting for a review of the new Clash album, *London Calling*.

Everyone goes a bit tense at this. Richard has commissioned a review of the album from a young freelance writer, recently recruited, named James Truman.

Everyone is now wondering, deadlines looming, where this James Truman is. As if on cue, the office doors swing open, and here's James, a baffled pasty-faced fellow in a black suit and white shirt, clutching a briefcase to his chest like he's protecting a baby from bandits.

James stands in the dull winter light, blinking like something with big ears they keep in the dark at the zoo. Richard now asks James for The Clash review. From his apologetic stammer, I presume he hasn't written it yet. Which duly turns out to be the case. James says if someone can find him a desk and a typewriter, he'll get cracking on the review right now. There isn't a free desk in the office, so I take him out to an adjacent garage where we keep the *MM* archive, an ancient stereo system, a rickety old desk and a typewriter. James sits down at the desk, puts a sheet of paper into the typewriter and in the top left hand corner of the blank white sheet types:

MM/JT
THE CLASH: LONDON CALLING

He stares for a moment at the sheet and breaks out in a sweat, probably cold.

I ask him if he's OK, and he nods, somewhat unconvincingly. I tell him I'll leave him to it, and I do.

About four hours later, John Barton and I get back from the pub. John's expecting to find James' Clash review on his desk, but it's not there. We go out to the garage, and there's James, sitting at the typewriter, surrounded by sheets of discarded typing paper, absolutely fucking tons of the stuff stacked up around him. I pick up a sheet at random. This is what's written on it:

MM/JT
THE CLASH: LONDON CALLING

I pick up another sheet, and another. What's written on them?

MM/JT

THE CLASH: LONDON CALLING

I look at James, who appears to be going into shock.

"I can't write this," he whimpers, an unfortunate position to be in with 1000 words expected in about five minutes.

He's going to fucking have to, no getting out of it.

"Oh, fuck," he says, and starts punching himself in the face.

"What's going on?" asks Richard Williams, joining us in the garage, where James is now banging his head on his typewriter, to Barton's ruthless glee.

Richard picks up one of the myriad sheets of paper surrounding James and looks at it quizzically. "MM/JT. The Clash: London Calling," Richard reads slowly, like someone coming to terms with a new language.

"What's this?"

It looks like the fucking *Shining* to me, unhelpfully, according to the look I get from Richard, who walks over to James, who flinches like he thinks Richard might hurt him.

"You can do it," Richard says, confidence draining from his voice as James starts to bleat like something lost on a mountainside, the weather closing in.

At around seven, James is *still* in the garage, stuck on sheet one of his Clash review. Barton and I are getting ready for the pub. Richard says he'll stay and wait for James and take James' review with him the next morning to the *MM* printers in Colchester.

What follows goes down in *Maker* legend. At about midnight, Richard tells James to go home, get some rest, finish the review – which he seems still not to have actually *started* – and drop it through his letterbox. Richard gets up the next morning, stumbles downstairs where he expects to find James' review on his doormat. Shit! No review. He gets dressed, opens the front door, steps out into the freezing dark, snow swirling around him as he heads down his garden path at the end of which there's a raw glow, a car, interior light on, someone hunched over a portable typewriter, up to his neck in paper. It's James, and unbelievably he's still on sheet one of his review and all he's written is "MM/JT. The Clash: London Calling".

Presumably resisting the temptation to throttle James, Richard gets in the car, says he'll drive to Liverpool Street station while James cracks on with his review, which of course he's still barely started when the 8:30am to Colchester pulls out of Liverpool Street, with James on his knees in a corridor typing furiously away, which is where Richard finds him a couple of hours later, the train now pulling into Colchester station. What's James written? Not much. Which means Richard has to drag him to the printers, where he locks James in a cubicle, from which through the long morning, afternoon and evening strange and unsettling noises emerge, James finally putting an amen to his review as the presses start to noisily roll.

Was it worth the wait? Not really. The next day *MM* and *NME* both come out, and we find Charles Shaar Murray has filed a magisterial review of *London Calling* and James' notice is entirely overlooked. What happens to James? He goes on to great things, fetching up in New York, where he becomes one of the most important people in American publishing. Way to go, JT!

SQUEEZE

Australia, February 1980

They come into view just after midday, two Letz Commodores, heading out of Brisbane, travelling south on Pacific Highway, heading for Surfer's Paradise on Queensland's Gold Coast. Ahead of them, the mountains of the Great Divide are massive, peaks lost in static banks of clouds. The Commodores race through rising waves of heat, sweltering ovens on wheels. A man on horseback watches us fly past from the top of a low hill then rides away. Road signs direct the two-car convoy to out-of-the-way places with exotic names: Ormeau, Eight Miles Plain, Tamborine. Crossing the Coomera River in the leading car, Chris Difford points at a sign for somewhere called Woolloongabba.

"Sounds like a fucking Ramones song," he says, tugging at the dripping T-shirt stuck wetly to his chest. I think this is pretty funny and laugh accordingly. Everybody else in the car just sits there, looking a bit glum. Squeeze have been like this since they arrived in Brisbane the day before, flying in from somewhere they can't be bothered talking about, surly, tired, miserable. A Channel 7 news crew meets them at the airport, but the band are hot, irritable and sulky. A local reporter asks Jools Holland if there are any similarities between audiences in America and Australia.

"People throw things at us wherever we play," he tells her.

And the venues, the reporter wants to know, are *they* similar?

"Well," Jools says, wearily, as Glenn Tilbrook swats at a fly and Chris Difford rolls his eyes, "they've all got stages."

Later that afternoon, Jools, Chris and drummer Gilson Lavis are sitting in the coffee shop of The Crest Hotel, staring through the windows at Brisbane. They've been in Australia for nearly a month, growing more homesick by the day.

"The thing about Australia," Difford reflects mournfully, "is that it's the other side of the world and *feels* like it."

Tour manager John Ley joins us with a fax from England, confirming Wreckless Eric as the support on their forthcoming UK tour.

"*Wreckless Eric?*" Jools asks, somewhat astonished.

"What's wrong with that?" Ley asks.

"Nothing, nothing," Jools says. "It's just that I thought Wreckless Eric was *famous*."

"If you feel that strongly about it," Difford says, "perhaps we could ask him if he'll let *us* support *him*."

That night, Squeeze play a show at Brisbane's Festival Hall, after which I end up with Glenn Tilbrook at the bar of some ghastly disco called The Top Of The State, apparently the swishest nightspot in town. We've bluffed our way in and, over the strongest drinks available, are regretting it. The place is full of macho Brisbane bruisers with perms, gold medallions and more hair on their chests than a koala bear's arse.

"Pommy bastard punks," one of them now growls menacingly at us. "Why dontcha fuck off?"

"Because I don't do requests," Tilbrook tells him, although not very loudly and not until he's well out of earshot.

The next day, we drive to Surfer's Paradise, tourist centre of the Gold Coast, a 40-kilometre stretch of coastline that runs from Southport to Coolangatta, where Squeeze are booked to play two nights at the Jet Club.

"Looks like Torremolinos out there," Jools says. We're sitting in the Sell Bar on Cavill Avenue, a lurid hybrid of Blackpool's Golden Mile, Carnaby Street and somewhere infernal from the pages of Dante. We're hiding in here from the sun. It's over 100 degrees outside, where the girls are sashaying by, naked flesh as far as the eye can see.

"You're always complaining," Difford tells him.

"It's because I'm English," Jools says. "That's what we're famous for."

"I know," Difford says. "Here we are, sitting under the palm trees, with the sun shining like we've never seen it before, there are tits everywhere – and what do we do?"

"Complain," Jools says. "Moan. Whinge. Like we always do."

"It was the same when I used to go to the Isle of Wight as a kid with me mum and dad," Difford recalls. "We'd get on the beach and everyone used to complain because the stones on the beach were too sharp."

"I love the British on holiday," Jools says. "Always complaining. Always finding something to moan about. But, I mean, this weather, it'd be all right if it was in England. I mean, if it was like this, you'd be out with your mates or your girlfriend. You'd get in the motor, drive down to some nice little pub, sit outside all afternoon and get really jolly."

He takes a sip of his drink, seems to be weighing something up.

"Actually," he says then, "this place wouldn't be too bad…"

"If," Difford says, reading Jools' thoughts, "it wasn't full of fucking Australians."

"Right," Jools says. "Dead right."

Feeling quite reckless, we decide to go to for a swim, sauntering down to the beach through crowds of pouting beauties and muscle-bound boys. Difford and I attempt to strike suitably manly poses as we stride into the ocean. Jools has forgotten his swimming trunks, so drops his trousers to reveal a pair of Marks & Spencer Y-fronts. They're blue with white piping.

"Do you think anyone will notice?" he asks Difford.

"Absolutely no chance," Chris tells him, looking over Jools' shoulder at the girls on the beach, who are pointing at us and cackling hysterically.

"It's going to be dreadful when we go back for the British tour," Difford says. We're sprawled out on the sand, the sun beating down on us, Jools still in the water – looking for his underpants, which he's lost to the crashing surf. "Our audience is going to take one look at us and go, 'Fuck me, look at this lot.' because some of us are going to go back looking a bit, you know, *bronzed*. And they'll think, 'What a lot of flash bastards. They've probably been pissing about in the fucking Bahamas all through the winter while we've been freezing back here." He rolls over, "Couldn't pass me the suntan lotion, could you?"

The night after the band's first gig at the Jet Club, Difford is sitting on the balcony of his hotel room. There's lightning in the mountains, far-off thunder, a stirring wind. We're talking about a track on the band's forthcoming album, *Argy Bargy*, a song called "I Think I'm Go Go" which articulates a sad disenchantment with pop celebrity.

"That's just how I feel at the moment," Difford explains. "This is a lonely business. Everybody thinks it's such a glamorous lifestyle. But it's not. Most of the time, you're hanging around hotel rooms feeling sorry for yourself. If you take it too seriously, and I have a tendency to sometimes, you find yourself walking out on the beach at night ready to say goodbye to the world. That sort of feeling creeps up on you now and again, especially towards the end of long tours. That's when you start writing songs about suicide.

"It all becomes such a chore," he goes on. "Especially when you're sitting around doing nothing, which seems to be most of the time. You're either travelling or you're sitting around the hotel waiting for the gig. Sitting around hotels and airports, I can't handle that at all. If I'm standing around too long, I start thinking of ways to escape. I've come very close to it on this tour. I feel really locked-up here. The other day, we were in Sydney airport. I was looking at the flights going out to America. And I looked over at John Ley's briefcase with my airline ticket in it. And I looked at my passport and I thought, '*Go!*' But I couldn't do it. If I had, the band would have punched me out and the promoter would have sued me. So I stayed."

Lightning flashes in the sky.

"But I'm not enjoying it," Chris says, quietly. "I'm not enjoying it at all."

DEF LEPPARD

Glasgow, February 1980

It's a Sunday night at Tiffany's Ballroom, on Sauchiehall Street, hardly a venue of dreams. That's Def Leppard on stage, making a noise like buildings coming down in an air raid. They're a riot of denim, bubble-perms, bare chests and skin-tight Spandex. There, for instance, is beefy vocalist Joe Elliott, and here's preening bassist Rick Savage. And this is Rick Allen, who will become the world's first one-armed drummer when he crashes his Corvette Stingray on the A57 somewhere between Sheffield and Derby in 1984. Completing a thoroughly bombastic line-up are ill-fated guitarists Pete Wills and Steve Clark. Wills is unsentimentally thrown out of the group at the height of their popularity while Clark throws himself into the role of heavy metal rock god with such ruinous abandon that he dies in 1991, ravaged by the drugs and alcohol for which, even at this early stage in Def Leppard's career, he's already developed a debilitating enthusiasm.

Anyway, the morning after the gig at Tiffany's, I meet up with the band at their hotel, where I'm shortly supposed to interview them, ears still ringing. At the time of which I'm writing, Def Leppard are being touted as the leading lights of something called the New Wave of British Heavy Metal, a phrase that journalist Geoff Barton comes up with to highlight the resurgence of heavy metal among young bands disaffected with what punk has become and the new wave music now replacing it, among them Iron Maiden, Saxon, Samson, The Tygers Of Pan Tang and, of course, Def Leppard.

Anyway, here they are in the foyer of their hotel, milling about rather aimlessly and talking among themselves. Joe Elliott finally announces that he and Steve Clark will do the interview, Wills, Allen and Savage then troop off with their road crew to see a movie, which, appropriately enough, we later discover, is *Apocalypse Now*. Elliott leads the way to his room, me following Steve Clark. The guitarist has started drinking already and looks like he won't stop until he falls over.

An hour later, in an accent as thick as a girder of Sheffield steel, Joe's just about finished a positively Dickensian account of how Def Leppard got together in 1977, which means I now know more about the childhoods, schooldays and adolescence of these five gritty Yorkshire lads than I ever imagined possible. What I want to know now, though, is why a band whose average age was around 17 when they formed had turned to something as old and hoary as heavy metal. In age and social circumstance – bored teenagers, working class – they surely had more in common with punk?

Elliott looks at me, aghast.

"We were *never*," he says with some feeling, "going ter be... *punk*."

He looks like he needs a moment to recover from the very thought, which is when Clark pipes up.

"We just did what we wanted to do," he says. "We never thought, 'Heavy Metal's dated, it's dead. If we want to be fashionable we'll have to form a *punk* band.'"

"It would have been *unnatural*," Elliott adds, as if punk represents something perverse and forbidden. "I mean," he goes on, "you get certain bands who'll say, 'We tried for 18 months to be *this* kind of band, we're not gerrin anywhere, let's be summat else and be *that* kind of band.' So they change their name and change their image and become something else. Like," he adds, "apparently, there used t'be a really weird heavy rock band called Black Widow. And apparently... apparently, some of them are now in *Showaddywaddy*."

He shakes his head in disbelief and we ponder this awhile, musing on the way things sometimes don't work out how they perhaps should, our silent contemplation broken then by Steve Clark, farting wetly.

Elliott, meanwhile, has somewhat recovered his composure and is now telling me that, yes, in certain circumstances, he can see why heavy metal might be easy to dismiss.

"It does annoy me, though," he says, "that the press will knock a band cos they're labelled heavy rock and heavy rock's just a fucking *joke* to some people. But if they took the time to be totally unbiased, and watched the bands, they'd see a lot of people who can really *play*.

Like Steve," Joe says, jerking a thumb in the direction of Clark, who's currently trying to light one of the two cigarettes he can obviously see in his mouth.

"Steve can really play," Joe says admiringly. "Not many people know this," he adds in whispered awe, "but Steve were trained *classical*."

"S'true," Clark says, with a belch that sounds like it's brought his breakfast into his mouth.

But didn't most heavy rock bands actually invite ridicule, with their light shows, lasers, dry ice, perms and sometimes brainless mysticism? And how far, anyway, are Def Leppard straying from classic heavy metal obsessions with, I don't know, sexual dominance, apocalyptic ranting about the end of the world, that sort of thing?

"All right," Elliott says. "So there are clichés in what we do. At the same time, I could run through thousands of punk songs that are all about the same punk clichés. There they are, singing '*I wanna be an anarchist...*' All that crap. So you get some heavy metal band singing about death and destruction and astral trips t'moon and all that. But we haven't got any songs about death and destruction."

Not one?

"Well," he says, "there is 'When the Walls Come Tumbling Down'. But that's the only one."

"If you listen to 'Walls'," Clark says, downing another pint, "you'll realise that it don't revive all those things about death and destruction that you had in, like, 1969. It's looking *forward*. We wrote that song before all this crap came around in Iran and Afghanistan. And if you listen to the words: 'All the people came together in fear of the end...'"

Yeah?

"Well, it *means* something," Clark splutters. "It's a *prediction*."

Oh.

"It's in the *future tense*," Elliott adds, speaking with the kind of deliberation he thinks might get his point across to someone he thinks is possibly too dense for the kind of complicated things we're discussing here. "If you ever get a chance to read the words to that song when t'album comes out, you'll see they explain exactly what would happen if there's a massive atomic war. I reckon that 90 per cent of those lyrics will prove to be about what'll happen."

He pauses for a moment to think about this.

"Give or take the odd thing," he says. "like the women being captured and chained."

"*That's* a cliché," Clark says, farting with gusto.

"Maybe," Elliott says, getting irritated by the guitarist, who's by now pretty sloshed. "But the bit about *'national suicide...'* You will get a lot of people killing themselves. And like, *'America fell to the ground...'* You're going to get buildings falling down. You're going to get kids left crippled, whether it's wi' atomic rays or whatever."

"Whole cities, *falling down,*" Clark says, dreamily, as if this is all he ever wanted to see.

"A lot of it'll be like that," Elliott says. "Of course," he adds, modestly, "I'm not saying that I'm some kind of messiah who can see into the future or anything like that."

Talking of which – the future, that is – how do Def Leppard see theirs? For a start, nothing short of world domination will do, their names up in lights, alongside Judas Priest, Michael Shencker, UFO, all the greats.

"They realised," Clark says of these bands, "that people don't want ter see Jimmy Page playing a 20-minute guitar solo wi' a fucking violin bow. At the same time, you don't want to go and see T'Damned, who don't play a guitar solo all night. People want summat in between. Summat between The Dooleys and Black Sabbath."

"The fucking *Dooleys?*" Elliott asks Clarke, bewildered. "Worra you talking about now?"

"*Us,*" Clark announces, spilling beer on himself. "We're The Dooleys wi' goolies."

"Why do keep bringing up the fucking *Dooleys,*" Elliott demands. "What have *we* got to do wi' the fucking Dooleys?"

"We're in't middle," Clark says, groping for meaning. "People are fed up wi' anarachy. There has to be a balance between bands like Rainbow, bands wi' ripped knees in't jeans and Genesis. And I think the balance is us. We can play, but we can still *roar.*"

Elliott looks at Clark, looks at me, looks confused. I'm about to ask Clark to elaborate, fascinated, but don't get a chance. He's collapsed on the bed, snoring and unconscious.

THE POLICE

Bombay, March 1980

We arrive in sweltering midnight darkness, a gaggle of tired hacks from *Melody Maker*, *NME* and the old *London Evening News*, here to report on a concert tomorrow night by The Police, making our way through a cackling swell of barefoot children begging rupees, to a taxi rank where complicated negotiations ensue to get us from Santa Cruz airport to our hotel in Bombay.

We're shortly driving towards the city, workmen toiling by torch-light on the road to Mahim Creek, to the south of which is the Dahravi Labour Camp, where 300,000 people live in one of the many sprawling shanty towns that surround Bombay, whose streets when we get there are full of homeless souls sleeping on the pavements, dogs sniffing at their heads, untidy bundles of bones wrapped in tattered sheets, an uncountable number.

We pull into the vast plaza of the Apollo Bunder, where the triumphal arch of The Gateway to India stands in the moonlight, the Arabian Sea palpitating behind it. And here's our hotel, the Taj Mahal Intercontinental, where the next morning in the Shamiana Coffee Shop ("The most outrageously colourful thing that ever happened to Bombay!"), we meet Stewart Copeland having breakfast with a somewhat moody Sting, who's flicking through a copy of The Times of India, a volume of Paul Scott's *Raj Quartet* on the table in front of him, clearly unread. Copeland scours the pages of a recent *Melody Maker*.

"The Jam are *number one?*" he says, incredulously. "Has everyone else stopped making records?"

Upstairs, in the original colonial wing of the hotel, The Police's manager Miles Copeland has pinned a handwritten sign on the heavy wooden doors of his suite: "Police Headquarters. Bombay Division."

A year ago, Miles had told me about a world tour he was plotting that would take The Police to Bangkok, Hong Kong, Bombay and Cairo. And here, against the odds, we are, with Egypt to follow.

"There was never any doubt we'd play these places, once we'd made up our minds," Stewart Copeland is now telling bumptious John Blake, the *London Evening News'* pop writer.

"It's a big market, potentially, I suppose," harrumphs Blake, clearly an expert on the vast sub-continent.

"Damn right, it's a big market," Copeland fairly howls. "A third of the world's population is waiting out there," he says, Blake's firm gaze turning to the window and the unimaginable millions beyond it.

"That's a lot of T-shirts," says a passing Sting. Blake nods sagely. Always eager to blend in, Sting is now wearing a turban.

"We figured that sooner or later some decadent, greedy, capitalistic Western rock 'n' roll band was gonna move in and exploit the shit outta them," Copeland continues. "And we simultaneously agreed it might as well be us rather than The Jam, The Boomtown Rats or a fink like Elvis Costello."

We take a stroll on the Apollo Bunder, where everyone's a hustler and everything's for sale.

"You want hashish, cocaine or heroin? Girls, you like girls, boys? Oh, yes. We make a very special deal."

We join a crowd around an old man who lifts a mongoose from one basket and a cobra from another, setting them each upon the other in mortal combat. The contest's brief but nasty, and I flinch at the look Sting gives Andy Summers when the mongoose bites a chunk out of the cobra's head and chews it.

Later, on our way through the hotel lobby to get a taxi to the sound-check for tonight's show, Sting and I meet John Scott, who two years ago sold his record shop in South Shields and, on a whim, flew to India where he now spends his days happily doing not much more than lounging on beaches, getting stoned. Could Sting put his name on the guest list for the concert? Sting makes a note of his name and off we drive, through wholly reckless traffic.

"It's strange talking to someone like that," Sting says, as the grasping hands of young children reach through the taxi windows. "That lifestyle he was talking about, sitting around all day getting stoned. It would satisfy absolutely none of my drives or ambitions. The whole hippy ideal is something I find completely foreign. I was never attracted to it. I never understood it. I've only ever been interested in material success."

So what are his ambitions?

"If I was specific," he says, "I'd sound crass. I mean, basically, I want gold records, money, fame and to enjoy being me."

The band start their sound-check and immediately run into problems, their four-man crew fighting a running battle with the spiteful inconsistencies of a capricious local sound system, that go on long into the evening and involve much baffled head-scratching as they try to identify the problem, the band stoically patient, but getting edgy.

"The fault is either here with these tweeters or there with those woofers," an elderly Indian gentleman informs me on the side of the stage, although I am sure we share the same mutual incomprehension of the electronic confusions being tackled. "But I am no expert," he adds, somewhat unnecessarily.

There's a big crowd outside the arena now, and only one gate for them to get through. It's past show-time and they're getting rowdy and restless.

"Just calm the fuck down," Miles Copeland shouts through the railings of the gate, against which hundreds of bodies are now dangerously pressed.

"They are used to being admitted at the previously announced time," frets Ratte, the elegant secretary of Bombay's Time and Talent Club, the charity organisation who are nominally the promoters of tonight's show, from which they will benefit handsomely.

"Yeah, well this is rock 'n' roll," Miles snarls back. "So they'd better get used to it if they want any more of it."

The concert that follows is hugely emotional, the crowd quickly overcoming its initial reserve and surging towards the stage, which many of them attempt to scale, the police beating them back with lathees, long wooden truncheons. By the end, they are lending their voices heartily to the call-and-response choruses of "Roxanne", an unforgettable moment that leaves me quite speechless and everyone around me close to tears, including Ratte and Miles Copeland.

I then notice John Blake, ruddy-faced under a spotlight, putting the finishing touches to a review he will shortly file for the *London Evening News*. He seems oddly unimpressed by the recent spectacle of Bombay learning to boogie.

"To be honest," he says, oblivious to the evening's magic, "I thought they were better last Christmas at Hammersmith. And," he adds, though no one's asked him, "I intend to bloody well say so."

THE POLICE

Cairo, March 1980

It's a tense moment. Rough hands shake me awake. I open my eyes – and the next thing I know, I'm staring down the barrel of an AK47 that someone in the uniform of a country I don't recognise is pointing in my face. I sit up slowly, voices being raised around me, a lot of them angry. I don't know who the people with the guns are, but they're sporting enough firepower to start a war.

Earlier that morning, we'd made it out of Bombay at our second attempt, two days after The Police had played an unforgettable concert there. Sting and Andy Summers, along with manager Miles Copeland and the road crew, had flown out to Cairo 24 hours ahead of us. I'm travelling with Stewart Copeland and a BBC TV crew shooting a documentary on the group's Far East tour. Our first stab at getting out of India goes badly wrong when, in the 4am chaos of Bombay airport, we're informed with a cheeriness that very nearly makes us homicidal that although our reservations are in order, our seats have been reallocated, apparently on a whim. We stamp our feet a bit, but we're generally too tired to argue and troop back to the hotel to sit out the day before heading back out to the pre-dawn bedlam of the airport. After a lot of shouting, we get seats in the first class compartment of a flight to Egypt and promptly crash out.

And, here we are in Oman, or somewhere, where an unscheduled stop is threatening to turn extremely nasty. The son of some local potentate has suddenly decided to fly to Cairo, had the flight we're on diverted and is now demanding our seats at gun-point. It's too much for Stewart Copeland, who makes a grandstanding speech about being American and therefore not much used to being pushed around by anyone – including petty dictators and their armies of jumped-up thugs with machine-guns.

At this point, the sinister-looking cove in aviator shades who's been acting as interpreter stops making with the bland apologies for disrupting our flight and makes it clear that if enough of our seats aren't vacated for the bandit notable and his surly henchmen, some of us are going to be very sorry indeed, possibly carted off to somewhere unpleasant where we'll be hung by our thumbs until our shoulders pop. Our seats are quickly vacated.

A couple of hours later, we land in Cairo, where there are more guns waiting for us. The city appears to be under siege or preparing for war. There are machine-gun emplacements and anti-aircraft cannons on the roofs of the airport buildings, tanks and troop carriers everywhere, soldiers wherever you look. The previous year, Iran had fallen to the Islamic followers of the Ayatollah Khomeni, which had precipitated the immediate flight of the deposed Shah, Mohammed Reza Pahlavi, erstwhile King of Kings, now an international fugitive, wanted by the Ayatollah's people. After spells in Morocco, Mexico and New York, the Shah's just been granted political asylum in Egypt.

Even as we're making our way through Cairo airport, he's holed up at the nearby Maadi Military Hospital, being treated for a cancerous spleen. Egypt's in turmoil, fearful of Iranian retaliation. There have been demonstrations by Islamic radicals at Cairo University. In the southern city of Assyut, anti-Shah riots led by Muslim fundamentalists sympathetic to the Ayatollah's revolution have been dispersed by gunfire and tear gas. At least one student has been killed.

"I can't believe it," Stewart Copeland complains as we head out by taxi to the Holiday Inn in Giza. "We come all this way, only to be upstaged by the fucking Shah. Sting's going to be seriously pissed, man."

That morning we had watched the sun come up in Bombay. This evening we watch it go down in Cairo, where we are sightseeing at the Great Pyramid of Cheops. That's the rest of the party – Sting, Summers, a trio of Copelands, assorted wives, children and the BBC film crew – galloping into the twilight on fiery Arab steeds. This is your fearless reporter, being trundled around the pyramids in what honestly must be described as a horse and cart. My driver is a 13-year-old malcontent who introduces himself as Frank. The diseased-ridden nag that's pulling our cart is introduced as Whiskey. Frank rolls a fat joint, full of extremely debilitating hashish. Pretty soon, we're getting on fine.

"American?" Frank now asks. I shake my head, unable to speak through the small bushfire of smoke from the joint Frank's given me. "Eenlish, then!" Frank decides, ignoring my tubercular coughing. "Good, *bloody* good!" he shouts, whipping Whiskey into a fast trot. "We go *tally*-ho!" And we do, circling the pyramids at some speed before heading off into the desert.

"I give you good time, Eenlish," Frank promises. I look at him suspiciously. "You are havin' good time, eh?" I tell him I am. "Then give me Eenlish monies," he says. I give him a quid. He looks forlorn. "You are not havin' good time. Whiskey," he goes on with positively thespian despondency, "Mr Eenlish no havin' good time." He looks at the note, shakes his head. I hand him another couple of notes. His face brightens. "Now I *know* you havin' good time," he beams. "Wan' see Sphinx, uh? Me an' Whiskey, we take you. We have jolly good time!"

Later, at the Ewart Memorial Hall, there's a noisy crowd waiting for The Police. Sting seems somewhat put out that the majority of the audience are young Americans. There are a few locals, but not enough for Sting, who's here to play for Egypt not a bunch of stoner Yank expats whose whoops and hollers send him into a bit of a snit.

The Egyptians applaud politely when The Police appear and then wonder what to do next. The Americans just get louder. Then they start dancing on their seats, which proves to be too much for the local authorities. An unidentified phalanx of bruisers sweeps down the centre of the hall, led by a little thug in a brown leather jacket. They wade into the Americans, order them to sit down. The Americans and the Egyptian security, bouncers, whatever they are, square off, punches are thrown. Ian Copeland, a Vietnam vet who is now The Police's agent, is quickly in the thick of things. He dives off the stage and emerges from a scrum of bodies with an arm locked firmly around the head of the angry little man who'd led the charge on the Americans. Sting now has something to say.

"Sir. Sorry, I'm afraid you'll have to go. You're *banned. Get out.*" He turns to the audience. "If he tries to move you or tries to tell you to sit down, tell him that I told you to tell him to fuck off!"

Well, everybody cheers at this, including the Egyptians. How stirring it is to witness the public humiliation of petty bureaucrats. Sting is immediately in his element, playing to the gallery, the moment's hero. He stands proudly erect at the microphone, chin out, obviously going to announce something of potentially staggering import. You can tell it's going to be significant in one way or another, because he puffs out his chest before opening his mouth.

"OPEN THE DOORS," he shouts then, "AND LET CAIRO IN!"

This sort of stuns everyone, and there is, in reply to Sting's windy exhortation, an uncomfortable lull in the general whooping – a throat-clearing pause in the hubbub. People exchange looks, more than few eyebrows are raised, there's a lot of sniggering and I have to stifle an urge to laugh like a fucking drain at Sting's impossible pomposity. There's a creaking then, as the magnificent doors at the back of the hall swing open, heads turning now in anticipation of spectacle, Cairo's teeming multitudes pouring in from the streets, a tide of humanity, seething and resplendent.

What do we get instead? Four little kids wearing not much more than rags, barefoot, who we had seen outside when we arrived. They step cautiously into the hall, see nothing that appears to interest them and walk back out. And so Cairo comes and Cairo goes. And Sting? He just stands there in the spotlight, looking frankly preposterous – a sight we quickly get used to, me and the world.

THE POLICE

Milan, April 1980

The day before the tear-gas and gunfire in Reggio Emilia, scary Cramps guitarist Bryan Gregory, a sinister stick insect in black leather with a peroxide quiff, walks up to me outside the Hotel Principe E Savoia – which The Police have commandeered as their Milan HQ – puts his mouth very close to my ear and whispers with husky intimacy: "Growl for me, Tiger."

Words, frankly, fail me. I head at a brisk pace towards the coach for the Palalido sports centre, where The Police are playing tonight, supported by The Cramps. Bryan follows me onto the bus and sits next to me.

"Can I interest you," he asks, "in a conversation about necromancy?"

Time goes by, and I guess at some point I nod off. Anyway, the next time I see Bryan he's onstage with The Cramps and 10,000 hysterical Police fans are jeering them very loudly and throwing things at them.

An orange bounces off Lux Interior's forehead and the Cramps' singer dives into the crowd. Someone bites a chunk out of his shoulder, hands claw at his naked back. He's thrown back on stage, covered in blood. The audience wants nothing to do with him. More fruit then flies at the stage, splattering against the equipment.

Andy Summers isn't amused. The Cramps are using The Police's expensive new PA.

"This is absolutely marvellous," Andy says, seething. "We pay a fucking fortune for the best PA we can assemble, hand it over to this shower and watch it reduced to ashes before we even get to use it. Fine. I've got absolutely no problem with that."

Lux, meanwhile, has gone down beneath a barrage of missiles.

"It's like the damned playing for the doomed," Sting says gloomily, turning away.

The next night, in Reggie Emilia, it gets worse.

The trouble starts in the afternoon. The Copeland brothers – Police drummer Stewart and manager Miles – are strolling through the streets around the Palasport stadium when they hear the sharp bark of orders, the ominous pounding of boot heels. Turning a corner, the Palasport is in front of them and they can't believe what they see. Thousands of fans have forced open fire doors along one side of the building and are swarming into the arena, pursued by a flying phalanx of riot police armed with batons and shields, who lay into the rioters with venom.

Meanwhile, Sting and I are standing by the side of the stage inside the Palasport. We're talking about Thomas Pynchon's *Gravity's Rainbow* – which Sting typically thinks only he has read – when there's a massive fucking bang and the plate glass doors at the back of the stadium just sort of explode, glass flying everywhere. Then the doors along the side of the stadium burst open, frames splintering and buckling. Hundreds of rock 'n' roll shock troops stream into the cavernous hall, pursued by the baton-wielding riot police Stewart and Miles had seen charging through the town.

We retire to the band's dressing room, where the next thing we know we're all hitting the deck as a volley of gunfire blasts through the night.

"Fuck me," Sting cries, incredulous. "They're *shooting* people now."

We can hear screams, the sound of running feet, a crowd advancing or retreating, another bloody riot. And now we're all coughing like coal miners, tear gas pouring into the dressing room from the battleground outside, the whole gang of us fleeing the dressing room, choking and spluttering.

"This is what I really like about Italy," Andy Summers says, leaning against a wall, trying to catch his breath. "They really try to make you feel at home."

"We'll get T-shirts made," Miles Copeland blusters. "I SURVIVED THE BATTLE OF REGGIO EMILIA!"

"Great," Sting says. "There's just one thing…"

"What's that?"

"We *haven't* survived it yet."

Another tear-gas canister goes off inside the stadium, there's more gunfire from outside.

"Just remember," Miles grins, looking for the BBC film crew who are touring with The Police. "This is all great for the movie."

"I will remember that," Sting says, "when they rush the stage and start tearing us to pieces."

"I don't know why you're so worried," Miles laughs.

"I'm worried," Sting says angrily, "because *I've* got to go out *there* to face that mob, while *you* sit in *here* and count the money."

Ten minutes later The Police are on stage and Sting is in an even greater strop.

"If you spit at me again," he's shouting at the crowd, "I'll come down there and break your fucking legs."

He wipes the phlegm from his face.

"It's feeble," he announces. "You spend all your energy rioting, and you've none left to dance. You people should get your priorities right."

What follows is fraught, ugly, hysterical, the crowd charging the barriers at the front of the stage, bodies being passed unconscious over the barricades, fights breaking out with security men, the police apparently having beaten a retreat in the face of the swelling mayhem.

Sting comes off stage and kicks open the door of the band's dressing room.

"What the *fuck* was going on?" he wants to know. "What's the matter with these people? Last night was bad. But *that* was ludicrous. People being crushed. Tear gas. *Riot police*. What the *fuck* are riot police doing at a gig?"

"They certainly weren't dancing," Andy Summers says.

"At least they weren't cracking heads," Miles offers.

"Not in here, they weren't," Sting says. "But what the fuck was happening *outside*? Outside, it sounded like World War-fucking *Three*."

On the coach back to Milan, Sting is calmer.

"Sometimes I think this is the best job in the world," he tells me. "Then I start wondering whether it's all worth it. I know I'll make a lot of money out of it, see the world. It's certainly more exotic than teaching in Newcastle. But tonight, you know, it makes it all seem so worthless. I don't mind being jeered, as long as I'm not *ignored*. I don't mind what an audience does, but *rioting* – leave it out. I don't want to be the focus for a fucking riot. It's nonsense. It doesn't even make great headlines – except for *him*," he says with a hoarse laugh.

Miles has his Sony headset on, couldn't have heard Sting but must have sensed someone talking about him.

"What's up now?" he asks.

"Nothing," Sting says, walking towards the back of the coach, where through the window you can see the moon hanging over the Alps. "Nothing at all."

ELVIS COSTELLO | THE SPECIALS | ROCKPILE

Montreux, July 1980

The rain follows us all the way from Lausanne, down through Vevey, into Montreux. We'd been rather looking forward to a weekend of Swiss sunshine here on the shores of Lake Geneva and accordingly packed a wardrobe more suitable for a holiday in the tropics, but we'd be better-equipped with snorkels and a life raft. We're driving through Montreux now, the rain still hammering down, intrepid tourists scuttling along the broad promenade that runs around the lake, hunched inside plastic macs and Day-Glo ponchos, past peeling posters advertising the 14th Monteux Jazz Festival. This is why we're here, of course. For the first time in its celebrated history, the Montreux Jazz Festival is hosting a series of rock shows featuring, over the next three nights, Elvis Costello and The Attractions, F-Beat label-mates Rockpile, Carlene Carter and Madness producer Clive Langer with his group, The Boxes. The Specials will also be playing. Since it all sounds too good to miss, I've whistled up *MM* photographer Adrian Boot and here we are.

We're in a small bar near our hotel, sampling the local wine, for which Boot seems to have quickly developed a nigh on insatiable thirst, when Jerry Dammers happens along and invites us for a drink further down the road – where The Specials are meeting shortly in a pub called The Mayfair. Well, we're up for this, and finish the bottle we're working on and follow Jerry out the door, Boot getting somewhat unsteadily to his feet, it must be said. Dammers is in great spirits, despite recent reports of unrest in the Specials' camp and the drawn-out sessions for their second album, *More Specials*.

"We spent two horrendous months in Horizon Studios in Coventry," Specials' bassist Sir Horace Gentleman tells us at the bar of The Mayfair. "Really, it almost killed us."

With the new album now almost finished, Dammers confesses the pressure is off and he can't stop raving about tracks like "Stereotype" and "International Jet Set". Jerry wants this out as a single, but Chrysalis are concerned that at seven minutes it'll be too long for radio play.

"I love it when they're worried," Dammers says, laughing. "It means they don't know what to do with us."

That night, Dammers, Horace, Roddy Radiation, Boot and I drive down to the lakeside casino where the festival is held, Boot at the wheel of the Golf hatchback we've hired for the weekend. Van Morrison's playing. We watch him from the bar, on video monitors. He sounds great, but looks like he'd rather be somewhere else. The moon, perhaps.

"Does he always look like he's enjoying himself so much?" Dammers asks, as the cantankerous Ulsterman appears on screen, a vision of scowling discontent. Van pops into the bar after his set, looking like someone who's walked in on their own funeral. He takes a quick look around and leaves, bad weather trailing behind him. The rest of us carry on drinking and are still knocking them back when the place starts shutting down around us and we have to leave. It's dark and windy outside. We appear to have lost Roddy and Horace, but Jerry's still in tow and we offer to give him a lift back to his hotel, although I'm not sure Boot should be driving since he seems barely capable of walking and is currently bouncing off lampposts, cars and suchlike, giggling all the while like someone who's mislaid their sanity. Anyway, after much comic confusion we find the Golf hatchback. Jerry gets in the back. I sit up front with Boot, who now drives off with a wild whoop, a great roar of the engine and abysmal clutch control.

We are now driving at some speed along what I take to be a small road running around the edge of the lake, which is lost in darkness to our left. We're going insanely fast now, Boot with his foot down on the accelerator, a mad look in his eye. Which is about when it hits me that what we're driving along is actually a fucking footpath – probably the promenade itself! – and that we'd better get back on the road before we run some fucker over. I'm about to tell Boot this when I see his mouth drop open and his eyes widen in utter panic. I look ahead and what's *this* looming out of what's left of the night? Some kind of fucking *tent*, it looks like, straddling the pathway we are currently burning rubber along like something flying out of hell with its tail on fire.

"Don't stop," shouts Dammers from the back seat. "Drive straight through!"

We hit the tent flaps at around 80mph, tearing them open with an awful crack and driving then down an aisle between rows of startled campers, most of them screaming, fright consuming them like a fireball, some of them diving for cover like refugees being strafed by Stukas, others sitting bolt upright in their sleeping bags or cots, mouths open, frozen in terror and utter disbelief.

"Morning everyone!" Dammers yells, leaning out the car window, waving his arms at the entirely gobsmacked campers as we burst through the opposite end of the tent, ropes and pegs flying behind us, by some miracle no one ending up under our wheels. We nevertheless spend a fitful night at our hotel, waiting for a knock on the door and a visit from the police that fortunately never comes.

The next morning, we find Jerry outside The Mayfair. He's with Suggs, from Madness, and they're polishing off the day's first round of drinks. Suggs has come over to see Clive Langer, with whom Madness are shortly due to start recording a new album.

"We've written the songs for it," Suggs says. "We're just working on the reviews."

A cloud passes over us then, bringing with it a brooding darkness, a sucking of light from the sky, which must mean that Elvis Costello is on his way, The F-Beat Mafia arrive in Montreux later that afternoon. We're sitting on the terrace of the festival's casino headquarters, when Costello's customised Greyhound tour bus pulls up outside. A small crowd gathers around its doors, stepping back sharply as they open in a gush of hydraulics, Jake Riviera leading his people off the coach.

One by one, they scramble off the Greyhound. Nick Lowe and Carlene Carter. Dave Edmunds and Rockpile. The Attractions. Then: F-Beat tour manager Andy Cheeseman, burly and officious in an NYPD leather jacket, easily picked out from the casino terrace.

Behind him: Costello and Big Jim Callahan, his personal security man, bodyguard in other words, a permanent fixture these days following death threats in America that Costello received after an infamously cantankerous incident that's almost ruined his career there.

Jake, Big Jim and Cheeseman force their way through the crowd, Costello in the centre of the huddle, while directions to the backstage enclosure are sought. The mood in the F-Beat party when we find them there is sour and edgy, full of ill-humour, bad vibes and the potential for violence. Sure enough, there's a nasty scene at the sound check. Costello starts by ordering the hall cleared of spying journalists, but a French photographer's been overlooked in the security blitz and Elvis goes berserk when he starts taking pictures. "Get the *film* off him!" he screams at his road crew, who swarm all over the continental lens man, who's thrown out of the building in a flurry of Gallic indignation. Then a festival lighting crew, up there in one of the galleries, turns a spotlight on Costello. He goes nuts.

"Tell that motherfucker to stop *now!*" he rants. But the lighting crew either fail to understand or are simply wilfully foolhardy. The spotlight remains trained on Elvis.

"Get those bastards *out of there*," he's screaming now, the road crew sprinting for the gallery like they've scented blood. "Get them all out. *All of them*!"

On stage, The Attractions keep their heads down, no telling who'll be the next target of Costello's jittery paranoid wrath.

That night, I walk back to the hotel where the F-Beat bands are staying with Dammers and Suggs and his wife, Bette Bright. Bette's raving about Costello's performance, particularly a brilliant new song called "Clubland", played for the first time tonight. Back at the hotel, Dammers has assumed the role of master of ceremonies. He's busy organising an outing to somewhere called The Hazyland Disco when Elvis walks into the hotel lobby, still wet from the show. He looks crumpled, damp and tense. In many ways, of course, he's still smarting from the fall out of the infamous set-to in America with Bonnie Bramlett and Stephen Stills when he made some ludicrously ill-judged remarks about Ray Charles for which the US press had crucified him. Always fraught, meanwhile, his relationship with the English music papers is at an all-time low. He thinks we're hounding him unmercifully and that any chance remark he makes now that might be overheard by a lurking hack is going to end up in the pages of something like *NME* or *Melody Maker*, who, of course, have sent me out here. He's not, therefore, entirely pleased to see me.

"You can fuck off, for a start," he says with a mirthless little grin. "Where's your notebook?" he goes on, verbally jogging my elbow, like a drunk at a bar looking for a fight. "Are you getting all this down?" he asks, grinning without humour.

Dammers, impatient, has already left for the Hazyland Disco. Elvis quickly follows in stomping pursuit. Jake Riviera now appears with The Attractions, Dave Edmunds and Rockpile drummer Terry Williams and we all set off for the disco, which turns out to be predictably garish. When we arrive, a seven-piece cabaret band's on stage. They're dressed in matching white silk body stockings and play what they hope might pass for soul music.

"Ah!" Jake gleams. "Dexys Midnight Runners!"

The cabaret band's followed by a dancer who quickly starts cavorting around the stage wearing nothing more than a G-string and a toothy grin. A waitress takes our orders for drinks.

Costello is hunched over a table full of beers, deep in conversation with Jerry Dammers. For a moment, everyone seems in good humour, earlier tensions dissipating as the F-Beat party begin to relax. Then I feel a hand on my shoulder. It's Elvis.

"I hope you're getting all this down," he says. It's an already tired mantra, but Costello seems intent on making the evening uncomfortable for as many people as possible. "Maybe you should be taping all this," he persists, his litany of provocation beginning to seem endless. "I'd hate you to forget any of this before you write it up for the paper," he goes on. He gives me a glowering *outside-now* kind of look and goes back to sit with Dammers.

"Good to see Elvis in one of his more cheerful moods," Dave Edmunds remarks, ordering another round.

The dancer simultaneously relieves herself of her G-string.

"BRAVO!" Attractions drummer Pete Thomas declares, applauding.

A couple of hours later, there are about 12 of us packed into Riviera's hotel room overlooking Lake Geneva. The drugs have just run out and people are getting twitchy – especially Elvis, who's on the prowl, walking the carpet deep into the night and early morning.

Something I'm talking to Dave Edmunds about catches his attention, annoying him.

"You've been hanging around all night," he says to me. "Why don't you just fuck off?"

"Why don't *you*," Dave Edmunds tells him, "*grow* the fuck up?"

Costello, however, appears to be beyond listening to anyone. He now turns on Adrian Boot, who's rummaging about in his camera bag, looking for some cigarettes.

"If you get a camera out of that bag," Costello says threateningly, "I'll break your fingers."

Boot holds up a pack of cigarettes, smiles weakly.

Costello looks disappointed, another opportunity for some sort of row or confrontation escaping him.

Jake's standing at the window. The sun's coming up over the lake. It's a cold grey dawn.

"Lake looks lovely this morning," Riviera says.

"Yeah," says Costello, standing next to him, looking down at all that water. "I think I might go for a walk on it later."

MONSTERS OF ROCK FESTIVAL

Castle Donnington, August 1980

We've got a map, but no idea where we're going. With *MM* photographer Adrian Boot at the wheel, we're driving down what we take to be something called Melbourne Lane – no more than a country track, something used by ramblers and the like – which we're hoping will take us to Wilson's Lodge, where we expect to find the backstage area for today's inaugural Monsters of Rock Festival at Castle Donnington. We've been driving down this road for an interminable while, the way in front of us mostly blocked by a stream of denim-jacketed scruffs, an already bedraggled army, toting tents and sleeping bags and other necessary paraphernalia towards the festival camping site. According to our map, Wilson's Lodge is apparently not far ahead, behind a Rolls Royce depot. So we follow the road, such as it is, along the perimeter of the main festival site, past the Rolls Royce depot, and carry on for another three or four miles. There's still no sign of the backstage area.

"If we go any further," Boot moans, "we'll be in the next county."

We go mile or two further and up ahead we can see a group of burly fellows in yellow slickers and T-shirts, leaning on a gate.

"What's *this?*" Boot bleats, as they signal us to slow down. "The fucking border guard?"

Turns out this is a crew of toughs from the security firm policing the festival. They wave us through the gate into a large compound that looks like the parade ground of some far-flung military base – Khe Sanh, or somewhere like that – with a low-slung breezeblock building that seems to have been pressed into service as a make-shift bar and cafeteria and not much else. There are a few photographers lurking about, looking suitably enough like war-correspondents in their flak-jackets and Wellington boots, most of them caked in mud.

Among them is heavy metal snapper George Bodnar, who's lucky to be here at all. The previous night, George tells us, festival headliners Ritchie Blackmore's Rainbow had staged a full-scale dress rehearsal, complete with pyrotechnics. Rainbow's intention was to end their show with the most violent explosion they could safely mount without blowing Donnington off the map. To this end, they'd brought in several tons of gelignite. Anyway, the rehearsal was apparently going well enough and Rainbow were roaring towards some typically ferocious musical climax or other when some unfortunate sod accidentally set the whole lot off with a bang you could have heard on the moon. The stage survived the blast, but only just. Judas Priest's entire back line was blown out, much of the festival PA went up in smoke and one of the massive lighting rigs was severely buckled. The explosion ripped through the tents and caravans in the artists' compound behind the stage, blasting people out of their lawn chairs and deafening the rest.

Undeterred Rainbow are still talking about going out tonight with a bit of a bang. Following last night's detonations, however, they've been obliged to ask all journalists and photographers covering the festival to sign a document accepting full responsibility for their own safety, indemnifying Rainbow and the concert promoters in the event of "injury or death, however caused."

Contemplating this, Boot and I make our way to the Arista Records mobile home, where there's going to be a reception for festival openers, the poodle-haired American rockers Touch. The boys from Touch duly appear. With their tans and curls, they look like professional tennis players. We quaff a couple of half pints of champagne from plastic beakers, just to be sociable, and decide to check things out in the crowd, which is when we run into festival publicity director, Jennie Halsall, who's festooned with walkie-talkies, radio transmitters, satchels and clipboards, and looks like a member of an SAS assault squad. She says she's heading for the stage and will drive us if we want a lift, which she recommends because it's a 30 minute walk, which seems incredible, Boot going ashen-faced on the spot. Jennie tells us if we don't want a lift with her, we can always catch the mini-bus.

"The *mini-bus?*" Boot wails, his disbelief growing by the moment.

"There's a shuttle," Jennie says. "The bus goes every 20 minutes from the Lodge."

We decide to go with Jennie, and here she is wrestling with the steering wheel of her Mini as it plunges into one pot-hole after another, waves of mud splashing onto the windscreen. It's been raining for the last week in these parts, so the whole area is a filthy sticky mess, a huge quagmire. We've now come to a series of concrete bunkers that look like the first line of an elaborate military defence system, something like the Maginot Line. We slide down an underpass, and through a complex system of tunnels, the walls of which are slimy with damp, the mud about a foot deep.

Jennie parks the car on the other side of the bunkers. We have to walk from here, and so go squelching off towards the stage, a vast crowd of grimy teens occupying a gentle incline, a lot of them apparently already unconscious.

"Look at that," Boot says, uncommonly jaundiced. "Up to their necks in shit and not a care in the world."

Touch are by now finishing their opening set and we decide to head back to the Arista caravan, where the label is hosting a post-show celebration for the band. We arrive expecting gaiety, but are greeted with scenes of catastrophe and flapping distress. A couple of girls from the record company are actually weeping. Jennie Halsall's on one of her walkie-talkies, jabbering frantically, like she's calling in the coordinates for an air strike, enemy activity on every front, lines starting to break, a perimeter broached, Charlie inside the wire, drop everything you've got on them, now.

What on Earth's *happened* here?

One of Touch has *swallowed a wasp,* that's what! He's been rushed to hospital. Will he pull through? Who cares? Boot and I fall out of the Arista caravan weeping with laughter and head for the backstage bar where I ask someone who looks like he might know when the next band, Riot, are on.

"They've *been on* for the last 15 minutes," he tells me.

We're so far from the stage we can't hear a band called *Riot* playing through 80,000 watts? The day gets better and better. I round up Boot and we head off to the stage, decide after about half a mile that we're not up to the walk and head back to the Arista bivouac where

269

Jennie Halsall radios for a bus that we have to hoof back at a marching clip to the backstage compound to catch. Eventually, something that looks like a cross between a tractor and a fucking milk float trundles into view, doing about three miles a millennium. It's meant to carry I'd say about six people. About three times that number clamber aboard, like refugees escaping a burning city. Most of the main tracks to the stage are now pretty much impassable, so we go by what I take to be the scenic route, a diversion that takes us so far out of our way that by the time we get to the stage Riot are just leaving it. We take the tractor, milk float, bread van, whatever it is back to the backstage paddock, where a mud-streaked photographer from *The Belper News*, a miserable old coot, is wondering what he's doing here.

"I've got a coontry and western concert t'go to t'night," he says, nursing a shandy. "There'll be about 200 people, a free bar and a bite t'eat. It'll be grand," he adds with an anticipatory smirk, "after this bloody shambles."

Apparently, Judas Priest are due on next, so we head for the pickup point to see if there's a mini-bus we can catch to the stage. There isn't. There's a fucking *lorry*. A dozen of us clamber in the back, where there's some kind of improvised seating and off we go. It's a bumpy ride. At one point, the lorry hits something that unfortunately turns out not to be Ritchie Blackmore and I spill most of a treble vodka. Fortunately, most of it goes into the pint of lager I'm holding in my other and, so all is not entirely lost. We get to the stage in time to see Judas Priest frontman Rob Halford riding onto it on a motorbike. I'm hoping he'll lose control of the thing and roar off the front of the stage and into the photographers' pit, but he brakes in time, hops off the bike and addresses the multitude.

"Who's from, uh...uh, north of Birmin'ham?"

The people from north of Birmingham make their presence known with a mighty roar.

"Who's from, uh... south of Birmin'ham?"

The people from south of Birmingham now weigh in with their contribution to the prevailing tumult.

"Coo-er," Ron Halford says, as if astonished. "You've coom from all over."

Earlier in the afternoon, we had watched a black Mercedes drive into the backstage compound at some speed, splashing through much standing water and spraying bystanders with mud. It was Ritchie Blackmore arriving to get primped up for Rainbow's headlining appearance. And that's Ritchie on stage now, wearing a catsuit, that probably fitted him when he bought it, and what looks like a dead cat on his head, Ritchie sporting the day's outstanding hair-do, rumoured unkindly by many to actually be an elaborate wig, something from a Restoration comedy or the wardrobe of a drag act. He's playing a version of Ye Olde English folk tune, "Greensleeves", through speakers as big as the Empire State Building as bonfires burn across the field and spotlights light up the night sky. We're actually only still here because we've heard that as part of Rainbow's spectacular finale, Ritchie's arranged to be shot into the air, as if from a cannon. We can't wait for *that*, but the moment never comes. The hydraulic system meant to launch the moody guitarist into space has broken down! This puts Blackmore in such a strop he smashes his guitar and sets fire to his amplifier. There are fireworks going off now, too, things blowing up on stage, smoke everywhere.

"Let's go," Boot whimpers. *"Please."*

As we struggle back to the car, Rainbow's drummer, ostentatious percussionist Cozy Powell, starts up a drum solo that incorporates all the loud bits of "The 1812 Overture". By the time he's finished, we're already nearly home.

OZZY OSBOURNE

Texas, March 1982

On the other hand, there's a fist, and on the fingers of that fist, in great big letters, he's tattooed his name: OZZY. And this is him, now, coming out of the hotel bar, the sun not even over the yard arm, San Antonio still coming to life at this relatively early hour, Ozzy with a drink in either hand, bleary-eyed beneath a greasy sheep dog fringe.

I'm in town with photographer Tom Sheehan to do a story on Ozzy. We introduce ourselves to the great man.

"Which one of yow's Allin Jownz?" Ozzy asks now, trying to get us in focus. "Yowr the one Tony Iommi whacked, intcher?" Ozzy continues, tail up for the bar, us following. And this was true. Four years earlier in Glasgow, Black Sabbath guitarist Tony Iommi had settled an old score by beating me senseless in a hotel car park.

"The last time I saw yow," Ozzy goes on, simultaneously trying to attract the attention of a cocktail waitress, "yow were flyin' across the bonnet of a car, covered in blood."

A waitress arrives to take our orders. Sheehan and I go for a Heineken each, a steady enough start to the day. Ozzy orders a mineral water, telling us he's had a rough old night: "I 'ad a few drinks, slapped the band about a bit and ended up in a canal."

The waitress returns with our drinks. Ozzy looks forlornly at his glass of water.

"Fuck it," he says. "Bring me a beer and large brandy. Y'know," he carries on, "what Tony did to yow, that was really *offside*. Yow was just a scrap of a thing. Really skinny little punk in a leather jacket and chains, as I recall. He was a *monster*, Iommi. Fists for fucking brains."

I ask Ozzy how the current tour's going.

"Grayyyt!" he announces, cheerfully. "Although the dwarf got hit by a lump of frozen liver the other night."

The *dwarf?*

"Yeah," Ozzy says. "We've got a dwarf on the road with us."

And what exactly do you with the, uh, dwarf?

"We *hang* him," Ozzy says, beaming. "During the ballad."

There's a choking sound from where Sheehan's sitting. I ask Ozzy what else has been happening on the tour. Well, he says, the night before last, he's not sure where, the police caught some fans trying to smuggle a cow's head into one of the concerts.

"It's been happening ever since I bit the head off that bloody *bat*," he says, wearily.

Oh, yes. The *bat*. This had been in all the papers. At one of the first shows on the tour someone had thrown a bat on stage. Ozzy grabbed it and bit its head off, much to the startled awe of his fans and the utter bewildered disgust of everyone else.

"I honestly *did not know* it was a bat," he claims. "You know, these kids're always throwing, like, plastic toys at me... so I just grabbed this *thing*, bit the head off and thought: *'Fuck me!'* The thing was *flapping*. I tell you, I really suffered for it later. I had to have these rabies shots. Real bad news, man. Terrible. Imagine someone injecting a golf ball into your leg. The syringe was like a bicycle pump. I told 'em, 'No more of them fucking injections. I'll take me fucking chances.' "

But Ozzy, what if you actually got rabies?

"Buy me a fucking *muzzle*," he says, knocking back the Heineken, reaching for the brandy. "If I start foaming at the fucking mouth, just fucking shoot me."

About two hours later, the table in front of us is fair groaning with empty bottles of Heineken and brandy glasses, and the three of us are really rather drunk. Which is when Sheehan announces it might be time for some pictures. As he correctly points out, if we stay here much longer, drinking at the rate we're drinking, pretty soon we won't be able to stand, much less walk and talk and all the other things we're going to have to do to successfully negotiate what's left of the day.

Sheehan wants to take some shots outside San Antonio's most famous historical landmark, the shrine of Texas liberty, The Alamo – a cherished monument, hallowed ground, an old adobe mission where 200 volunteers, fighting for Texas independence, died holding off a

Mexican army of thousands to win freedom for the Lone Star State. Ozzy's up for it, but says he's got to change first. He's back in about 10 minutes, dressed in a baggy blouse, a straw Stetson and ill-fitting women's culottes with white socks that stop short of his knees. And on those knees, I notice now, are two tattooed smiling faces, whose eyes appear to blink when the skin around them wrinkles.

We pile into a waiting cab, make off at some speed through the mid-afternoon traffic, pull up outside the Alamo. Ozzy throws a commendable variety of poses for Sheehan, attracting a few suspicious looks from the tourists who have come to the Alamo to pay their respects to the martyrs who died here in the name of freedom. Fortunately, there's not much of a crowd, just some geezers who look old enough to have had immediate relatives behind the Alamo walls when the *deguello* blew and the cannons roared. Everything seems to be going smoothly enough under the circumstances, when Ozzy announces he needs to piss rather urgently. I'm looking around to see if there's anywhere convenient, as it were, for him to go when I realise he's actually already going. There's a shrill scream, the piercing, skin-shredding high-decibel caw of a wounded Valkyrie. I look around to see a man and woman, the latter with her hands to her mouth, which is hanging open like she's waiting for someone to feed her. She's clearly speechless. Her husband or whatever he is looks like he's well on his way to a seizure of some kind.

They're staring at Ozzy, who's just pulled down his culottes and, bare bum to the wind, is currently pissing quite torrentially all over the front of the shrine of Texas liberty. We'll be lucky to get out of this in one piece.

"That's the man, officer, *that's him*." This is another appalled tourist, eyes bulging, face crimson with immeasurable hostility, pointing at Ozzy. Ozzy by now has pulled up his pants and clambered halfway up the venerable adobe mission, where he's lurking in an alcove like a transvestite gargoyle, looking down on a group of clearly unamused Texas Rangers.

"Get *down*, boy, and get down *quick*," one of the Rangers tells Ozzy, the Ranger's hand on his pistol hip, hovering. Ozzy climbs down, grinning like a loon. The irate tourist tells the Rangers he'd seen Ozzy – with *his own eyes* – urinating, yes, *ur-eye-nayting*, on the Alamo. The Rangers flinch as one at the sacrilege.

274

"This *true?*" one of them asks Ozzy, almost afraid that it might be.

"There's the STAIN!" bleats the tourist, pointing with trembling fingers at a darkening patch on the Alamo wall, provoking gasps of horror from the small crowd that's gathering around us. The San Antonio Police Department turn up just about then, guns out. Ozzy wants to know what all the fuss is about.

"Mister," a Ranger tells him, "when you piss on the Alamo, you piss on the state of Texas. *That's* what all the fuss is about."

"Fair enough," Ozzy says, finally contrite.

"I mean," says the Ranger. "Would you piss over Buckingham Palace?"

"Actually, I did once," Ozzy tells the startled Ranger, who wants to know what happened next. "I got arrested," Ozzy admits. Which is what's about to happen to him now.

"Name?" barks an SAPD patrolman, booking him.

"John Osbourne," Ozzy tells him. "But me mates call me Ozzy."

The cop takes off his hat and gives Ozzy a squinty once-over.

"You ain't the guy who eats *bats* are you?" he asks Ozzy, who nods eagerly, thinking he's maybe off the hook here.

"Mister," the cop says then, "we are taking you *in.*"

Sheehan and I have been trying to keep our distance from all this, innocent bystanders and all that. But one of the Texas Rangers is now giving us a closer look.

"Split up," Sheehan says, actually talking out of the side of his mouth, like a gangster or something. "Take these," he adds, the sharp-witted lensman palming me the roll of film he's just quickly ejected from his camera, me peeling off even as the Ranger starts quizzing Tom. Now one of the SAPD patrolmen is walking towards me with a vaguely threatening look, asks me if I know anything about what's been going on here and if I know Ozzy or have anything to do with him. I assume an expression of wholesome innocence, not as easy as it sounds, shrug my shoulders, start babbling in an accent I hope sounds suitably Scandinavian – I'm thinking Swedish, keeping my fingers crossed that the SAPD man doesn't by some coincidence have relatives in Gothenburg or Helsingborg. The cop regards me as he might regard a cross-eyed idiot and waves me on. The Texas Ranger's got no greater sense out of Tom, whose quick-fire, cor-blimey-cockernee banter has completely baffled the Ranger's interpretive powers.

Anyway, Ozzy's being marched to a waiting police car when a cab comes roaring around a corner and out pops Ozzy's manager – Sharon Arden, not yet married to Ozzy – a shrill woman with a slightly demonic air, prone to hysterics and a lot of blunt language. Sheehan and I hang back as she tears into the patrolman, who ignores her and pushes Ozzy into the back of the police car, driving off with him and leaving Sharon fuming. She's still swearing like a docker when she notices Sheehan and me and furiously berates us for leading Ozzy off the reservation when he was under strict instruction to not leave the hotel under any circumstance while she had her hair done, or something. She seems tempted for a moment to let him rot in whatever cell he's been thrown in, but then makes a sort of high-pitched whining noise that sounds like something coming apart in outer space, presumably when she realises there's now a fair chance that Ozzy might miss tonight's show at the San Antonio Convention Centre and how much that will cost her.

We have to get him out, then, and so head off to the Bexar Country Adult Detention Centre which, when we get there, is a place of raw terror and tremendous noise, full of pleading wives, mothers and many howling children. Sharon marches up to the nearest desk and starts shouting at everyone in a uniform, worrying the cops with the promise of an almighty ruckus to come if Ozzy's not released in time to play tonight's show, his fans likely to get somewhat out of hand, many thousands of them. Calls are made, there's mention of a lawyer in New York, money being wired to cover whatever it's going to cost to spring Ozzy. When we're told this is likely to take some time, Sheehan and I go off for a drink and a little shopping, Tom picking up some nice western duds at a nearby thrift shop. When we get back to the detention centre, there's a great deal of mechanical clanking, gates being opened and shut, and here comes Ozzy, being marched out of a holding cell and into the chaotic maw of the facility's main reception area. He seems a little dazed, but otherwise in surprisingly good spirits.

"They put me in a cell with a *murderer*," he's telling anyone who'll listen, as if this is one of the most wonderful things that's ever happened to him. "He'd just killed his wife," Ozzy goes on. "Bit her throat out. He was covered in blood, but seemed nice enough."

Late the next afternoon, we're in Dallas, in the bar of the Fairmount Hotel (the scene, a few years earlier, of the CCBS annual convention I'd attended with Bob Geldof and Johnnie Fingers). Ozzy's talking about an earlier brush with the law that ended up with him behind bars for considerably longer than the couple of hours he'd spent the day before in San Antonio. He was 16, growing up in Aston, a grim Birmingham suburb. Unemployed, he drifted into petty crime, mainly shoplifting and burglary. He was finally nicked trying to get a stolen colour TV – that turned out to be too heavy – over a garden wall. The TV fell on the hapless Ozzy, pinning him to the ground, where he was arrested and subsequently sentenced to three months in Winson Green prison.

"In actual fact," Ozzy now tells me, rolling up a sleeve, "this tattoo was done by a guy who was in there for beating three prostitutes to death."

Apart from the convenient tattooing facilities, what else did prison have to offer?

"Nothing. Nothing at all," he says. "I tell you, when they sent me down, it frightened the shit out of me. When you go in there, it just degrades you. It's like you're no longer human. They give you a number and that's your life. That's your only identity. You're not a man anymore, you're prisoner 1237486. I experienced some wild things in there. When I got out, I sat down and cried my eyes out. That place was like a sewer. I don't believe people should be put in luxury cells with colour tellies and maids, but there's a point where you have to draw the line. To be locked away from your loved ones is one thing, to be forced to live in absolute filth is another."

He mentions a recent conversation with someone and how he complained about the severity of UK tax laws, and was told that taxes went to good causes, like the state. This argument did not sit well with Ozzy.

"I said, 'What's the state ever done for me?' Three months in Winson Green. That's all the state's done for me. Put me in jail and caused my mother and father countless years of misery. I watched my father die of cancer at the age of 63. I looked at him and I thought, 'You poor bastard. What have you seen of this world? You've seen a war. You've seen poverty. You've scrimped and saved through your tiny little life only to end up in a fucking closet in the death ward of a hospital. I thought I'd rather die of a fucking overdose than end up like that. At least that'll be the way I want to go. After being in prison, I knew I wouldn't go back and I knew that I wouldn't be told how to

277

live, what to do, when to work, when to have me tea break. I saw my father going through all that. The man never missed a day's work in his life, and he dies in this closet. There's no dignity in it. And there's millions like him. Why don't they have a state funeral for somebody like that, instead of some arsehole who's probably ripped the country off and led us into war."

So was rock 'n' roll the only alternative to prison?

"Actually," he says, "I never really thought about becoming a singer. I always wanted to join the Merchant Navy or the Army or something. I went to enlist once, but they wouldn't have me. The guy looked at me and said they wanted subjects, not objects. I didn't even get through the door. I thought, 'Great. If they call me up for the next war, I'll just tell them to fuck off."

And then we are talking about his audience and how Ozzy thinks they're madder than he is.

"I do believe that 90 per cent of the audience is sicker than I'm even *alleged* to be. I mean," he says, "there's a point in the show where we throw liver and offal at the audience and the kids'll be clamouring to get a piece in the face. I fail to understand it, really," he goes on, sounding genuinely bewildered. "Why, in this day and age, do people like to see so much gore? I mean, I'll give it to 'em if that's what they want. They're paying money to see me, so I'll do whatever they want me to. But I often say to myself, 'If I was in the front row and some prick on stage threw a great big piece of shit all over me, I'd get up there and punch the guy out.' That's why I get the dwarf to throw the liver. He's too small to hit."

Did he ever think things were getting out of hand?

"I dunno," he says. "There's just a point where you know you've gone far enough. Like at the beginning of this tour, we were going to sell *tour humps*, instead of tour T-shirts. T-shirts with HUMPS! And *club-feet!*" Chuckles consume him at the very memory. "But then I said to Sharon, 'What if we had a son and he came home from a concert covered in shit with a hump on his back and a club foot?' It'd be a bit bizarre. 'Where the 'ell 'ave you been?' 'T'see Ozzy Osbourne!' 'Gerrup those bloody stairs!' "

Then Ozzy's complaining about the relentless pressures of touring, the wear and tear. Mention is made of Alex Harvey, recently dead from a heart attack on tour in Belgium.

"Whorra *bummer*," Ozzy says of Alex's passing. "But there you go. I suppose the same thing's going to happen to me one day. It's the price you pay, I suppose. The death rate in rock 'n' roll is phenomenal. You live at 100 miles an hour, 24 hours a day and your body can only take so much stress."

So what does he do, you know, to wind down after a tour?

"Do you know what I *really* like doing?" he asks, flushed with sudden enthusiasm. "Fishing and shooting," he beams. "Enjoying the countryside"

And what exactly did he like shooting?

"Rabbits," he says. "Pigeons. Pheasants. Vans. Policemen."

We'd been talking earlier about a song from his *Blizzard of Ozz* album, an eco-anthem called "Revelation (Mother Earth)". Wasn't all this talk of hunting, shooting and killing somewhat contradictory to the song's general sentiments?

"Not at all!" he insists. "I eat what I shoot. I don't just go *bang!* I don't leave the bodies to rot. I go hunting for *food*. I don't just *kill*. There is a purpose. I mean, if there's a crisis, a food shortage or a war, I'll know how to survive. Most people wouldn't. 'Oh, the butcher's closed. Where am I going to get some meat?' You won't hear *me* whingeing. I'll be out with me gun. There's so much hypocrisy about all this," he's now complaining. "Like, this guy was interviewing me once and he's got this big fat greasy steak in front of him on his plate. And he says, 'Don't you think biting a dove's head off is cruel?' "

This was reference to Ozzy turning up at a record company meeting with a couple of doves he'd originally intended to send fluttering among the label executives and their various minions. This would perhaps have startled them, but Ozzy now wanted to freak them out, which he did, by biting the head off one of the unfortunate doves, leaving him with a mouth full of blood and feathers.

"So he asks me if biting the head off a dove is cruel," Ozzy goes on, "and he's tucking into this *rump steak*. I said, 'Listen, mate, you're the one who's eating a cow's arse on a plate.' I said, 'Don't you realise that *food* used to hop around a field, *mooing*. Minding its own business. And now you're eating its *arse* off a plate.' He couldn't accept the idea that I might've bitten the head off the dove to show up all these hypocrites. You've met these people, these record company executives

279

in their satin tour jackets. They're a pain in the arse. That's why I did what I did."

Was there a stunt he's pulled, an outrage committed, that he actually regretted?

"I've done some *terrible* things to animals," he says, suddenly rather serious, a little contrite. "When I worked at the slaughterhouse, I used to do some *grotesque* things. I was just a kid then," he goes on, somewhat wistfully. "I'm sure everyone's done something at that age they regret. Like, I once sawed a sheep's head in half."

It was dead, I hope.

"No!" he laughs. "It was *alive*. It wouldn't have been any fun if it had been *dead*."

In which case, I presume you used, I don't know, something quick and effective, like a high-powered chainsaw, something like that, to get the job done quickly.

"It was a hacksaw, actually," Ozzy recalls, making a slow, deliberate sawing motion that leaves me feeling rather nauseous.

"The look on your face!" Ozzy now roars, laughing, doubling over, clutching his sides, all that. "It's a killer."

His delight in my obvious squeamishness makes him delirious with laughter to the point where I can only join in, both of us haw-hawing like a proper pair of bravos.

"One thing's for sure," he says at the height of this hilarity, rather dashing the passing thought that he's been winding me up, "that sheep weren't laughing…"

MORRISSEY

Reading, February 1984

Later, when he cheers up, we start talking about death and dying –
last breaths, the lights going out, the darkness that in the end takes us
all, chucklesome stuff like that. For the moment, though, Morrissey,
in a bleak little hotel room in Reading, where tonight The Smiths are
playing at the University on a UK tour to promote their just-released
debut album, is sitting on his bed, knees tucked beneath that singular
chin, telling me about his troubled teenage years – something we are
going to hear a lot about in the months to come, as The Smiths continue their popular ascendency and everybody wants to know everything about him.

When he was 18, he initially remembers, his voice an undulation
of moping vowels and world-weary sighs, he wanted only to retreat
from the world and its daily grit. He lived then on a diet of sleeping
pills, incapable at times of even getting out of bed to face the day, lost
in barbiturate dreams. It had been a bleak old time, by his detailed
account, Dickensian in its gloom and debilitating isolation.

"I can't ever remember deciding that this was the way things
should be," he says. "It just suddenly seemed that the years were passing and I was seeing out from behind the bedroom curtains. It was the
kind of quite dangerous isolation that's totally unhealthy. Most of the
teenagers that surrounded me, and the things that pleased them and
interested them, well, they bored me stiff. It was like saying, 'Yes, I see
that this is what all teenagers are supposed to do, but I don't want any
part of this drudgery.'

"I can see that talking about it might bore people," he continues. "It's
like saying, 'Oh, isn't life terribly tragic. Please pamper me, I'm awfully

281

delicate.' It's that kind of boorishness. But to me, it was like living through the most difficult adolescence imaginable. But this all becomes quite laughable," he goes on, indulging in a little titter to emphasise the point he's making. "Because I wasn't handicapped in a traditional way. I didn't have any severe physical disability, therefore the whole thing sounds like pompous twaddle. I just about survived it, let's just say that."

As I was saying a moment ago, The Smiths' first album has just come out and they're very much the current centre of attention as far as *Melody Maker* and the rest of the music press are concerned. Which is what Morrissey always knew they would be.

"I had absolute faith and absolute belief in everything we did, and I really did expect what has happened to us to happen," he says with a quiff-wobbling emphasis. "I was quite frighteningly confident. I knew also that what I had to say could have been construed as boring arrogance. If the music had been weak, I would have felt silly and vulnerable. But since I *absolutely believe* everything I say about The Smiths, I want to say it as loud as possible."

How long had he subscribed to the not disagreeable notion that the Smiths were so totally special?

"For too long!" he fairly shrieks, making me jump. "And this is why when people come up to me and say, 'Well, it's happened dramatically quickly for The Smiths,' I have to disagree. I feel as if I've waited a very long time for this. So it's really quite boring when people say it's happened perhaps too quickly, *because it hasn't.*"

As for what people wrote about him, did he recognise himself in what he read?

"Perhaps in a few paragraphs," he says, a pained expression on his face as he apparently recalled all those column inches, acres of recent newsprint. "But most of it is just peripheral drivel, and a misquote simply floors me. And that happens so much, I sit down almost daily and wonder why it happens at all. But the positive stuff one *always* wants to believe, and the insults one always wants *not* to believe. When one reads of this monster of arrogance, one doesn't want to feel that one is that person.

"Because," he continues, "in reality, I'm all those very boring things, shy and retiring. But when one is questioned about the group, one becomes terribly, terribly defensive and almost proud. But in daily life, I'm almost too retiring for comfort."

So what do you do when you're not working?

"I just live a terribly solitary life, without any human beings involved whatsoever," he says, apparently resigned to nights in by the fire, a glass of sherry on the mantelpiece, the wireless murmuring in the background, a kettle coming to the boil, nothing but the weather for company. "And that to me is almost a perfect situation. I don't know why exactly. I suppose I'm just terribly shy. Privacy to me is like a life support machine. I have mounds of people simply *bounding* into the room and taking over. So, when the work is finished, I just bolt the door and draw the blinds and dive under the bed.

"It's essential to me. One must, I find, in order to work seriously, be detached. It's quite crucial to be a step away from the throng of daily bores and the throng of mordant daily life."

Are you afraid of relationships, of letting people get too close to you or you to them?

"It's not really fear," he says by way of considered reply. "I just don't really have a tremendously strong belief that relationships can work. I'm really quite convinced that they don't. And if they do, it's really quite terribly brief and sporadic. It's just something, really, that I eradicated from my life quite a few years ago, and I saw things more clearly afterwards.

"I always found it particularly unenjoyable," Morrissey says, and he's talking now about sex. "But that again is something that's totally associated with my past and the particular views I have. I wouldn't stand on a box and say, 'Look, this is the way to do it, break off that relationship at once!' But, for me, it was the right decision. And it's one that I stand by and I'm not ashamed or embarrassed by. It was simply provoked by a series of blunt and thankfully brief and horrendous experiences that made me decide upon abstaining, and it seemed quite an easy and natural decision."

The week we meet, the papers have been full of other people's opinions about The Smiths. What does Morrissey himself have to say about the album?

"I am ready," he says, "to be burned at the stake in total defence of it. It means so much to me that I could never explain, however long you gave me. It becomes almost difficult, and one is just simply

283

swamped in emotion about the whole thing. It's getting to the point where I almost can't even talk about it, which many people will see as an absolute blessing. It just seems absolutely perfect to me. For me," he announces with a flourish that nearly sets the curtains on fire, "it seems to convey exactly what I wanted it to."

JOHNNY MARR

Reading, February 1984

After our marathon conversational stint, Morrissey meets up with
the rest of The Smiths and we all pile into a van and drive to the gig,
which turns out to be predictably fantastic. We then head back to the
motel, where we are relieved to find the bar still open and manned
by a blessedly insomniac night porter who tells us he'll keep serving
us until he runs out of beer or we keel over, whichever comes first.
Morrissey quickly disappears in the direction of his room, a book
under his arm. What's left of The Smiths, meanwhile, mix eagerly
with a crowd of fans who've followed us back to the motel, things
getting quickly rowdy. At some point, I find myself in a corner of the
bar with Johnny Marr.

I had earlier thought Morrissey was a danger to donkeys and their
back legs, but Johnny's gift for the proverbial gab is staggering. The
briefest mention of The Byrds, for instance – for whom we have a
mutual, if hardly unique, affection – precipitates a veritable tsunami
of fact and opinion about West Coast music. We've been chatting
a while when he notices that out of instinct I've turned on my tape
recorder. Too much of what Johnny has to say is too good to be lost
to what experts describe as posterity.

"Are you interviewing me?" he asks then.

I guess I am.

"Oh, great!" he laughs, and then we're talking about the way in
which the world, when it looks these days at The Smiths, seems only
to have eyes for Morrissey. Was this a problem?

"Nah," he says, sinking another one, the night porter already on
his way to our table with fresh drinks, which he is encouraged to keep

coming. "Just because Morrissey ends up on the covers of the music papers, that doesn't mean we're jealous of him. That would be petty. That's just a disgusting trapping of old rock star attitudes. The Smiths are beyond that, honestly."

Then Johnny's recalling the first time he met Morrissey, turning up at his front door, ringing the bell and waiting for an answer.

"I was pretty confident he'd like me," he says. "But I was a bit worried in case he thought I looked too outrageous. I had this really silly haircut – this *quiff*. It looked like I had a French loaf sticking out of me head. I was afraid he'd think I was some kind of Gene Vincent freak. All I knew about him was that he'd written a book about The New York Dolls, so I was quite prepared to spend a bit of time talking to him about them. But after about three minutes of being in his flat, I realised that would be so irrelevant. We just seemed to have so much else in common, it was amazing.

"I remember when he answered the door, I just laid this heavy jive on him. I just spoke even faster than I am now, like 300 words a second. I just said, 'This is how Leiber and Stoller got together', and he just invited me in. I dare say he'd come into contact with people who wanted him to be in groups before, so I wanted him to take me seriously, so I said, 'Look, the time is right for a fantastic new song writing partnership...' The idea that we wouldn't get on just didn't enter my head. Before he even heard me play guitar, we had ideas for about four songs. I was just singing melodies and he was already coming up with ideas for lyrics. When I walked into his room, he just said, 'What music do you like?' And I told him, and after every single group I mentioned, he just went, 'Yeah...' I couldn't believe it. I could've gone in there with this spiel and if it hadn't worked out I would never have done it again with anyone else cos I really opened up and he did the same, I think. He just got this amazing vibe off me.

"From then on, we kept in contact all the time. We just had this tremendous belief in ourselves and since that day my life has totally changed, and I know Morrissey's has, too. Right from the beginning, we knew it was going to be brilliant.

"One of the first lyrics he showed me was for 'Suffer Little Children'. That impressed me massively. It's probably a self-indulgent little story, but the first time we ever recorded our songs, we went into this little studio in Manchester one night and started recording at about 11:30

and went straight through until 06:30 the next morning. We did 'The Hand That Rocks the Cradle' and 'Suffer Little Children' in, like, two takes. I played guitar and bass and this drummer who was a friend of ours just stumbled his way through. But when we played the tracks back, we were just overwhelmed. By 'Suffer Little Children', especially. The more we listened, the more touched we were. It was the first time me and Morrissey realised what we could do together.

"Like, all the time we'd been writing together we knew we had the conviction and the confidence and the ability and the talent to put these gems together, but this was the confirmation of it all. Listening to that playback of 'Suffer Little Children', I really heard for the first time the beauty of Morrissey's voice. We've never," he says then, trying to attract the barman's nomadic attention, "looked back."

R.E.M.

Athens, GA, June 1985

"You've heard of Fellini? Wow. Cool," says Michael Stipe and I'm not sure if he's easily impressed or being somehow facetious. We're having breakfast in a small coffee shop in downtown Athens. Stipe is talking about his favourite books, films, music, paintings, that sort of thing. For reasons I'm unaware of, he's dressed like a Depression-era hobo, someone who's been riding the rails, a boxcar poet or dustbowl troubadour, in grubby jeans with a big hole in one knee, a threadbare jacket, a shirt that looks like he's been using it to clean windows and a battered hat, its brim pulled rakishly low. It's a look that I presume is meant to somehow match the music on R.E.M.'s new album, *Fables of the Reconstruction*, their third, due out soon, the follow-up to *Murmur* and *Reckoning,* which have made the band darlings of US college radio. *Fables of the Reconstruction* is a departure of sorts from both, a record that when he first thought about it Stipe wanted in some way to tap into the currents of a vanishing America.

"A lot of what I was listening to, going into this album," Stipe says, "was, like, cassettes recorded in Tennessee, in the mountains. Appalachian folk songs, field recordings, literally someone with their tape recorder, recording an old man with a fiddle, with a woman in the background with her hand on the stove. That sort of image, I think, really infected the way I wanted it to sound. I also had the idea of it being a storytelling record. I was fascinated by the idea of the old men sitting around the fire, passing on these legends and fables to their grandchildren. And, you know, that little boy sitting over there, building a tepee out of sticks, listening to these stories, taking in all these old legends and tales.

"I'm real saddened," he goes on, "by what's happened to this century, to the world. America's become like a dumping ground. Its culture is dying and when the culture dies, so does the country. I guess that's why I'm so drawn to these romantic ideas of traditions being passed down by way of storytelling, by way of folk music, country music, hillbilly music, the music of the people. Somehow, that has to be preserved."

We leave Stipe to however he's going to spend the afternoon – practising the banjo, picking cotton, shucking some corn, tar-papering his shack, shoeing a mule or goin' fishin' down at the crick with Huck and Tom – who knows? Bill Berry's waiting for us, meanwhile, at the bar of the Georgia Hotel, an old timey place, the drummer upset with some label wonk who's complained about R.E.M.'s refusal to include a lyric sheet with the new album. "That would be like going to the movies and getting the script to the film with your ticket," he says, exasperated. After spending a pleasant afternoon with Bill, we follow his directions to East Broad Street, to meet Peter Buck at his favourite bar. As you join us, the guitarist is chuckling at the idea that R.E.M. had been at all concerned about recording their new album in London or that working in England would in any way affect their songwriting.

"I was only worried about the weather," Buck laughs, "which was miserable. You lived up to your reputation, fully. It rained every single day it wasn't snowing. But, hell, it's not like we thought that coming to England we'd start coming out with sea-shanties or, you know, Boy George-type stuff. What did you talk to Bill about?" he then wants to know.

One thing that had come up, talking to Bill, was how much he disliked playing the larger venues R.E.M. were moving into the more popular they got. He'd been particularly wound-up by some dates they'd played with The Police. Peter's on this in an instant.

"I really love playing bars, basically," he says, which isn't all that surprising since he seems to spend so much time in them anyway. "I like to see who I'm playing for. We've played those big arenas, man, and we hated it. We opened six dates for The Police and it was miserable. I remember sitting in Philadelphia and it was like 105 degrees. They were carrying kids over the barriers. It's one in the afternoon and you can't even walk around outside, it's so hot, and we had to go on in 10 minutes. And I'm going, 'Man, I just don't wanna go on, let's just break up the band.' It was no fun. We'll never do that shit again. As soon as the show was over, it was like, 'Hell, let's go get drunk!' Shea Stadium with the Police was kinda fun, because no one in New York really knew who we were at the time and we only played 20 minutes – that's all they wanted us to play – and it rained during our set and so everyone was screwing around with their clothes off when we played, which was kinda neat. But every other date was kinda, sheeesh..." He shakes his head at clearly unhappy memories. "There were all these moronic Police fans sticking their middle fingers at us, booing us because all they wanted was to see Sting."

The bar gets rowdy pretty quickly and Peter suggests we go back to his place – a new house he's just bought, his first. He moved in recently, but when we get there it looks like he hasn't had time to unpack much apart from the albums that line a couple of walls.

"You know," he says, shirtsleeves flapping, getting some beers from the kitchen, picking up the conversation we'd started at the bar, "the most fun I ever had was when we first started touring, before we had any records out, before anyone had even heard of us. We'd pull into some town and if we were lucky we'd open for the local hot-shit band and blow the fuckers offstage. In our own naive way, we were kinda arrogant. We were like head-hunters. Sometimes we'd open for some cool bands, but usually we opened, you know, for just some nobodies who weren't very good and we'd go in and say, 'Man, let's blow them offstage.' The whole idea was to walk on and do, like, a 50-minute set that was like a hurricane blowing off the stage.

"We wanted to present these people with something that was just undeniable. By the time we were finished, we wanted them to think that everything else was irrelevant. I just loved that challenge. And we did it every night, man, in those bars. Man, we must've played, like, 200 bars, all over the South. We'd go in and there'd be maybe 30 people if we were headlining on a cheap drink night – we always tried to play cheap drink nights, because that would draw 'em in – and by the end of the set, we'd be able to go, 'See – now tell your damned friends about us.'"

Buck sounds nostalgic for that time, but dismisses the thought.

"God, no. I'm not nostalgic," he says, getting more beers from the fridge. "When I think back, I just remember all the garbage we had

290

to go through. The five people to a bed, not being able to afford hotel rooms, sleeping as we drove overnight, driving all night, all the time, to get to the next show on schedule. Not being able to bathe. Not having money for food. We went for four days once in New York without any of us eating. On the fourth day, we borrowed 20 dollars off someone and went to McDonald's and had a feast. So, no... being broke, starving and evicted. I'm not nostalgic for that, at all. I just kinda miss the fun of turning up in these real small towns, not knowing what the hell was going to happen. It was always an adventure, and that's what kept us going. Whatever happened was just one more story for us. We played this gay bar once and they advertised us like, 'Come see the young boys in the band, they're really cute.' So all these queens turned up, leching after the band, not really listening to us at all. And backstage, they're all asking for our phone numbers and stuff. I just cracked up. I just thought, 'What a great way to make money.'

"Christ, we played some weird places. Weird bars where the audience had to check their guns in at the door, where crazy drunken guys would come down front and yell and scream at us and threaten to kill us. Mind you, we were pretty rowdy ourselves, kinda like The Replacements, getting drunk and falling offstage and fighting people in the audience, punching some guy if he was bothering us, that sorta thing. They weren't real pleasant places, but we were never in a situation that I thought was incredibly life-threatening. None of us were ever beaten up and at least we weren't playing those places you read about in Alabama where they have chicken wire in front of the stage."

This sounded like the Spit Club in Houston, a lot of pretend-punks throwing bottles at Joe "King" Carrasco the night I was there, rich kids getting their kicks. Buck recognises the scene.

"That's kinda trendy trouble," he says. "I mean, if those kids came out to some of these bars in the South and tried that, you'd never see 'em again. They'd be buried out back somewhere. Not everywhere in the South's like that. Athens, here, is a nice, cultured, quiet town. But if you're maybe playing the wrong bar in somewhere like Charlotte or Augusta, you don't pull that kinda stuff. If you do, you'll get, like, five guys who'll pull you outside into the parking lot and smash your head in. But hell, you know, I'm just a sweet-natured middle-class kid. I never got involved in anything like that."

Somewhere in the neighbourhood, a dog is barking. A car door slams. Peter Buck is talking about what he calls R.E.M.'s sense of mission, a fundamental belief that as bad as the world is, it's still worth fighting for.

"I guess that's just the kind of people we are," Buck says. "We're not overly optimistic. When you look around the world, you can't be. There's still too many countries where people are being slaughtered right and left and there's still a lot of just outright savagery. But you don't just give in to that. The world sucks, but whining about it isn't gonna make it any better. I hope R.E.M. does sound uplifting, that would be a great compliment to pay our music. There are too many professional whiners. You can't ignore what goes on around you, but you have to look beyond that. You don't want to get like Jackson Browne and get really obsessive about your problems. You listen to Jackson Browne and you just go, 'Jackson, you're rich and you're handsome and you're still relatively young, will you just shut the fuck up! Be happy for once.'

"Music should reach out to people, you can't afford to be so introverted. I think that anything that touches people is doing a service, whether people understand why it's moving them or not. We always wanted our music to have heart. That's why we sometimes sound a little weird or cranky, because we always try to leave the heart in what we do. We wanted our records to be like doors to other worlds. We wanted to say, 'Here's the door, on the other side there's different rooms, another world.' We don't have any answers for anyone. We're just saying, 'This is R.E.M., this is our music, this is the door. Why not open it and walk through to the other side, maybe take a look around and see if you like it.'"

Out in the street or in someone's backyard, that dog's still barking, the day has long since turned to night, the way it's prone to, and it's started to rain. Buck goes off to get more beer, a manifesto delivered.

VAN MORRISON

London, June 1986

The first time I try to interview Van Morrison, in his trailer backstage at Knebworth in 1974, it ends badly after, as I find out later, he
mistakes me for someone who's written unflatteringly about him in
Melody Maker and he works himself into a complete and unnecessary
strop. Van's almost pathologically rude and won't listen to a word
of explanation. The upshot is I eventually storm out of his caravan,
slamming a door behind me, with Van shouting something at my
retreating back.

A few years later, I review Morrison at the Self Aid concert in Dublin,
which is headlined by Elvis Costello and U2. Van's brilliant at the show,
at which he previews material from his forthcoming new album, *No
Guru, No Method, No Teacher*. Just before the album comes out, I get a
call from an old friend named Kellogs, who I'd first met when he was tour
managing the Be Stiff tour, the one on the train. I'm surprised to learn
that Kellogs now manages Van. I'm even more surprised when Kellogs
tells me Van is doing a day of press – mostly European – to promote the
No Guru album, and after being shown the Self Aid review, Van's agreed
to do one with me. This is both exciting and fairly terrifying news.

Whatever, a few days later I'm scuffling nervously outside the
door of the Phillipe Suite at the Chesterfield Hotel in central London,
waiting to be ushered into the great man's presence. Kellogs shortly
introduces us. I offer my hand in nervous greeting. Van promptly
ignores it.

"You've got 30 minutes," he says brusquely. "What's your first
question?"

My mind of course goes immediately blank and all the finely-honed questions I'd prepared are suddenly vapour. I mumble something about the new album that, on reflection, isn't even a question, but which anyway gets Van talking, for which I am grateful.

"It's a *struggle*," he says of the writing and recording process that even after 20 years he clearly finds difficult. "Always has been. I think when you get past your second album it all becomes something of a routine. So you have to struggle against that, find a way of making what you do sound fresh and new each time.

"It's more difficult now than ever," he goes on. "I find it difficult to know what to say nowadays, or who I'm saying it to. When I started singing, you know, my audience, they were usually the same age as me and they had at least half the same problems I had... but now, I dunno. The 80s are such an extreme period for everybody. As far as what space I'm in, I can't really find it. I deliberately try not to cater for the commercial market, so I can't see myself in competition, you know, with second or third generation rock stars. I find myself at this point out on a limb, basically. A lot of people who were writing when I came through originally as a singer-songwriter have disappeared, a lot of them have ended up as MOR entertainers. So it's kind of left people like myself without an obvious slot, you know. It's like people don't quite know what to make of me anymore, he says," shrugging his shoulders and moving uneasily in his chair.

At Self Aid, he was introduced as a "living legend", which made him sound like a relic.

"I think that's absolute *rubbish*," he seethes. "I don't feel that way about myself at all. It's just something these silly little boys in the rock press come up with, this stupid thing about age. I think that's just part of the mass stupidity that seems to have gripped people at the moment. It's like, if you're over 28, you should be singing ballads or you should be dead. It's ridiculous."

How had he got involved with Self Aid?

"They asked me to do it and I said yeah," he answers curtly. "See, I kept being asked why I didn't do Live Aid, right? And the only reason I didn't do Live Aid was because I wasn't asked. I figured the next time someone asks me to do something like that, I'll do it so I don't have to answer a lot of stupid questions about why I *didn't* do it"

At Self Aid, he'd prefaced one new song, "Town Called Paradise", with this aside: "If Van Morrison was a gunslinger, there'd be a terrible lot of dead copycats out there..."

"What provoked *that?*" Morrison snorts when I bring it up. "This constant frustration, people *constantly* asking me what I think about every Tom, Dick and Harry that's sorta copied me – and what I think about that is that. I've had enough of it. I mean, it's OK if it happens, like, once. After that, after two, three, four albums, when after *four* albums people are *still* just ripping me off, it starts to get like a monkey on my back.

"And you know, I'm carrying these *Paul Brady* monkeys and these *Bruce Springsteen* monkeys and these *Bob Seger* monkeys, and I'm just *fed* up with it. I just wish they'd find someone else to copy. In the old days, they'd have called it a form of flattery. But I don't find it flattering at all. I mean, find someone else to copy, or else send me the *royalties*, you know."

And what did he think of Springsteen?

"Not my scene, you know," he says dismissively. "I'd rather listen to the source than the imitation. That's where *I'm* at."

Was he merely miffed at Springsteen's huge commercial success?

"No," he says firmly, "not at all. I'm perfectly happy with what I've got. At the same time, I don't see why something *I've* invented, *I've* developed and worked hard to come by should be ripped off, year in and year out, by these people."

We go on to talk at some length about specific tracks on the new album, Van getting himself completely worked up when I ask if "Ivory Tower" is a reply to his critics. He rants almost incomprehensibly about window cleaners and brickies for I don't know how long and mid-tirade suddenly stops in his tracks, as if he's got so wound up he's given himself a stroke.

I ask him what the matter is, and why the inexplicable silence, mid-sentence.

"Your 30 minutes," Van says then. "It's up."

He's not wearing a watch and there isn't a clock in the room, but on cue, incredibly, the door opens and Kellogs appears.

"Your man there," Van says, not really looking at me, "will show you out."

And he does.

EDDIE GRANT

Barbados, October 1986

Not long before the wind comes up over the ocean and whips the sunbeds across the lawns and into the swimming pools, I stroll down to the far end of the Haywards Resort Hotel complex, towards the sound of the calypso band and the chatter and munch of hungry guests tucking into a lavish barbecue.

I'm here in the tropics to meet the splendid Eddy Grant, recently back in the higher reaches of the UK charts with a greatest hits collection. Back in the days when record companies knew how to spend money, everyone waited with great anticipation for Eddy to put out anything at all that might be worth talking to him about. Since he could never be bothered to quit his paradisiacal retreat on Barbados, it meant for years that not without a hint of regularity several lucky members of the UK music press would find themselves packing up the beach towels, suntan lotion and cheerful holiday slacks and flying out to sun-kissed Barbados. This year, the post-cards are on me.

It's not all frolics, cocktails and sea-breezes out here, however. Sitting around a swimming pool for hours, skimming through the new Elmore Leonard and knocking back cold beers is something of an uncommon perk – but after being boiled to a shining lobster-pink and made somewhat senseless by a remorseless sun, things can get a tad tricky for the hapless holidaymaker more used to dreary overcast skies with occasional showers.

The evening of our second day on the island, for instance, a group of us are watching a spectacular sunset from an attractive patio bar, enjoying our cocktails and generally feeling on top of the world.

Which is about when I feel myself starting to glow like a nuclear accident, some kind of Chernobyl meltdown apparently imminent. Even my hair is hot. In fact, I am burning up like tree bark in a forest fire.

Perhaps a cold shower's in order, so I announce that I'm off to my room to take one. I don't get far. I'm off the patio and half-way across the adjoining dance floor when the room begins to spin around me like the carousel in Hitchock's *Strangers on a Train*. There's nothing but crashing surf in my ears. Someone is walking towards me, saying something I can't hear. And then I'm swaying like I've taken a heavy calibre round in the chest. It feels like I'm falling through space in a suit of lights. The next thing I know, I'm on the floor and after that everything goes black for a moment, possibly longer.

When I open my eyes, people I don't know are standing over me.

"Is he drunk?" someone asks.

"Heart attack," someone else decides, attempting to give me the kiss of life, which makes me sit up with a start, frightening everyone.

"It's only *heatstroke*," another voice chimes in. This is Eddy Grant's English PR, the dapper and moustachioed Keith Altham, a celebrated veteran of the British music press who as a reporter in the Sixties for *New Musical Express* hung with Jimi, The Who, the Stones, The Beatles, Small Faces, everyone.

"For God's sake, get him a drink," he now orders one of the waiters, who rushes off to the bar, reappearing moments later with something festooned with umbrellas and other bits of paraphernalia peculiar to the more exotic kind of cocktail.

"When I told you to get him a drink, I was thinking, you know, of a glass of *water*," Keith admonishes the waiter who's already given me the cocktail, which I have now come around enough to enjoy.

Altham hasn't lost a journalist yet on one of these much-loved trips and he's not about to start now. He grabs the drink off me and hauls me to my feet, looks at me like a corner man checking to see if there's any light left in his fighter's eyes, reckons I'll live, but insists, all the same, that I have an early night. He then instructs two flunkeys to escort me to my room, presumably to make sure I don't stop off at every shorefront bar on my way to my bed.

The next morning, I'm feeling much more chipper. Just as well, really, as somewhere along the line, and probably after a few rum punches too many, I appear to have volunteered to take part in a hotel tennis tournament. My opponent? Ilie Năstase, the former Wimbledon favourite. In his heyday, of course, the flamboyant Romanian was a volcanic Centre Court presence, as fiery as Connors and McEnroe, who followed shortly in his tempestuous footsteps. He's here to play in a tournament for ageing tennis pros and have a knockabout with the likes of me for the amusement of our fellow guests.

On the morning in question, Ilie turns up in immaculate tennis whites. I'm wearing a Clash T-shirt, baggy black shorts, Converse sneakers and fluorescent purple socks. Ilie looks at me like I've just insulted his mother, probably a capital offence in Romania. He invites me to select a bat – or "racquet", as the professionals call them – and join him on court. He then suggests we limber up and smashes a ball over the net between us. The ball hits me on the shoulder, nearly dislocating it. Ilie says something to the throng of sun-tanned beauties bouncing around in bikinis behind him and eyeing him adoringly. Then he points at me and they all laugh. I knock a ball back at him, but it doesn't make it over the net. Cue much laughter from the sinister Romanian and his beach whores.

Ilie now wants me to kick off – or "serve" as the pros have it. I toss a ball in the air, take a swipe at it and inevitably completely miss the falling ball, which then hits me between the eyes. Ilie indicates via a series of guffaws that such is my hopelessness that he will now serve. Something whistles past my ear. This is the ball, which has come at me with such velocity it could have taken my head off. He aims another ball at me and I manage to get the racquet to it but succeed only in knocking it out of the court and straight into an adjacent swimming pool.

"You are pathetic," Ilie is shouting at me now. "A *dog!* This is for sure. You are hittink the ball like a *potato*. I am not playink any more. This is too bad."

He starts walking away, swiping the air with his racket, a man in escalating dudgeon, simperingly pursued by his tan-limbed harem.

"You never put me down, Ilie," I call after him, Jake LaMotta on the ropes in *Raging Bull,* bloody but unbowed, all that. "You never put me down."

But Ilie's not listening. Head thrown back, he stalks imperiously off the stage, in the manner of a once-proud lion of the theatre reduced now to bit parts as butlers, valets and other assorted menials, all the great roles now being played by someone else.

And Eddy Grant? Brilliant bloke, wore his charm like a crown.

TOWNES VAN ZANDT

London, October 1987

The first time I set eyes on the great Texan songwriter Townes Van Zandt, he's standing in what looks like churlish weather outside the shack he currently calls home in a place with apparently nothing going for it called – I believe – Franklin, just down the road a ways from Nashville.

Townes is giving a big howdee to a film crew making what turns out to be the celebrated 1976 documentary *Heartworn Highways,* which profiles great new country artists like Townes, his friends Guy Clark and Rodney Crowell, as well as the young Steve Earle, among others. Townes is already pretty plastered and greets the film crew with a huge grin, a Winchester rifle in one hand and a bottle of bourbon in the other. His dog, Geraldine, swarms around him, tail wagging. He's carrying a gun, Townes explains to the baffled film crew, because his property, such as it is, is currently under attack from giant rabbits. As evidence of the infestation, he points out the holes he says they've dug in his yard, big enough for a man to fall into, which is what Townes does now, tumbling head first into a deep pit. The film crew back off. Who are they dealing with here? But this is nothing new for Townes, who's been disappearing down holes of one kind or another for years.

At the time of which I'm writing, Townes should be a country superstar. But albums like *For the Sake of the Song, Our Mother the Mountain, High, Low and In Between* and *The Late Great Townes Van Zandt* are hard to find, out of print, caught up in litigation. Major labels won't touch him, of course. Townes already has a reputation for the kind of behaviour best described as erratic. He is in fact

300

a hardcore drinker, already well on his way to the full-blown alcoholism that will kill him. For nigh on a decade, following 1978's hopelessly despondent *Flyin' Shoes,* there's been nothing but silence from Townes, a protracted hush broken only by the release earlier this year of a new album, *At My Window,* which now brings him belatedly to London.

I meet him at the Columbia Hotel on the Bayswater Road, the bar of which he seems to have mistaken for his room. He's playing The Mean Fiddler in Harlesden tonight and isn't meant to be drinking. But he's in desperate need of a cold beer, at least, after a Pernod binge the day before. Soon we are knocking back shots of tequila with beer chasers and Townes starts reminiscing about what for him are the old days, playing rough old places like the Old Quarter in Houston. I draw up a chair and light a pipe.

Townes draws a vivid picture of the Old Quarter – fights most nights, Mexicans with knives, rednecks with shotguns, a lot of stabbings, the occasional shooting, but otherwise pretty uneventful. Certainly not as bad as a place in Odessa, the name of which he can't presently remember.

"When we arrived," he says, a couple more shots lined up on the bar in front of him, "we thought it was gonna be a cowboy bar, which would have been *hell.* Turned out, though, it was a *Mexican* bar, which wasn't so bad. See, cowboys like to fight and if things get out of hand, somebody will pull a gun and shoot someone. Mexicans don't carry guns. They carry knives. They can be nasty, no doubt about it. But, on the whole, I always figured it was safer in a place where they carried knives rather than guns.

"Anyway, we were third on the bill, and this place, it was like an old aircraft hanger, with this big glistening mirror ball, biggest one I ever saw, revolving over the dancefloor. There was me, a full-blooded Indian named Jimmy Gray playing bass, a friend of mine from Kentucky named Rooster playing guitar, Cody the Cajun fiddle player and our road manager, Harold. There was this constant crashing of beer bottles and all these Mexicans screeching, 'Y VIVA ROCK 'N' ROLL!' We played the fastest version of 'Wabash Cannonball' you ever heard and got the hell off stage.

"We were followed by this… I don't know what he was, a black guy, Creole maybe, half-French and half-black. Anyway, he's wearing this big cape with sequins all over it and he sang the weirdest stuff you ever heard in your life. The Mexicans dug the hell out of him. Meanwhile, we've been paid by the promoter and I'm trying to figure out how we're going to get out of this place without someone relieving us of our money.

"In the end, I just got Harold to bring the car up to the dressing room and we made a dash for it. I said to Harold, 'If anybody tries to flag you down in this parking lot, run 'em the hell over.' Harold would have done it, too. He was a good old boy. I remember we had a 1500-mile drive after that show. Cody tried to sleep on the hood of the car. I climbed out on the roof. It sure was a long drive."

And then we're talking about movies, a mutual love of westerns, toasting anything by Sam Peckinpah, which is when Townes just sort of mentions in passing that a girl he'd been married to had been murdered. This happened some time ago but as soon as it's mentioned now, Townes starts slipping into some dark place he clearly doesn't benefit from visiting too often.

"She was hitch-hiking down from LA to San Diego," he says. "Someone picked her up, stabbed her 17 times and threw her out of the car. She crawled to a house and a woman answered the door and she managed to say my name and that she was Lesley Jo Richards from Houston. And then she expired. I got a phone call about four in the morning from a friend in Texas. The next day, I had to finish the album I'd been working on. There was one more song to record, a song called 'You Are Not Needed Now'. I got halfway through the song and, although I didn't want to break down, I just told the engineer I had to go. I went down to Long Beach, where my friend Guy Clark was living, and I stayed there for four or five hours and then I said, 'I'm going to the mountains.' Guy said, 'Man, it's late at night and I don't think your car will make it that far.' I said, 'Man, I'm *going*.' And I left and lived in those mountains for six or seven summers."

There follows, predictably, what might be described as an ominous silence. I suspect a lot of unfinished business lies here and duly ask Townes what he would have done if he'd ever run into him, the man who murdered his wife.

"I would have staked him out over an ant hill, cut off his eyelids and skinned him alive," Townes says in answer to that, making a sign to the barman that we could do with two more drinks.

LOU REED

London, February 1989

Lou Reed's record company has booked a suite for this afternoon's interview with *Melody Maker* at a high-end boutique hotel in Holland Park, a prissy place that seems to have its own volume control, turned down low. There's dreamy piped music, barely audible in the pillowy hum. The staff talk to each other like they're secret agents, whispered secrets exchanges between them followed by a quick scan of the hotel lobby, just in case. The air is scented with something flowery that makes my eyes water. This seems less like somewhere you might check in for a relaxing weekend, making full use of the spa facilities, than it does a funeral parlour or a Swiss euthanasia clinic specialising in assisted suicide with optional alpine views. You wonder what they would have made of Lou rocking up here in his debauched rock 'n' roll animal heyday, shooting up in the resident's lounge, a transsexual lover in tow and constant calls to room service demanding this, that and whatever, no need to re-stock the mini-bar, thanks, just put up a whiskey still in the en suite bathroom.

Oh, but those were different times. The Lou Reed I meet today is much reformed, off drugs and booze for many years now, his hard-won sobriety harrowingly documented on songs like "Underneath the Bottle" and "The Last Shot" from *The Blue Mask* and *Legendary Hearts*, two of the many overlooked albums Lou records in the 1980s when not many people are listening to him. When he eventually appears in the hotel suite and asks where the mini bar is, it's only to dig out a jar of some kind of coated nut that's taken his fancy. He's dressed typically in black, with lots of leather, but the neat little gold-rimmed glasses he's wearing give him a collegial air, the look of a writer-in-residence at an author's retreat in Idaho or Montana. These days, it should also be noted, Lou is politically and ecologically concerned, an active member of Amnesty International – in support of whom he toured America in 1986, alongside U2 and Sting – and a regular at benefits in New York for a variety of good causes and charitable concerns. He's lined up with the good guys, ready to fight the good fight, an upstanding citizen, firm in his opposition to Republican America, the blight of Reagan and Bush, who at the time has just succeeded the addled Reagan in the White House. The just-released *New York* – the album we're here today to talk about – is full of angry songs about what the city and America have become in these grim days.

He settles himself into a chair across the table from me, pours himself a mineral water.

"May I?" he says, lighting a cigarette he's just taken from the pack I've just put down.

I thought you'd quit.

"I'm working on it," he says, taking a long drag.

I remember you once saying you had no attitude without a cigarette, something like that.

"I remember saying a lot of things," he says.

We make a little more small talk while I try to remember how to work the rather new-fangled tape recorder I've just bought, which appears not to have a start button, and vaguely mention the consensus of opinion that *New York* is full of the best songs he's written in years.

"A *consensus?*" he snaps. "Among *whom?*"

Er, critics. People who've written about the album.

"*Critics?*" Lou lets out a long sigh, a world-weary, here-we-go-again sort of sigh, pitched somewhere between a dying breath and a gas leak. "Lo and behold! The critics! Listen," he says, "I think all my records are great. I think all of them have had something really terrific on them."

I try to be delicate. Wouldn't he admit some of them were perhaps not, you know, as good as they could have been?

"No," he says, sounding pretty sure about this. "I *wouldn't.*"

He lights another cigarette and looks at me through the smoke between us.

"This album is the result of all the other ones," he says. "And on this particular record I was able to assemble a team of people who could help me get the sounds I've been working on for these many years, which is essentially an old Fender guitar fed through an old Fender amp, but then it's hot-rodded a lot and has to deal with overload and distortion and tempering with harmonic feedback..."

My heart sinks at this point. Lou is notoriously obsessed with vintage recording equipment and prone to windy digressions on such that, allowed to run on unchecked, are likely to eat up all your interview time. So here he is, explaining *New York* and all its angry, brilliant narrative urgency merely in terms of its production, valve amps, wood guitars, Neve mixing desks, volume intensity, acoustic laws and parallel walls of sound. Fascinating stuff, I'm sure, if you're a boffin. But I feel like screaming. It's the songs I'm interested in here. I try to attract Lou's attention, but it's like trying to flag down a train I eventually throw myself in front of. Babbling something about how the dark subject matter of *New York* and its nightmarish images of squalor, poverty, disease, drugs, death and despair seems less documentary storytelling than melodramatic exaggeration, I hope a contrary view will catch his attention, even if it's not what I really think. It does.

"You think I'm making this shit *up?*" he asks, irate, but at least no longer banging on about directional microphone techniques, fold-back speaker systems and effects pedals. "Listen," he goes on. "This album is not Lou being negative. Or picky. Or so terribly selective that I've focused on this narrow corridor of negativity. I just write about the things that are happening around me. And it's just terrible what's happened to New York in eight years of Reagan being in the White House. It's just terrible. Especially when you realise it needn't be that way. Something could be done. And the fact that nothing's been done makes me *mad*. The Reagan administration was the most corrupt American government in modern history. And now we've got George Bush."

Meaning it's not going to get any better?

"Right. It's not going to get better. Not at all. Bush is as cute as Reagan. What's he been in – a week? And already you've got all these fundamentalists and right wing fanatics ready to march on Washington to try to undo the abortion decision, which is 16 years old now, I think.

It's unbelievable. They really want to roll the clock back. The Reagan legacy is a three trillion-dollar debt and a war he waged against people who couldn't fight back. Women. Children. The poor. People who are sick. People who are dying of AIDS. The attitude of someone like Bush on AIDS is somewhere along the lines of, 'Well, they deserve it.' And he thinks it's confined to these so-called degenerates in New York. I don't know what he's going to say when it creeps around his little house and comes in with the fucking postman."

It's been made clear to me that I'm only going to get an hour with Lou and there's not much of it left. In fact, I'm being told I have time for only one more question, preferably something that'll keep him talking for a while yet. I decide to bank everything on *New York's* closing track, "Dime Store Mystery". It sits slightly apart from the rest of the album and I'm hoping it might have a life and back story of its own, not least because it's dedicated to Andy Warhol.

Bingo! It turns out to be Lou's favourite song on the album and he has a lot to say about it. I'll see you later.

"'Dime Store Mystery'," he begins. "I'd been trying to write that song for 10 years. I had the title and I'd keep starting it, but I could never finish it. Something would happen and it would leave me. And I could never get it back. Every once in a while, my wife would say to me, 'Lou, remember "Dime Store Mystery"? Why dontcha finish it, hon-ee?' And I'd say, 'I would if I could, but I have no idea what it's about.' Actually, I did have an idea what it was about, but it was in general, nothing specific, and that won't take you far.

"So for 10 years, all I've got is a title and a vague idea for a song that would take place in a dime store, which is like a cheap department store. And the store would be symbolic of a 10-cent mystery, a cheap mystery. Not a profound mystery. One that doesn't matter in the end. Anyway, I'm writing the album and I'm on the last song, and lo and behold! What do I write down in my notebook? 'Dime Store Mystery'. I thought, 'Oh, my God. Why does this title keep coming back to haunt me?' I still didn't know what it was going to be about, but something obviously wanted me to write it. So I had a crack at it. And the results were zero. Less than zero. Profoundly zero, zero, zero. I thought, 'Oh, Christ.'

"So one night I'm watching TV and Marty Scorsese was on a show called *Nightline*, talking to this guy about his film, *The Last Temptation of Christ*. I hadn't seen it then. Later, Marty had a special screening for his friends so we didn't have to walk through the picket lines. Did you *see* those lines when the movie came out? I mean, for crying out loud! Things like that remind you there are some real *savages* out there. So, anyway, Marty's explaining in a very articulate way how he sees the movie, what he was trying to do here. And it's a fascinating movie. Takes all the poetry out of the language, so you're not faced with these neat little golden maxims. Christ is talking like a human being. It was really interesting, the idea of trying to imagine what Christ might have been thinking when he was up there on the cross. Was he tempted to say, 'Hey guys, knock it off. I was only kidding. This is all a terrible mistake. Maybe I should have gone off with Mary, had a family. This has gone too far.'

"Meanwhile, he's still hanging from the cross and things aren't looking too good for him. And you realise this is just a way to get closer to him, take a look at him, possibly interpret him for modern times. I'm not a Christian, so it's infinitely more passionately felt by Marty, this idea, than it is by me. But Marty's passion is contagious. He's a great artist and that's what great art is about – the contagion of passion... *Whoo!* I like that. The contagion of passion! Anyway, I'm listening to Marty talking about the character of Jesus and I started taking down what he was saying, verbatim. 'Goodly nature... godly nature... human nature...' And it just struck me – 'Dime Store Mystery'. Smack. Got it. Finally, I wrote this song and I said, 'Well, that's it. Finished. I can't fucking believe it. Over and out, right?' Then I woke up Sunday, six in the morning, with a neon sign in my head blaring out at me this one message: 'YOUR SONG STINKS. YOU GOTTA REWRITE IT. THIS IS NOT YOUR LANGUAGE AT ALL. THIS IS TERRIBLE. TERRIBLE. TERRIBLE. GO OVER THERE NOW AND REWRITE IT.' I really hate rewriting, but I know it's gotta be done. So I have another go at it, and in the rewriting I suddenly end up with this verse about St Patrick's Cathedral, which is where they had the wake for Andy. Then this kind of generalisation thing about Christ went into this specific thing about Andy, and I had the song."

How were you affected by Warhol's death?

"I don't know," he says. "How do you measure something like that? He had no right to die before talking to me first. Put it that way.

I mean, how dare he! It was like, 'Hey, whaaat? Die? You can't do that!' You know, I haven't met that many great people. But there are two great people I've known, and my life has been much the greater for knowing people that brilliant. One was Delmore Schwarz. The other was Andy Warhol. And I was unhappy from a selfish point of view that I wouldn't get to talk to him anymore. He was perfect. He was perfect all the way up to the end. Just hilarious. He was one of the smartest guys I've ever met in my life.

"We were talking earlier about what I thought about doing TV commercials for Honda and American Express and people saying, 'Lou! That's so uncool. How could you sell yourself like that?' Well, those ads, what I got paid for 'em, partly financed this album. So fuck you. I had no qualms about doing either. Andy wouldn't have thought more than 10 seconds about doing them. When I was with Warhol, he did all kinds of commercial art jobs just to keep the Exploding Plastic Inevitable and The Velvet Underground going. Like, in the early days, we always needed money because we weren't making any ourselves and Andy wanted to try things in the show like a bubble machine. We said, 'Andy, are you *sure*? A BUBBLE MACHINE?' And he said, 'Yeah! The lights will hit the bubbles and it'll look fantastic.' So we said OK. But it didn't work. It was so hot in this room where we played and the air was so heavy, the bubbles never got more than four inches off the floor. There were these very tired, very weary bubbles that just went pop and disappeared. Anyway, how we got the money for the bubble machine in the first place was that someone offered Andy $10,000 to paint a pig—a live pig. Andy said sure. He got a Magic Marker and he painted this pig. The pig was gorgeous by the end. It was that pig's best day. And Andy got the money and we got the bubble machine. Thanks, Andy."

Our hour's up. Lou's now going to spend five minutes with *Melody Maker* photographer Tom Sheehan.

"Let's make this quick, uh, Tom?" Lou says, putting on his shades.

The eternally-dapper photographer asks Lou to give him a bit of shoulder.

"I'm not a model, Tom," Lou tells him. "If you want me to pose, it'll cost you 500 bucks an hour."

"Over 'ere," Sheehan says, "we send our bands to acting school to learn how to throw a few shapes for the camera."

"It's a pity you don't send 'em to music school so they can learn how to play," Lou says.

"Step forward, Lou. Just a gnat's cock."

Lou takes a step forward.

"'Ang on, Lou," Sheehan says. "You've gone too far."

Lou laughs.

"Tom," he says. "That's the story of my life."

NEIL YOUNG

London, October 1989

"The first thing you have to understand about me," he says, getting close, his eyes, you'd have to say, blazing, "is that no one tells me what to do. It's just not gonna work. I'm not gonna listen, simple as that."

He's almost in my face now.

"What I'm saying here, I guess," he goes on, staring at me pretty hard, "is that I don't give a damn. Never have. Never will."

He holds the stare for a long, long moment. This is unnerving, to say the least.

"I do what I do," he says at last, the room breathing again, "and I always have done. It's all I can do. I can't do anything else. A lot of the time over the last 10 years, I know what I've done hasn't been the kind of thing people wanted from me. It hasn't been the Neil Young people wanted to hear. I had a battle every time I went out. It was an uphill battle with every album, from the beginning to the end. I was fighting the record company. I was fighting general reactions to what I was doing that weren't really all that encouraging. Still, what I was doing was what I wanted to do. So I did it. And what I did, it wasn't what people wanted from me. I knew that."

So you have a keen sense of what it is your fans and record company want from you?

"Not really," he says. "But I knew what I was doing wasn't what people wanted to hear. At the same time, I couldn't give them what they wanted, so it didn't really bother me."

Why couldn't you give them what they wanted?

"I didn't *want* to give it to 'em."

In other words, you wouldn't bend to their expectations.

"Hell, no. I hate that kind of attitude. I'd never do that. It's not me. I'm not gonna do that. I know some people are convinced I've spent the last 10 years systematically destroying my career, taking this music my audience thought was so super-valuable it shouldn't even be touched and just ruining it. But you have to do that sometimes, however painful it is. It clears the horizon, gives you a new beginning. You can't stand still. You don't stop, ever. If you stop, you're dead. You know, what I am – I'm a musician. Not a superstar. I'm a musician. That's what I am. A writer and a musician. The more I play, the more different things I do, the better I get at what I do.

"I'm *not* going to grow if I just give people what they think they want to hear from me. I'm not gonna grow, sitting in a mansion. I'm gonna die. That's not what I want to do. So I keep going out there. And I don't care what people think. I just want to keep going, keep the blood flowing.

"Hell," he says after a well-judged pause, timed to give weight to what he says next. "That's my job."

My first impression of Neil Young is that Neil Young does Neil Young as well as Lou Reed does Lou Reed. Which is to say gruff contrariness comes easily to him, Neil as much as Lou relishing a reputation for cantankerous intransigence, grizzled singularity, a legendary unwillingness to compromise. He's standing across the room from us when we walk in, his back to the door. It's a plush hotel suite, lots of dark wood, thick carpets, too much brass, furniture you can't move. He turns, strides purposefully in our direction. He's wearing a long coat that appears to be made out of an Indian blanket, ripped jeans, an Elvis Presley T-shirt under some kind of blouse. His thinning hair is showing signs of grey and is otherwise ratty and uncombed, which makes him look a bit wild, especially when he breaks into a wide and unexpected smile that makes me think of Jack Nicholson, gurning madly in *The Shining*.

"You're late," he loudly scolds us, a brash admonishment intended presumably as a joke that it's not easy, in the circumstances, to find remotely funny. He's just kept us waiting for nigh on three hours, for no better reason than it's the kind of thing he can get away with, effectively to remind us of our lowly place in his world. Ever since *Harvest* put him somewhere he didn't want to be, Neil's made a lot of noise about the paltriness of fame and its various gaudy trappings. But there's something about his aloof condescension, an ear cocked for a lapdog's bark, that suggests there are some perks of an otherwise shunned superstardom he hasn't quite brought himself to give up – chief among them, treating people badly without apology. The message couldn't really be clearer. His time is more important than yours. "Take a seat," he says.

There are two straight-backed chairs in the middle of the room, facing each other, one for Neil, one for me. We sit, knees nearly touching. When we lean forward at the same time, we almost bump heads. He's in London for a one-off solo show tonight at the Hammersmith Odeon that coincides with the release of the career-reviving *Freedom*, for many fans the first Neil Young album since 1979's *Rust Never Sleeps* that they can listen to without wanting to jump in a hole. The Eighties have been no kinder to Neil than they have to Bob Dylan, Lou Reed or David Bowie. They start with Neil leaving long-time label Reprise for a new deal with David Geffen, who's buying up musical talent like real estate for his new label, Geffen Records – the big bucks portfolio soon boasting John Lennon and Yoko Ono, Joni Mitchell, Peter Gabriel, Cher and Neil. Unfortunately, his five Geffen albums are the worst-received and poorest-selling of his career. Geffen end up suing him for deliberately making uncommercial records.

"Geffen was just a mismatch," he says now. "It was a bad marriage. It just didn't work out. And it got to be a personal thing. It was a bad deal. But they're a great company," he adds, trying not to sound too bitter. "They're an efficient organisation. They've got some great groups, and they've sold a lot of records. Unfortunately, none of them were mine."

The Geffen albums cover diverse musical ground – rockabilly, country and western, flaccid hard rock, menopausal raunch, heavy-handed redneck satire and, most controversially, the much-ridiculed synth-pop of *Trans*. They're mostly regarded as dismal, jaded, oddly detached, as if he's sent a small part of himself out into the world to make them, while a larger, hurting part of himself becomes elsewhere increasingly distant, brooding, inconsolable. What isn't taken much into account at the time, mostly because he can't bring himself to talk about it, is the extent to which these records have been affected by the emotional impact on Neil of his children Zeke and

Ben, who have different mothers, both being born with a rare, non-hereditary form of cerebral palsy, Ben a non-verbal quadriplegic. The odds against both children being born handicapped are off the scale, baffling doctors. There's suddenly a lot of grief, resentment and anger to deal with.

"There was a lot of pain," he says, prompted by a passing question about *Trans*, a lot of the hard bluster going out of his voice, a surprising softness creeping in, a little huskily at times. "I just withdrew. I cut myself off from virtually everything. I closed the door. You can only feel so much and then you have to deny it. You can't deal with it. That was a heavy thing for me. I dealt with it for a while, as best as I could. But then I just had to cut myself off from everything. I just closed that door. I was cut off from everything. Because, you know, what had happened was a real private thing. I couldn't share it. And when you say those records I made then, they sound kinda detached, that's basically why. The door was closed. I couldn't get out and no one could get in. You know, there are times when you want to sing your heart out, and there are times when you want to disguise yourself and not let everything out. Some things, I don't know, they're too painful and they maybe shouldn't be let out. But they have to come out anyway, and they come out in a hidden kinda way. You know, they're not explicit. You can't recognise what's happening.

"I think a lot of those records, they'll be better understood when more time has passed. Like *Trans*, that was a real personal record, as personal as anything I've ever done. I did that album for my son, Ben. He's a non-oral child. And the setting for *Trans* is a hospital where there are all these people, bionic people, machines and robots, half people, half machines. They all work in this hospital, and they have this little baby and they're trying to teach the baby how to communicate. That's what they're doing.

"There's one guy, he's made out of stuff like that guy CP30 in *Star Wars*. He's all kinda brass-looking and his face is a computer key-pad, so whenever anything happens that needs figuring out, he starts hitting himself in the face. There were all kindsa characters. I had these nurses that sang, they were like clones of The Supremes. And, anyway, what they're all trying to do is make this baby communicate. That's what all the words are about. But you can't understand the words

313

because all the vocals are being put through Vocoders and machines. But that was the point, you know. That's the point I was making. How difficult and painful it can be to communicate, which is something we often just take for granted."

It must've been frustrating that so little of this was picked up on at the time.

"Oh, shit, yeah," he says. "No one knew what I was doing. Nobody could understand it. The record company was pissed off at me. Everybody was pissed off at me."

And how do you cope with that kind of uniformed rejection?

"It makes me mad, angry."

And how does that anger manifest itself?

"It comes out in my music," he says. "Eventually, you'll hear it."

Right about now, there's a hand on my shoulder. It's Elliott Roberts, Neil's manager of the last 25 years, sharp featured under a plume of silver hair, looking airy and rich in a billowing white shirt and black leather trousers. He brings his own kind of theatre with him into the room, a hint of LA hustle that makes you think of palm trees and cocaine, A&R meetings in hot tubs, quite a life.

"You guys!" he says, clapping his hands together lightly, like he may be summoning a servant or two, putting a little chuckle into his voice to go along with a headshake presumably meant to indicate his astonishment, at what I don't know. "It's always the same when you get together," he goes on, unbearably hearty, either mistaking me for someone else or not really bothered about who I am and merely going through some well-oiled routine. "I know you could talk all night, but sorry, but we have to break this up now," he says, although we're only 25 minutes into an allocated hour, a mean return on the three we were kept waiting.

"That's OK," Neil says. "We're just finishing up here."

This is news to me, as I've just been saying something to him about how hardy veterans like himself, Dylan and Lou Reed spent the Eighties looking for a voice to match the times. As Lou and Dylan had found that voice on *New York* and *Oh Mercy*, so had he on *Freedom*.

"There's something to be said for that," he says, already on his feet. "We've come through a lot, people like Dylan, me, Lou Reed. And what that shows me is that creativity is reliant on some force, something out there that sweeps through us, that's completely out of our control. I don't know what it is, when it's coming or where it's going. I don't know how long it's gonna stay. But whatever it is, it seems to affect a lot of people. And it's not the first time it's happened. If you look back, there was a period when I put out *Tonight's the Night*, *Zuma* and *American Stars 'n' Bars* in one year. The same year Dylan made *Blood on the Tracks*.

"So I believe there's some wind blowing around, you know," he says, trying to make sense of his hair before stepping in front of Tom Sheehan's camera for the three minutes Tom's now got to take some pictures. "You don't always know when it's there. But if you're receptive and something's happening, you'll pick up on it, that's for sure."

R.E.M.

Athens, Georgia, December 1991

There's a sign outside the motel advertising a seasonal parade of lights on Thursday evening. Christmas is coming, but it doesn't feel much like it here in Athens, home of R.E.M. It's nearly December and at 75 degrees, it's hot enough to make your shirt stick to your back and your tongue itch. No one can remember weather like this so late in the year.

On the first floor of R.E.M.'s HQ on West Clayton Street, their then-manager Jefferson Holt is finalising travel plans for a flight the next day to Los Angeles where he and Mike Mills will accept a Billboard award on behalf of the band.

"They've voted us the best international urban post-modernist non-dance absolutely non-rap rock band or something," says Jefferson, whose office recently has been piling up with awards. It's been that kind of year for R.E.M. with their *Out of Time* album breaking them internationally – a good enough reason for *Melody Maker*, the band's original UK champions, to put them on its Christmas cover.

Downstairs in the basement at West Clayton Street, there's an office for R.E.M.'s fan club secretary. It's a small room, cluttered with band memorabilia. On one wall, there's a poster for an early British show at the Queensway Hall, Dunstable. Tickets were priced at a not unreasonable £3.50. "BAR! SNACKS! FREE PARKING!" a blurb on the poster generously adds. A note taped to a computer terminal says, "FEED CAT", a civilised priority. On another wall, there's a sign that reads: "The Omni Atlanta April 1&2/89 – Sold Out!! Cheers, Charlie." It's a message from the concert promoter and framed above it, literally, is the shirt off his back.

At the rear of the fan club office, there's the group's rehearsal space, a small studio. This is where we find *Melody Maker* photographer Kevin Westerberg, preparing for his photo-session with the band. He's stripped down to braces, vest and pants, barefoot, with his hair tied back. The room is in almost total darkness and Kevin is hunched cross-legged over a flickering candle, taking a light reading.

Michael Stipe suddenly bursts through the door. He's totally hyper, like he's been up all night on a caffeine drip. He's wearing a greasy baseball cap, grubby T-shirt, slightly soiled jeans and construction worker's boots. He looks like he's come to mend the plumbing or unblock a drain.

"Am I disturbing you?" he asks Kevin.

"Oh," says Kevin, startled. "I was... uh... just chanting."

"Hey, cool! OK!" Stipe beams. "Go ahead. I didn't mean to interrupt."

And with this, he's gone.

"I hope he realised I was only joking," Kevin says, vaguely perplexed.

We're joined now by Peter Buck, Mike Mills and Bill Berry. They're wearing serious frowns and sporting an air of uncomfortable concern. Seems they've just run into Michael, who's outside in the street unloading his car.

"I don't *believe* it," Buck says. "He's got a Santa suit, some kinda *bear* costume and an Uncle Sam top hat. I think he seriously wants us to *wear* 'em."

He does, too. And here he comes, struggling through the door with a whole pile of shit in his arms.

"Are you serious?" Bill asks. "You want me to wear *this?*"

Bill's holding up a bear suit, mouldy, moth-eaten, a little rank.

"If you don't want to wear it, I will," says Stipe. "I'll take my shirt off and wear the bear suit. That'll sell some copies of *Melody Maker* for Allan."

No one looks very enthusiastic.

"Come *on*, guys," says Stipe. "This is for a holiday cover. Let's get *wacky.*"

"Michael," Buck says, exasperated, "you probably think this is a good idea now but you know these shots will haunt us for years if they print them. And you know," he adds, giving me a bit of a stare, "they will."

"Peter, just wear the Santa outfit, *please*," Stipe says, trying to mollify the spectacularly disgruntled guitarist.

"Does this suit me?" It's Bill, looking absolutely fucking ridiculous in a bear cub hat.

"It's not *bad*," Stipe tells him, with a startlingly evil little grin. "But I think the *ears* should be sticking up. Does anyone have any tape?"

"Correct me if I'm wrong, but didn't Santa have hands?" Buck asks, looking for pockets in his Santa suit.

"Aren't you going to wear the pants, Peter?"

"No, Michael," Buck says, poutily. "I'm *not* going to wear the pants. I don't want to even *discuss* the pants."

"Are these ears sticking up enough?"

"Looks great, Bill," Stipe says. "Mike, do you want to wear the Uncle Sam hat?"

"Not really," says Mike, stiffly. "I hate the stars and stripes."

"Me, too," says Buck.

"That's our *flag*, man," Stipe mugs. "You can't say that about our *flag*. We're Americans and we should be proud."

"I just think it looks dumb," Mike says, heading for a sulk.

"Awwww, c'mon," Stipe coos. "Look at *Bill*. Bill's dressed up as a *bear*. Peter's dressed up as Santa. You can wear the American flag. It's just another stupid costume."

Mike puts on the hat.

"Are you happy with that?" Kevin asks.

"No," says Mills, sharply. "I'm not happy with it at all."

Michael has stripped off his shirt and clambered into the bear suit. He's still wearing his baseball cap. Kevin asks him to take it off.

"I think the cap should stay," he says. "I think the cap is very *Stipey*."

He starts chuckling, the chuckle turning into a creepy cackle. It's curiously disturbing.

"Did you say your cap was very *Stipey*, Michael?" Bill asks, a tad bewildered.

"Yeah, I guess I did," Stipe smirks, a worrying glint in his eye. "I actually think the cap is *fantastically* Stipey."

And with that, Kevin's flash goes off and the room is flooded with light.

WARREN ZEVON

London, September 1992

The former golden boy of West Coast rock is backstage at a dingy north London venue, standing in dim light at the far end of a corridor down which he might have swept in his Seventies heyday, flanked by a pampering entourage.

We find Warren Zevon tonight in somewhat reduced circumstances, however. He's just played a show at a sparsely-populated Town & Country, drawing extensively on his breath-taking back catalogue of songs that, when they were originally recorded, featured luminaries galore, including fans like Bob Dylan, Neil Young, Bruce Springsteen, Jackson Browne, members of The Eagles, Fleetwood Mac, The Beach Boys and R.E.M. Those glory days have long-since ridden out of town, taking with them the lavish recording budgets and advances that bankrolled them. Tonight, he didn't even have a band.

"They're gone," he says of those high times now past. "This is who I am now."

From the cut of his duds – a Prada overcoat, a cashmere scarf that looks like it might have cost as much as a small car – he's not exactly on his uppers. But in the gloom of this dank corridor, water from a dripping pipe gathering in a puddle at our feet, he looks like someone used to much better than this dire moment.

"I don't have a band," he's telling me now, sounding a bit raw about it, "because my records don't sell and I don't have any money."

How much would he need to put a band on the road? He looks at me with an eyebrow raised and a pirate's grin.

"How much money do you *have?*" he asks, laughing when I tell him not enough, actually, for my cab fare home.

"That's too bad," he says as a light bulb somewhere further down the corridor flickers and dies. "I guess that means we're both shit out of luck."

I should perhaps remark here that I am only fairly recently a Zevon fan, my present infatuation occasioned by R.E.M.'s Peter Buck, as a timely flashback will explain: It's June 1985, and I'm in Athens, Georgia, to interview R.E.M. for a *Melody Maker* cover story ahead of the release of their third album, *Fables of the Reconstruction*. Michael Stipe's asleep in that ditch over there after a long night shoot for the video R.E.M. are making for "Can't Get There From Here", a track from the new album. It's about 3:00am. The film crew's packing its gear. Bill Berry and Mike Mills have just split. Peter Buck, meanwhile, is knocking back a beer and telling me, among other things, that in a couple of days he, Bill and Mike are heading for Los Angeles to record an album with the singer-songwriter Warren Zevon, who's currently being managed by an old college friend of Peter's, Andrew Slater.

Warren Zevon? I'm frankly shocked. At the time of which I'm writing, Zevon for me is part of a discredited West Coast culture of cocaine and excess, self-regarding balladry and narcissistic wimpery, the kind of bollocks punk was meant to have killed off. I mean, *Warren Zevon!* I have a vague memory of seeing him, perhaps 10 years earlier, supporting Jackson Browne – an influential early mentor – at London's New Victoria Theatre. The only song of his I can think of is "Werewolves of London", which I've always thought of as a novelty record.

Anyway, Pete listens to me rant and listens some more when I start ranting again, getting a second wind after becoming momentarily breathless.

"Allan," Peter says then, "just listen to the fucking records and get back to me."

I tell him I will, and I eventually do.

Back in London, I track down Zevon's back catalogue, which turns out to be surprisingly slim – just six albums since his 1969 debut, *Wanted Dead or Alive*. What I eventually end up listening to blows my mind, as they used to say. I've been expecting the winsome murmurings of some flaxen-haired minstrel, and here's this apparent cross between Randy Newman and Lee Marvin – a laconic song writing genius with an already legendary taste for vodka, guns and drugs. His talent is matched only by a capacity for self-destruction that's provoked one critic to describe him as "the Sam Peckinpah of rock 'n' roll". Spread across these albums are songs about mercenaries, murder, Mexican revolutionaries, rough sex, rape, necrophilia, hula boys, Elvis Presley, baseball, heroin, heartbreak, unpaid hotel bills, incestuous hillbillies and hard-drinking losers.

Los Angeles at the time Zevon is making these records is a place of notorious debauchery, lorded over by a decadent rock aristocracy. Zevon is the cynical laureate of its dark abandon, an unflinching chronicler of its gory charms, a brilliant noir poet, with more in common with James Ellroy than James Taylor. It's fair to say, in fact, that apart from an enduring admiration for Bob Dylan, Zevon's main influences are literary. Zevon is a fan and friend of Ken Millar who, as Ross MacDonald, has written some of the best post-Chandler California noir. He also strikes up a lively friendship with the great American novelist, screenwriter and occasional film-maker Thomas McGuane – Chet Pomeroy, the slightly unhinged former rock star in McGuane's disturbing and hilarious *Panama* is surely based at least in part on Zevon's riotous antics and singular talent for mayhem. Later, Zevon becomes close to writers Carl Hiassen and Dave Barry. Hunter Thompson, with whom down the years Zevon raises more than a little hell, is also a fan and not shy about it either.

"Warren Zevon is a poet," Thomson writes. "He has written more classics than any other musician of our time, with the possible exception of Bob Dylan. He is also a crack shot with a .44 Magnum and an expert on lacrosse. I have learned not to argue with him, about hockey or anything else. He is a dangerous drinker and a whole different person when he's scared."

I'm back in Athens in December 1991 to do another story on R.E.M. It's a couple of nights before Christmas and Peter Buck is knocking back margaritas at a bar called Gus Garcia's.

"Told you so," he laughs. I've just spent the best part of the last half hour describing my Damascene conversion to all things Zevon, much to Buck's amusement. R.E.M. have somewhat fallen out with Zevon since the release of *Hindu Love Gods* the previous year, an album of cover versions they'd knocked off during the sessions for *Sentimental Hygiene*, the record R.E.M. were about to go off and make with him on my last visit. Things have really happened recently for R.E.M. This year's *Out of Time* is on its way to making them international superstars. Things for Warren haven't gone so well. He's somehow survived the fearsome alcoholism that nigh on cost him his life and career, but *Sentimental Hygiene* doesn't sell and he's dropped by Virgin after its follow-up, the hugely expensive *Transverse City* – Warren's *Heaven's Gate*, as one wag puts it – recorded with another stellar line-up, principally a band that includes Jerry Garcia on guitar, Little Feat drummer Richie Hayward, Jefferson Airplane bassist Jack Casady and featured soloists David Gilmour, Chick Corea and Neil Young. There are three more albums, followed by a five-year silence, so complete many people presume Zevon's either retired or died. Then, in remarkably quick succession, in 2000 and 2002, come *Life'll Kill Ya* and *My Ride's Here*, whose songs are mostly about death. Which everyone thinks is very funny until Warren, suffering from acute breathlessness, after a lifetime avoiding doctors, visits a specialist who tells him he's suffering from mesothelioma, a rare form of cancer that also killed Steve McQueen. He's given three months to live, during which he records a final album, *The Wind*. All this is to come, however.

Back in the Town & Country's gloomy corridors, Zevon is getting ready to split. He's about to go, when I mention that my wife, Stephanie, also a big fan, had been looking forward to seeing him but is at home ill. I ask him if he'll sign something for her.

"Let's do it," he says. I give him my ticket and he holds it against the wall, starts writing something.

"Is it terminal?" he asks.

What?

"Your wife is ill," he reminds me. "Has she got anything terminal?"

Uh, no... why?

"Because I was just about to write 'Get well soon' and I didn't want to sound facetious," he says, and with an unforgettable smile and a brisk handshake, he's off.

I'm sitting in a bar called O'Lunney's, down there on West 42nd Street. I'm thinking about Bob Dylan and where he might be right now (holed up in a hotel room, you like to think, with a beautiful woman, drugs, a couple of guns and an old guitar) and what his record company have planned for him tonight. I'm talking, of course, about something called "Columbia Records Celebrates the Music of Bob Dylan", a big old ding-dong being put on tonight to commemorate the 30th anniversary of his recording debut. Madison Square Garden's been booked for the event, which sold out quick enough to break box office records, the show also going out live to America's pay-to-view audience at $20 a pop, with an estimated global audience of 500 million for its subsequent broadcast in a further 68 countries.

This means bucks aplenty for someone, which perhaps explains why the locals are somewhat cynical about the whole thing. New Yorkers I know are calling it "Bob Aid". This has a horrible ring to it, as if Dylan's become a needy case, fallen on hard times, a dosser with a dog on a string in need of a hand-out, a food parcel and a couple of warm blankets to keep out the coming winter chill. However it's been sold to them, a lot of Bob's old cronies have enthusiastically signed up for it. Neil Young, George Harrison, Eric Clapton, Johnny Cash, Kris Kristofferson, Roger McGuinn and Tom Petty are all scheduled to appear alongside Lou Reed, Pearl Jam's Eddie Vedder, Stevie Wonder, Chrissie Hynde, Sinead O'Connor and a lot more performing their own choice of songs from Dylan's vast repertoire.

Columbia have attached enough significance to the concert to fly in journalists from all over the world, most of whom are presently laying rowdy siege to the press gate at Madison Square Garden to collect their accreditation – a colourful panoply of laminates, name tags, wrist bands and colour coded passes. A cab drops off a group of European correspondents as near as the driver can get to the venue and we're immediately engulfed in an unfolding mayhem, a rising edge of panic, the world's press growing as frantic as passengers on a sinking ship who are squabbling over the last places on a lifeboat. Klieg lights are blazing. There are television crews from all the major US networks, people with cameras on their shoulders and clipboards in their hands, shouting into walkie-talkies, adding to the general shriek.

A vicious little wind's blown up out of nowhere. My hair's a mess and I'm dying for a drink, which means I want to get inside as quickly as possible and find the nearest bar. Instead, we're stuck at the arse end of a queue that's moving so slowly it might as well be not moving at all. After the slow passing of several millennia, we eventually negotiate this outer cordon, only to find ourselves in another long queue for the lifts that will take us up or down – I'm not quite sure which – to wherever it is in the vast auditorium we'll be sitting. Needless to say, this queue isn't going anywhere in a hurry, either. I feel like pushing someone off a cliff.

Next thing anyone knows, I'm leading a breakaway group of mostly European scribes up some stairs, at the top of which are two huge service elevators, their doors open onto interiors full of dirty light, hanging chains and clanking machinery, reminiscent of the vast cargo hold of the ship in *Aliens*. We take the elevator on the left, without a clue where it's going. There's a big red button. I press it and the faithful crew who've followed me look a wee bit fearful at the grinding of invisible gears, a fearsome amount of creaking and the shriek of metal. The lights flicker, producing a strobe-like effect that puts the wind up a couple of Belgians, one of whom begins to whimper. The lights then go out altogether, causing further alarm, even as the elevator stops with a shuddering jolt. Its doors open with apparent reluctance and much rusty growling on a floor not visibly numbered. I have no idea where we are, but suspect it won't do to let the others know.

"This way," I fairly shout, striding down a curiously empty corridor. We take a right turn, a left turn, then go right again. The corridors remain deserted, as if everybody's blown town in an emergency evacuation (leave everything you can't carry, including the children!), news of which has yet to reach us. Just as it seems we've been doomed to wander this infernal maze until we are old, I spot ahead an open door through which I can see beer, wine, sandwiches, fruit, cold meats, flowers in a vase, the latter a thoughtful touch. We are delivered!

I'm about to neck a much-needed Heineken when a hand as big as Minneapolis grips my shoulder, a bone or two close to cracking. Amazingly, it's someone I know: Big Jim Callahan, minder to the stars, last encountered, I believe, working as a bodyguard for Elvis Costello.

"Jim!" I declare, like a hearty party host. "Have a drink," I add, indicating the table behind me with an imperious wave. Big Jim gives me a pat on the head that nearly flattens it.

"Out," he says, adding for unwanted emphasis: "Now." This seems a bit churlish of the usually sporting Big Jim, until I read the sign on the door that Jim is pointing at now with what passes for a smile. It says: 'BOB DYLAN – PRIVATE HOSPITALITY SUITE.'

Well, not long after this unfortunate misunderstanding, suitably chastened, but with two beers I manage to sneak into my bag when Big Jim's back is briefly turned, I'm in my seat in Section 110 of Madison Square Garden, gritting my teeth as John 'Cougar' Mellencamp does something to "Like a Rolling Stone" for which he deserves a spell on a chain gang. It's the start of a long evening that ends many hours later, with Dylan, natty in a black matador outfit, delivering a dignified "Song For Woody" and a tempestuous "It's Alright Ma (I'm Only Bleeding), then fronting an all-star version of "Knockin' on Heaven's Door", after which the stellar cast begins to disperse. Bob for a moment looks like he's going with them, but stands instead alone in the spotlight for a paralysing "Girl From the North Country". He finishes the song, looks around. The recently packed stage is empty. To what looks like his surprise, everyone's gone. And then so is he.

NEIL YOUNG

London, October 1992

"The doctor will see you now."

This is Neil Young, in town to promote his new *Harvest Moon* album, calling out from the hotel room where he's spent the afternoon entertaining a succession of journalists, all of them beckoned into the greatness of his presence with the same booming declaration, Neil making said announcement in a peculiar accent presumably meant to imply some kind of comic intent on his part, but not exactly side-splitting.

Neil is looking his usual self, I'm pleased to note when I am ushered into his presence. Which is to say, he looks like he's just been shot out of a cannon, wearing someone else's hair for a joke.

"I hear you were at the Dylan show in New York last week," he says, in a low voice, ominous as thunder rolling down a valley. "Did you enjoy it?" he asks.

Most of it, yes. Was it good for you?

"It was great. Met a lotta old friends and it was a lotta fun."

Bob had looked a bit bewildered, I thought.

"Hell," Neil laughs. "Bob *always* looks like that. Don't worry about Bob."

I ask Neil what he thought of the crowd's treatment of Sinead O'Connor, who'd provoked their wrath a few nights earlier by ripping up a picture of the Pope on a TV chat show. The wee Irish songbird had been set to favour us with a rendition of Bob's "I Believe in You", but had been mercilessly booed and finally howled down entirely by the enraged New York mob, blurting out a couple of verses from Bob Marley's "War" before quitting the stage in a mucky flood of tears, fleeing then into the sheltering arms of the impossibly noble Kris Kristofferson. "Don't let the bastards grind you down," Kris had told her, giving the screaming horde a flinty look, the sort you might see in a bar, just before the chairs start flying.

"She got a good reaction," Neil says, by way of surprising reply.

From where I was sitting, it was like she'd provoked a 20,000-strong lynch-mob. She'd left the stage in tears, puking spit. Did Neil really think this could be described as a Good Reaction?

Neil now gives *me* the kind of look Kristofferson had given Madison Square Garden.

"It was a *New York* reaction, OK?" he snaps, a grizzled veteran of the rock 'n' roll wars. "It was a *strong* reaction. They were booing her, but at least they were reacting. It wasn't like they didn't know she was *there*. I'd say that was a good reaction."

She seemed pretty distraught.

"I'm surprised by that."

I've also just heard that after talking to God, or at least someone who knows him, she's decided to quit the music business.

"Well," Neil says, and you can tell he's not really impressed, and may not even be at all interested, "she's gotta do whatever she thinks she's gotta do."

Would he have taken that kind of hostility in his legendary stride?

"Absolutely. Shit, I've been booed for my music. Bob was booed for going electric. I was booed for coming on and singing with a Vocoder and synthesisers. I was booed here in London. I was booed in Germany, Spain, France, Italy, everywhere. Wherever I went, they booed me. But they never made me run."

And what's it like, facing down a hostile mob like that?

"It doesn't bother me," he says, playing the crusty old geezer here, the unyielding loner hero. "I just keep on going. It's just a moment. It passes. And how often do you get a chance to play when people are booing? It doesn't matter. The thing is, she's supposed to know what she's doing. So don't ask me to feel any sympathy for her."

God forbid!

"I think she really blew a really great chance to be brilliant. She let the audience get the best of her. I don't want to pass judgement on her and the things she's said or done. I'm sure she has plenty of good reasons for the things she does. More power to her. You want to protest,

327

go ahead. Be my guest. But there's a time when it's gonna come back on you. You have to be strong. You have to be prepared to take that. She let it beat her."

And that's never happened to you?

"Uh-uh. I *love* things like that. There's nothing more creative than a volatile situation. You can turn *that* into anything. If she'd just sung that song, 'I Believe in You'. Do you know the lyrics to that song?"

Er, yes. I do, I tell him, hoping he won't ask me to sing them for him.

"It's such a beautiful song. Imagine a girl who looks like her singing that song with her beautiful voice with the crowd booing. It would have been *perfect*. She could have got so *into* it, man, and by the end they would have been standing and cheering. *That's* what would've happened. But they put her to the test and she just wasn't up to it."

Didn't he think it was strange that a Dylan audience would act with such illiberal contempt?

"Aw, *come on,*" he groans, like I'm some pampered, knicker-wetting, bleeding heart, tree-hugging softy. "These were the same people who booed, *Bob,* man. Remember that. They did it to Dylan. They booed him. The *same* people. The people who booed him in 1965 or 1966 were at that show. These people now have become successful enough to pay $130 for a show like that. There were probably a lot of them who tried to howl down Dylan. It shouldn't have come as a surprise to *anybody.*"

There's a moment's silence, and I change the subject.

Neil's handsome new album, *Harvest Moon,* is worlds away from the guitar firestorms and feedback apocalypse of the previous year's epic *Arc Weld.* His record company are especially thrilled by it because it reminds them of Neil's last big money-spinner, 1972's *Harvest,* to which the new album, in their words, is a sequel.

Was he happy with it being so described?

"They can call it whatever the hell they like," he says, snippily "I just make these records," he adds testily. "It's not my job to describe them as well."

When we last spoke, he actually said that for 20 years people had been pestering him for a follow up to *Harvest,* and now the time was right to deliver it.

"Did I?" he muses. "I wonder what I meant?"

It sounded like you were going to record a follow-up to *Harvest*. Not a great deal of ambiguity there, surely?

"Whatever," he says, and I can tell by the drift in his voice that he's heading for somewhere I'm not going to reel him back from, his eyes now wandering in the direction of the door, that wooden thing in the wall, that I am very shortly walking through, the doctor already getting ready for his next appointment.

New York, April 1994

"You know," Eddie Vedder says, his voice trembling, hoarse, a whisper, "I always thought I'd go first."

Neither of us says anything for a moment after this. It gets so quiet between us, I'm sure I can hear my heart beating, an insignificant pulse. Eddie stares at the floor, looking for secrets in stone.

"I don't know why I thought that," he says finally. "It just seemed like I would. I mean, I didn't know him on a daily basis. Far from it. But in a way, I don't even feel right being here without him. It's so difficult to really believe he's gone. I still talk about him like he's still here, you know? I can't figure it out. It doesn't make any sense. I remember when he got sick in Rome – I didn't realise then it was actually a suicide attempt. I was in Seattle. I went out to grab something to eat and saw the headlines. That he was in a coma. I just freaked out. I went home and made some phone calls, tried to find out what was going on. Then I started pacing the house and started to cry. I just kept saying, 'Don't go, man, just don't fuckin' go... just don't go.' I kept thinking, 'If he goes, I'm fucked.'"

We're backstage at New York's Paramount Theatre, somewhere deep in the vast ugliness of Madison Square Garden, where Pearl Jam will shortly be playing the last show of their current American tour, a comparatively low-key gig for them, originally intended for fan club members. Nine days earlier, Kurt Cobain had turned a shotgun on himself in Seattle, with predictably dire results.

"I don't know how we've got through this last week," Eddie says, dragging a rickety metal chair across the floor of this whitewashed cell. We could be patients in an institution, waiting for some unpleasant treatment, a leather strap in the mouth, the crackle of electricity. "It's been so fuckin' hard, man," he goes on, although I think by now I've got the general picture. "So hard. For a number of reasons, I didn't want to continue this tour, Kurt's death being one of them. But we decided to pull together, make it through this last week and then forget it for a while. I don't know where we go from here. Maybe nowhere. I think this is going to be the last thing for a long time. I'm just going to live in a cave with my fuckin' girlfriend. I don't think I'll be showing my face for a while. I just don't know. I'm having a really tough time right now."

His voice is full of dust and gravel, worn out, almost gone. He seems at once tired and ready for some kind of action, a physical demonstration, perhaps, of his raw sense of grief, bewilderment and anger. His mood shifts and lurches from painful introspection to livid anger. One minute he's talking in a hushed, faltering whisper. The next, he's shouting, ranting, swearing. One minute, he's hunched in his chair, small, crouched, turning in on himself. The next, another fuse has blown and things are flying across the dressing room. To describe his current mood as volatile would be an understatement. You were expecting something like this, of course, Eddie's response to Kurt's suicide always likely to include a great deal of tragic roaring and brooding self-examination. They were meant to be enemies, of course, arch rivals. This was the convenient narrative, the proclaimed drama often fuelled, you'd have to say, by Kurt's many toadies – the two biggest new stars in American rock in irreconcilable conflict, Kurt saying a lot of sour and ugly things about Eddie and his band.

"There was a lot of stuff that got said, but none of it really matters now. I like to think he may have had second thoughts about some of the things he said," Eddie says, although he admits to the indelible hurt he felt when he saw a headline in a Seattle magazine, a small-circulation coffee house rag, when Kurt went into a coma in Rome. It said, starkly: "WHY COULDN'T IT HAVE BEEN EDDIE VEDDER?"

Funnily enough, this is exactly what Kurt's widow Courtney Love told British music magazine *Select* at the time. Eddie looks stunned when I mention this.

"Oh," he says, the wind gone out of him, deflated. "That's nice. That's really nice. That makes me feel really good. I wonder why she didn't mention that when I phoned her last night and offered her any help or support I could give her." Eddie sort of stews over this for a couple of minutes. "I don't really know any of these people," he says then. "I don't know Courtney. I'd never talked to her before. But someone said I should call her and I thought maybe I should. I mean, all this shit that comes up and all this bullshit that flies back and forth in the press that gets italicised and trumped up to make it a bigger deal than it really is, when that's all said and done, there's feelings I have for these people. And the ones that are alive, I need to let them know how I feel."

We've slipped into another protracted silence, Eddie with his face screwed up and breathing heavily.

"Fuck it fuckin' all," he suddenly snaps, standing up, grabbing a chair and throwing it hard against a wall, which it hits with an almighty crash, Eddie looking around as if for something he might tear apart with his bare hands and sharp teeth. He picks up the chair, sits down with a sigh, something in him, for the moment, spent.

"You know, all these people," he says, "all lining up to say that his death was so fucking inevitable? Well, if it was inevitable for him, it's gonna be inevitable for me, too, if this continues. That's why this could be our last show in fuckin' forever as far as I'm concerned. Kurt's death has changed everything. I don't know if I can do this anymore. People like him and me, we can't be real. It's a contradiction. We can't be these people who just write these songs. We have to live up to the expectations of a million people. And we can't do that. And then there's a cynical fuckin' media on top of that. Fuck that, fuck them. All along the line, they question your fuckin' honesty. No matter what you say, no matter what you do, they think it's an angle. They think it's all a fuckin' game. They don't know what's real and what isn't. They just think it's all some kind of fuckin' angle. And that makes it so hard for somebody who's just trying to be honest. So fuck it. Fuck it all."

He stops for breath and you can feel exhaustion and something close to hysteria coming off him in waves. You wonder for a moment if he's all talked out. He isn't.

"Another thing," he says, voice rising again, like he's trying to get someone's attention across a crowded room. "Although we were very different people, there was probably a lot we had in common. We

332

had similar backgrounds, things that happened with our families and shit. I think that's something that comes out in what we wrote in our songs, definitely. It is kinda similar sometimes. But what makes it more similar is the way people responded to what we wrote and sang about, the intense identification. I think it was maybe a shock to both of us that so many people were going through the same things. I mean, they understood so completely what we were talking about. And this was shit we thought only he and I were ever gonna have to deal with. Because we kinda wrote those songs for ourselves, really. Then all of a sudden, there's all these people who connect with them and you're suddenly the spokesman for a fuckin' generation. Can you imagine *that!*" he shouts. "A... spokesman... for... a... generation," he goes on, and you're not sure if he thinks this is sad, terrible or too funny for words. "It's just so fucking weird. You write about this shit and you're suddenly the spokesman for a fuckin' generation," he laughs, and it's a bitter, scary laugh, nothing funny about it at all.

"Think about it, man," he says, shaking his head, baffled and alarmed. "Any generation that would pick Kurt or me as its spokesman must be really fucked up, man, really fuckin' fucked up. And I don't think it's fair for anyone to criticise me or Kurt or anyone else for not wanting any fuckin' part of it. We got into this because we wanted to be in a band, play music, make records. End of fuckin' story."

Right about now, *Melody Maker* photographer Steve Gullick turns up with his own tale of woe. He's been told by someone of dubious authority that he can only take pictures of the first two numbers of Pearl Jam's show, no flash, from an obscure vantage point on the far side of the stage.

"Fuck that," Eddie tells him. "Take as many shots as you like, from where you like, for as long as you like and if anybody gives you any shit, tell 'em to talk to me about it."

Steve also wants to take some pictures of Eddie here in the dressing room. Eddie says sure and goes to fetch his guitar.

"Let's go in here," he says, back in the dressing room, walking into the shower stall and turning on the shower, water now drenching him. Then he borrows my lighter and starts burning the cork from one of the bottles of wine we've just emptied. He uses the burned cork to draw black circles around his eyes, deep in the sockets, and a large cross on his forehead that makes him look like a member of a sinister cult, someone who might slip into an unprotected home, slitting throats and scrawling Beatles lyrics on a wall in blood.

"This going to make you look ever so weird," Steve tells him, Eddie in his viewfinder.

"Let me be as weird as I fuckin' like," Eddie tells him. "It's my fuckin' life."

THE AFTERGLOW

It's May 19, 2015, a warm, sunny morning giving way to a slightly overcast afternoon. I'm standing with a crowd of people outside St Stephen's Church in Twickenham, southwest London. We're here for the funeral of Bobby Irwin, a veteran of many sessions and tours with Van Morrison. For nearly 40 years, Bobby's also been Nick Lowe's drummer of choice and one of Nick's closest chums. I'd known Bobby for almost as long as Nick knew him, coming across him first in 1978, on the Be Stiff tour, when all the bands travelled on a specially chartered train and much hilarious chaos predictably ensued. He was drumming at the time for the singer Lene Lovich, shortly to have a big hit with "Lucky Number" and also playing in a snappy power pop band called The Sinceros, who recorded a couple of albums for Epic that nobody bought. He played for a while after The Sinceros split with American country singer Carlene Carter, who was then married to Nick Lowe – me and Tom Sheehan joining them once on an uproarious tour of Holland that was nothing but laughs and great music. Bobby was also part of the wild party that accompanied Nick in 1982 to Texas, where we all ended up joining something called the Confederate Air Force as full colonels, a trip that came with much colourful lunacy attached. I lost touch with Bobby when he moved to San Antonio in 1985, but we were neighbours in Twickenham from 1992, when he came back from Texas to work with Van and Nick.

There are a lot of familiar faces in the crowd who've come to see Bobby off, most of them from the old Stiff days. Nick is here, of course, elegant in his maturity, dressed in an immaculately cut black suit, crisp white shirt and tie, a handkerchief plucked regularly from the breast pocket of his suit jacket to dab his eyes, tears coming quite freely. With his black horn rims and silver thatch combed into a generous quiff, he cuts a rather smarter figure now than the often-bedraggled coked-up boozer of the Stiff era and Rockpile years. Jake Riviera is also here, heavy and slow moving after a recent serious illness, in need of a stick to get around, but still recognisable as the two-fisted firecracker of yore. Paul Conroy, who after a stint as Stiff's General manager went on to run Virgin Records, where he signed The Spice Girls (a change from working with Wreckless Eric, at the very least), seems meanwhile to have barely changed at all, apart from a few grey hairs. Dave Robinson, who started Stiff with Jake, also looks well, what's left of his hair slicked back, a satanic-looking goatee beard giving him the look of a Mexican bandit. I spot Dr Feelgood manager Chris Fenwick, who 20 years after the death of Lee Brilleaux still has a line-up of the Feelgoods on tour for most of the year. He's just booked them for a summer season on a Mediterranean cruise liner, with first class accommodation, all they can eat and drink and a free berth for Chris.

I wonder what Lee would have thought of all that.

"I'm sure he would have had an opinion," Chris laughs. "Pity he's not here to give it. But we go where the work is," he says. "Always have. The money for the cruise is tasty and the free berth for me is the gravy on the potatoes. Who's complaining?"

Clearly distraught, Nick delivers a funny and tearful eulogy, speaking from a pulpit with Bobby's casket in front of him. When Nick breaks down, sobbing quite uncontrollably, his young son, who's been sitting in one of the front pews, climbs up beside him in the pulpit, hands Nick a handkerchief for his tears. At that point, there isn't a dry eye in the fucking house. It's probably the toughest gig Nick's ever played.

Bobby was a bit of a sailor, so someone's now reading from John Masefield's poem, "Sea Fever" – "All I ask is a merry yarn and a laughing fellow rover, And a quiet sleep and a sweet dream when the long trick's over." And suddenly it's not just Bobby I'm missing. Even before the Great Cull of 2016 that took, among others, David Bowie, Leonard Cohen, Merle Haggard, Prince, Guy Clark, George Michael, Leon Russell and George Martin, a lot of the people featured in this book were dead. So I think of Lou Reed, Lee Brilleaux, Warren Zevon, Mick Ronson and Lemmy, all lost to cancer. I think of Joe Strummer, Alex Harvey and John Peel, and their hearts giving out on them. I think of Kurt Cobain discharging a shotgun into his face. I think of Jimmy and Pete from The Pretenders and how they couldn't get enough of anything until they took too much of everything and were both dead by 1983. I get quite glum.

We follow Bobby's casket out of the church. The sun's shining again. The sky's clearing. Let's put some birdsong in here, too; a sweet tune from a branch atop one of the nearby trees – elms, oaks, whatever they are. The crowd's breaking up now, most of them heading for the pub across the road at the kind of enthusiastic clip Bobby would have appreciated. A few of the less nimble among them look like they won't get to the fucking bar until closing time at the rate they're going, but they can't be faulted for effort. I find the writer and broadcaster Mark Ellen working the edge of the dispersing throng and head off for a drink with him and pub rock veteran turned rock biographer Will Birch. The gloom begins to lift. A little cheer returns to the afternoon.

It's not like the old days. But until something else comes along, it'll do.

A NOTE ON THE TYPE

The text of this book is set in Linotype Sabon, a typeface named after the type founder, Jacques Sabon. It was designed by Jan Tschichold and jointly developed by Linotype, Monotype and Stempel in response to a need for a typeface to be available in identical form for mechanical hot metal composition and hand composition using foundry type.

Tschichold based his design for Sabon roman on a font engraved by Garamond, and Sabon italic on a font by Granjon. It was first used in 1966 and has proved an enduring modern classic.